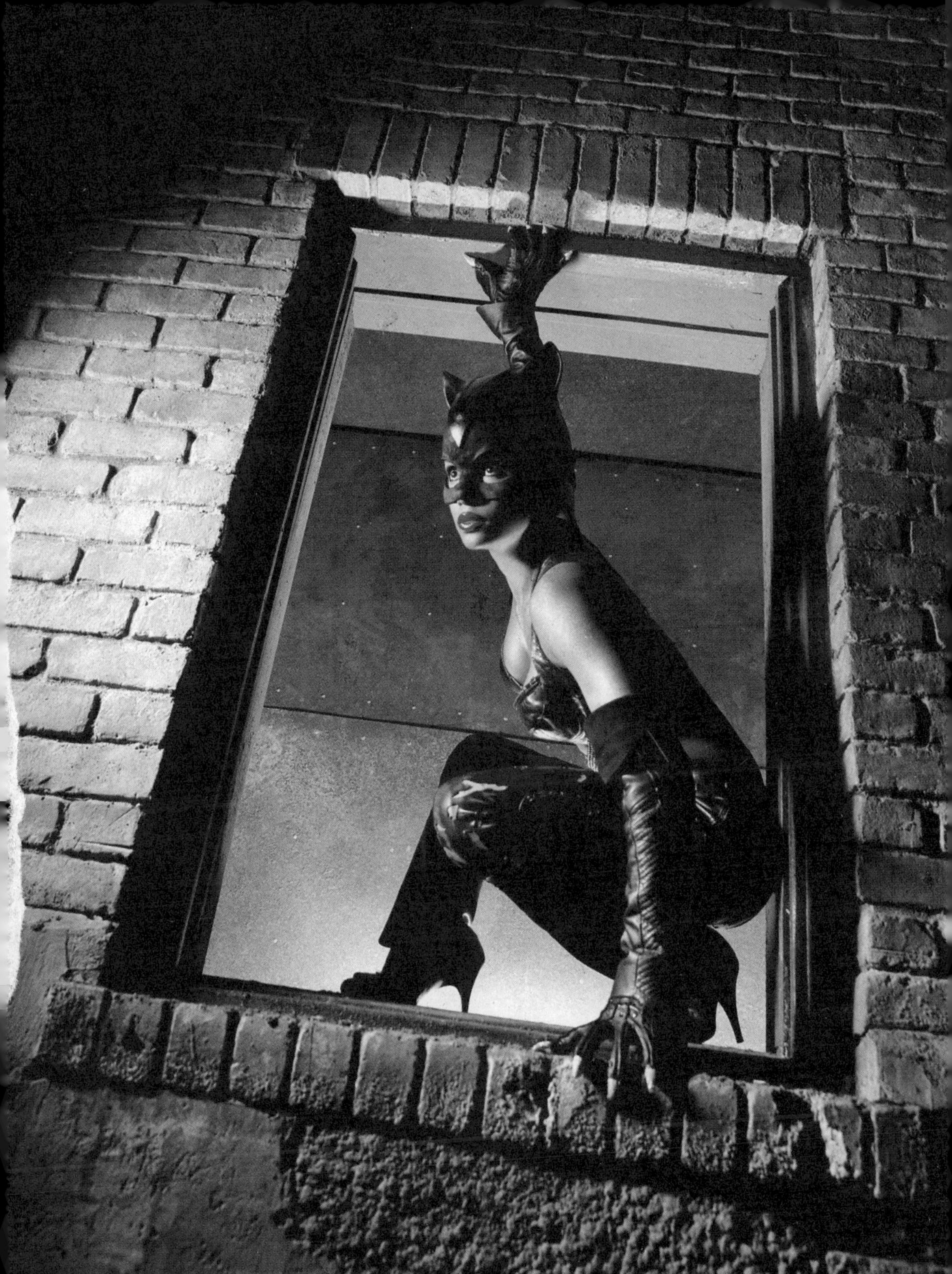

# CATWOMAN™

THE MOVIE & OTHER CAT TALES

Dan DiDio VP-Editorial. Tom Palmer, Jr. Dennis O'Neil Matt Idelson Editors-original series
Jordan B. Gorfinkel Nachie Castro Assistant Editors-original series Anton Kawasaki Editor-collected edition
Robbin Brosterman Senior Art Director Louis Prandi Art Director Paul Levitz President & Publisher
Georg Brewer VP-Design & Retail Product Development Richard Bruning Senior VP-Creative Director
Patrick Caldon Senior VP-Finance & Operations Chris Caramalis VP-Finance Terri Cunningham VP-Managing Editor
Alison Gill VP-Manufacturing Rich Johnson VP-Book Trade Sales Hank Kanalz VP-General Manager, WildStorm
Lillian Laserson Senior VP & General Counsel Jim Lee Editorial Director-WildStorm
David McKillips VP-Advertising & Custom Publishing John Nee VP-Business Development
Gregory Noveck Senior VP-Creative Affairs Cheryl Rubin Senior VP-Brand Management Bob Wayne VP-Sales & Marketing

**CATWOMAN: THE MOVIE & OTHER CAT TALES** Published by DC Comics.
Cover and compilation copyright © 2004 DC Comics. All Rights Reserved. Originally published in
single magazine form in CATWOMAN: THE MOVIE, CATWOMAN (first series) #0, CATWOMAN
(second series) #11 and 25. Copyright © 1994, 2002, 2004 DC Comics. All Rights Reserved.
All characters, their distinctive likenesses and related elements featured in this publication are trade-
marks of DC Comics. The stories, characters and incidents featured in this publication are entirely
fictional. DC Comics does not read or accept unsolicited submissions of ideas, stories or artwork.
Printed in Canada. First Printing.
DC Comics, 1700 Broadway, New York, NY 10019. A Warner Bros. Entertainment Company.
ISBN: 1-4012-0336-1
Photographs by Cliff Watts.

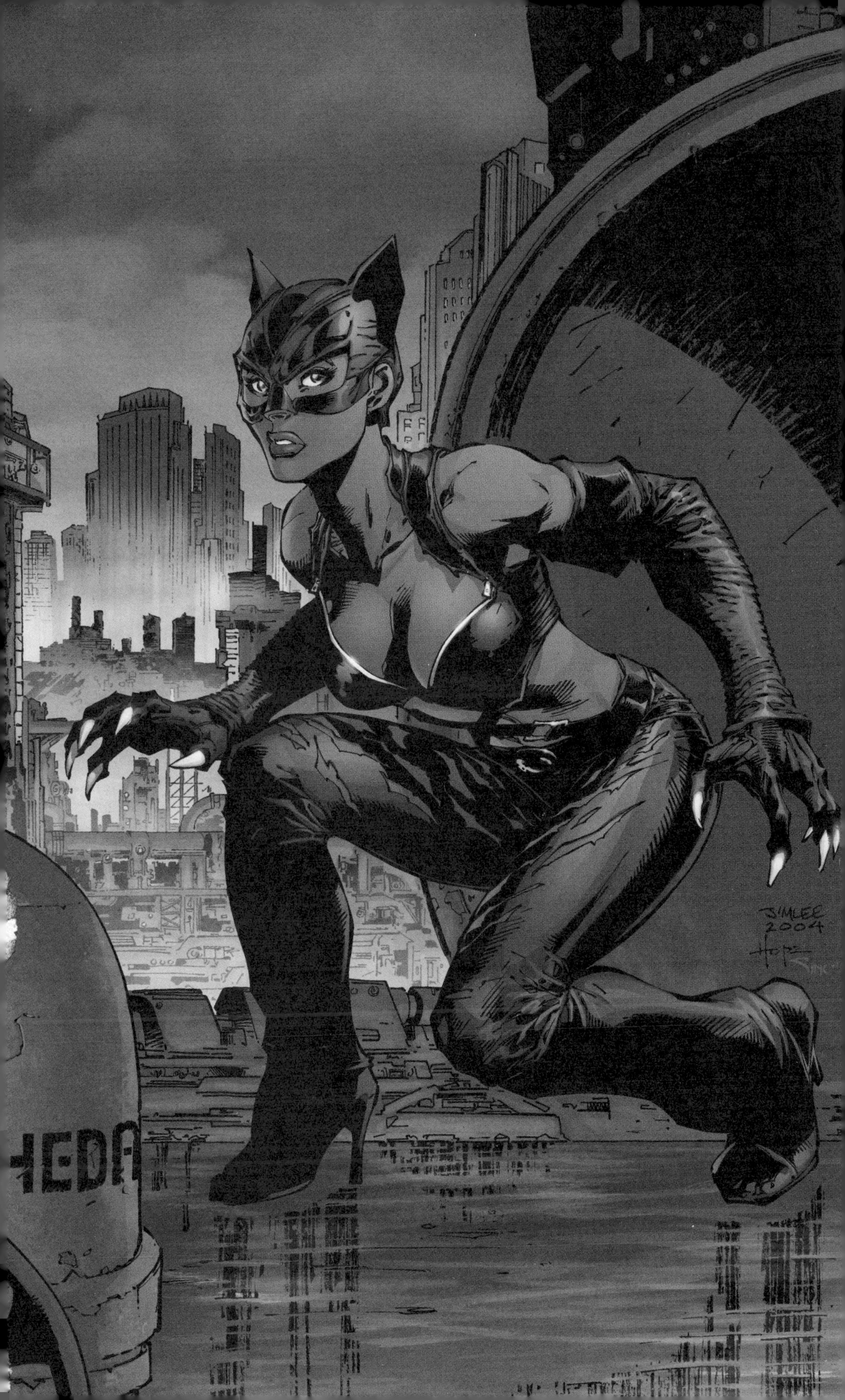
JIMLEE
2004
HEDA

# CATWOMAN:

## THE MOVIE

**Chuck Austen** Writer
**Tom Derenick** Penciller
**Adam DeKraker** Inker
**Zylonol** Colorist
**Jared Fletcher** Letterer
**Jim Lee** Cover Artist

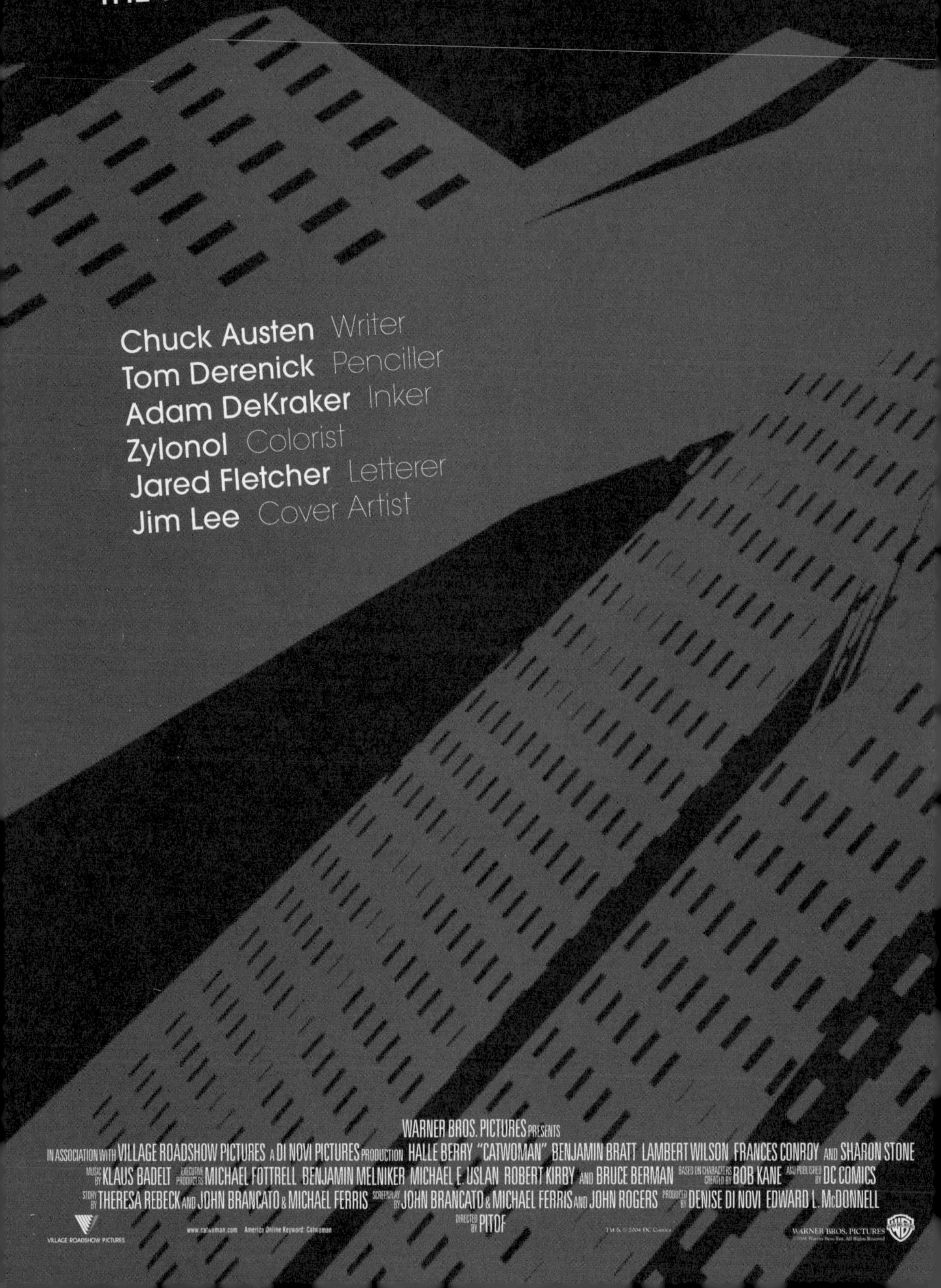

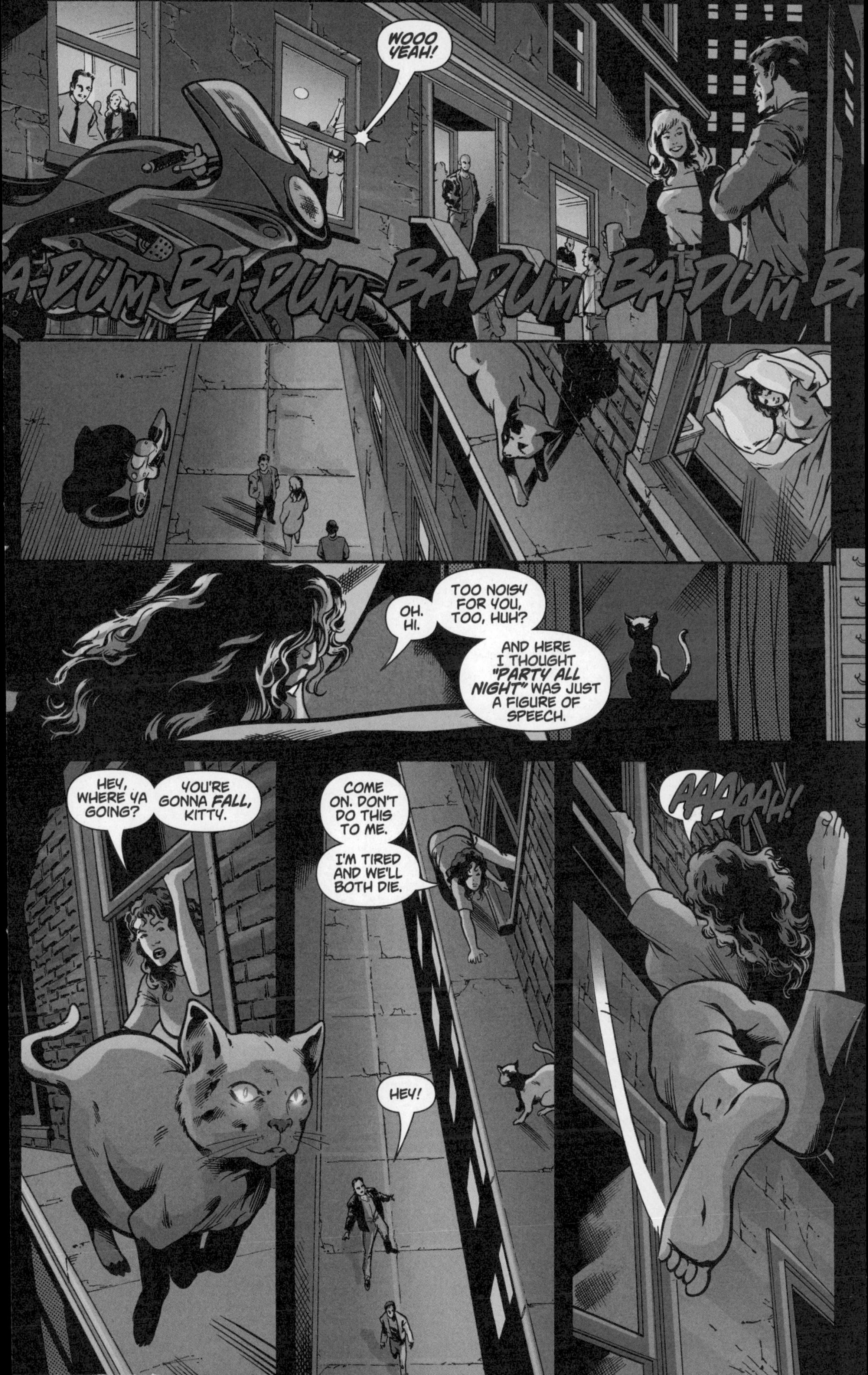
WOOO YEAH!
BA-DUM BA-DUM BA-DUM BA-DUM
OH. HI.
TOO NOISY FOR YOU, TOO, HUH?
AND HERE I THOUGHT "PARTY ALL NIGHT" WAS JUST A FIGURE OF SPEECH.
HEY, WHERE YA GOING?
YOU'RE GONNA FALL, KITTY.
COME ON. DON'T DO THIS TO ME.
I'M TIRED AND WE'LL BOTH DIE.
HEY!
AAAAAH!

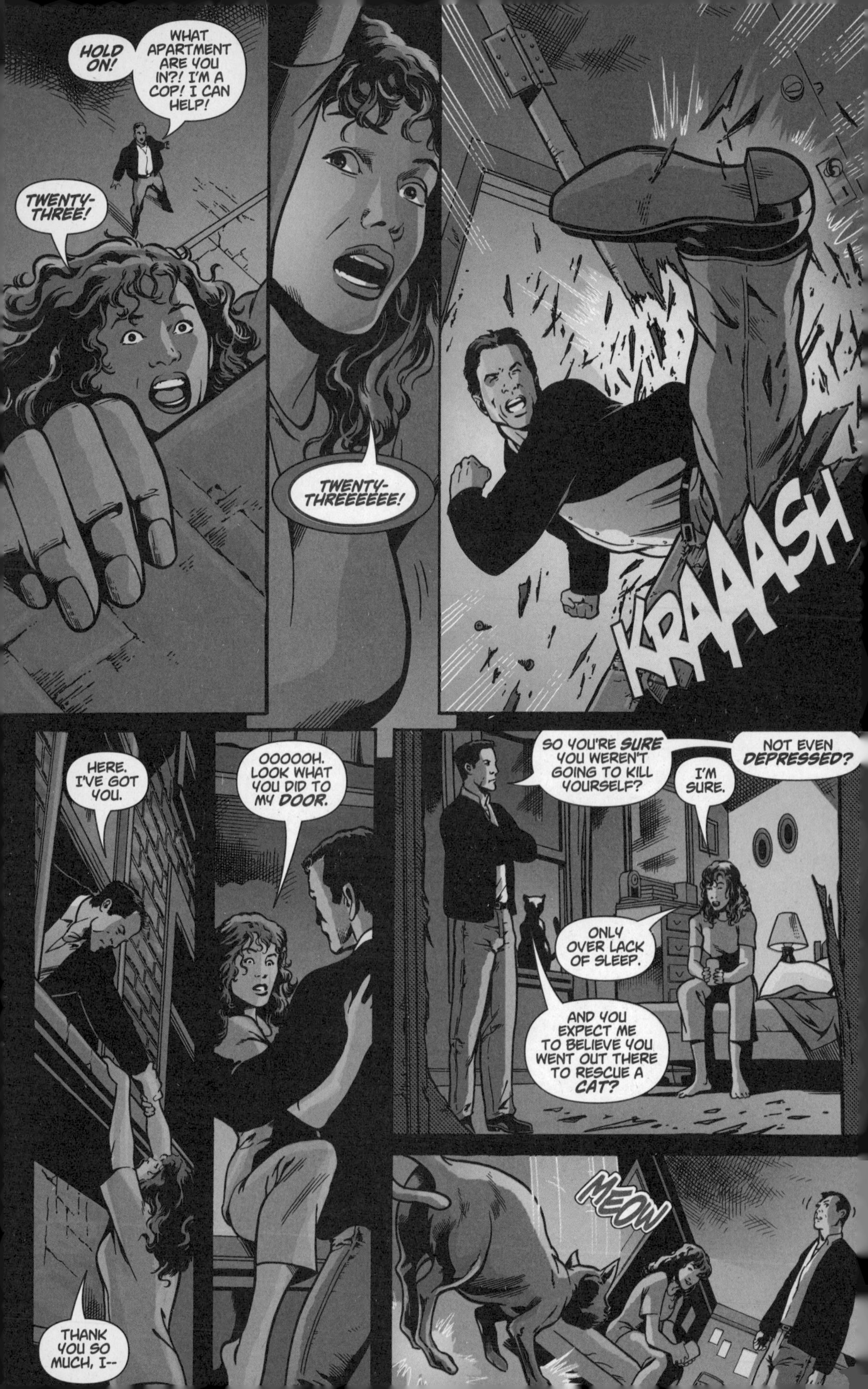
HOLD ON!
WHAT APARTMENT ARE YOU IN?! I'M A COP! I CAN HELP!
TWENTY-THREE!
TWENTY-THREEEEEEE!
KRAAASH
HERE. I'VE GOT YOU.
THANK YOU SO MUCH, I--
OOOOOH. LOOK WHAT YOU DID TO MY DOOR.
SO YOU'RE SURE YOU WEREN'T GOING TO KILL YOURSELF?
I'M SURE.
NOT EVEN DEPRESSED?
ONLY OVER LACK OF SLEEP.
AND YOU EXPECT ME TO BELIEVE YOU WENT OUT THERE TO RESCUE A CAT?
MEOW

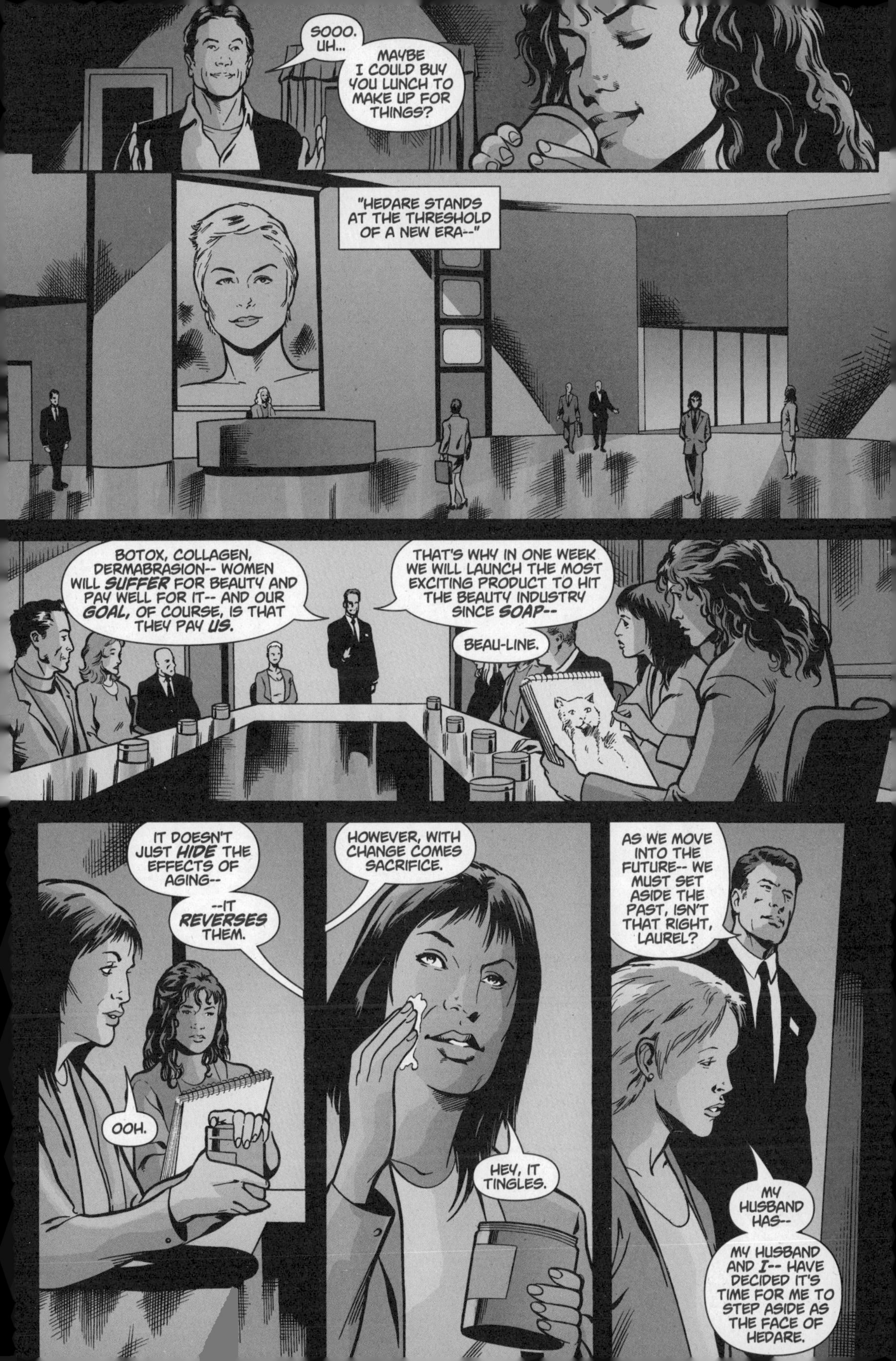
SOOO. UH...
MAYBE I COULD BUY YOU LUNCH TO MAKE UP FOR THINGS?
"HEDARE STANDS AT THE THRESHOLD OF A NEW ERA--"
BOTOX, COLLAGEN, DERMABRASION-- WOMEN WILL SUFFER FOR BEAUTY AND PAY WELL FOR IT-- AND OUR GOAL, OF COURSE, IS THAT THEY PAY US.
THAT'S WHY IN ONE WEEK WE WILL LAUNCH THE MOST EXCITING PRODUCT TO HIT THE BEAUTY INDUSTRY SINCE SOAP--
BEAU-LINE.
IT DOESN'T JUST HIDE THE EFFECTS OF AGING--
--IT REVERSES THEM.
OOH.
HOWEVER, WITH CHANGE COMES SACRIFICE.
HEY, IT TINGLES.
AS WE MOVE INTO THE FUTURE-- WE MUST SET ASIDE THE PAST, ISN'T THAT RIGHT, LAUREL?
MY HUSBAND HAS--
MY HUSBAND AND I-- HAVE DECIDED IT'S TIME FOR ME TO STEP ASIDE AS THE FACE OF HEDARE.

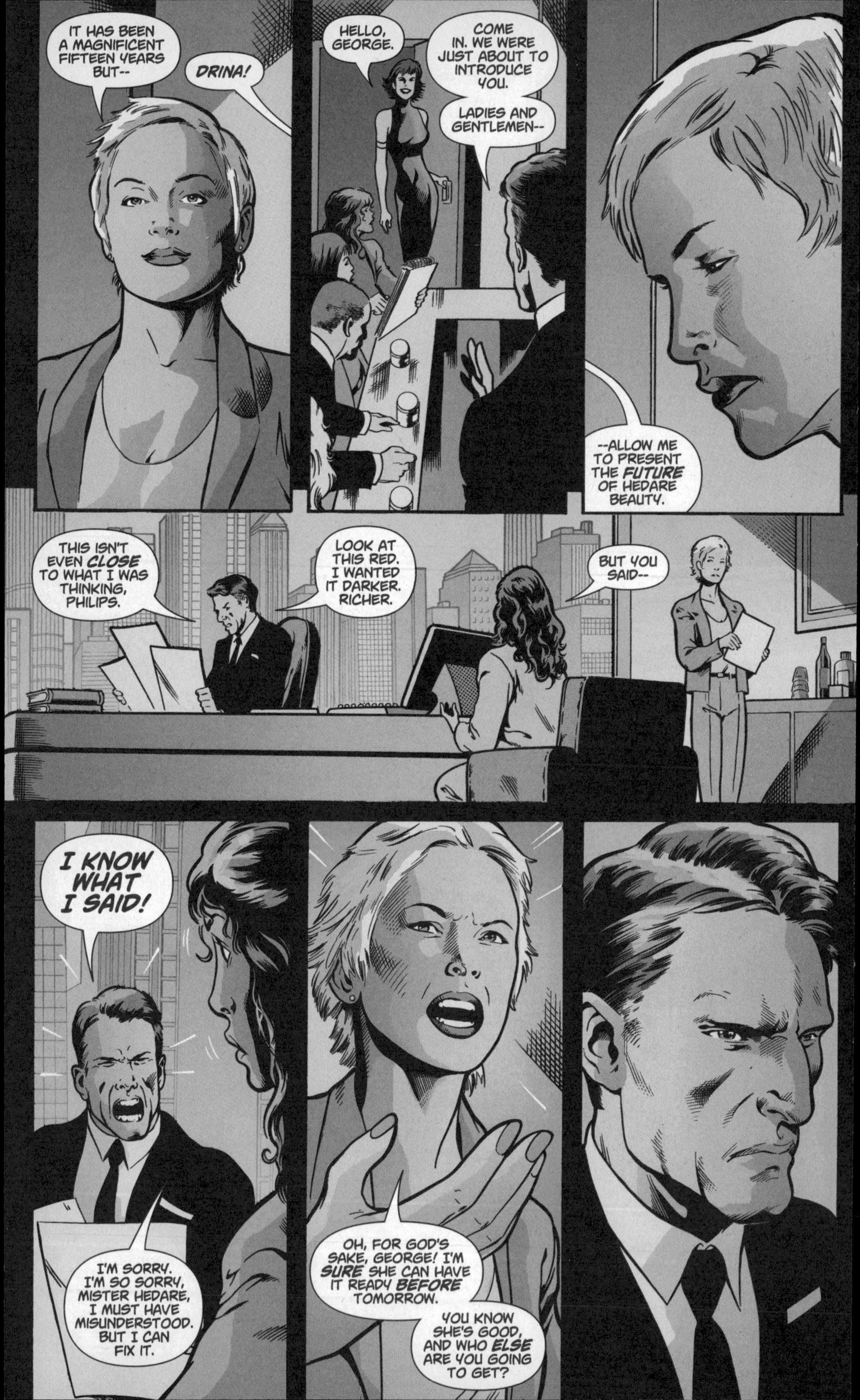
IT HAS BEEN A MAGNIFICENT FIFTEEN YEARS BUT--
DRINA!
HELLO, GEORGE.
COME IN. WE WERE JUST ABOUT TO INTRODUCE YOU.
LADIES AND GENTLEMEN--
--ALLOW ME TO PRESENT THE FUTURE OF HEDARE BEAUTY.
THIS ISN'T EVEN CLOSE TO WHAT I WAS THINKING, PHILIPS.
LOOK AT THIS RED. I WANTED IT DARKER. RICHER.
BUT YOU SAID--
I KNOW WHAT I SAID!
I'M SORRY. I'M SO SORRY, MISTER HEDARE, I MUST HAVE MISUNDERSTOOD. BUT I CAN FIX IT.
OH, FOR GOD'S SAKE, GEORGE! I'M SURE SHE CAN HAVE IT READY BEFORE TOMORROW.
YOU KNOW SHE'S GOOD, AND WHO ELSE ARE YOU GOING TO GET?

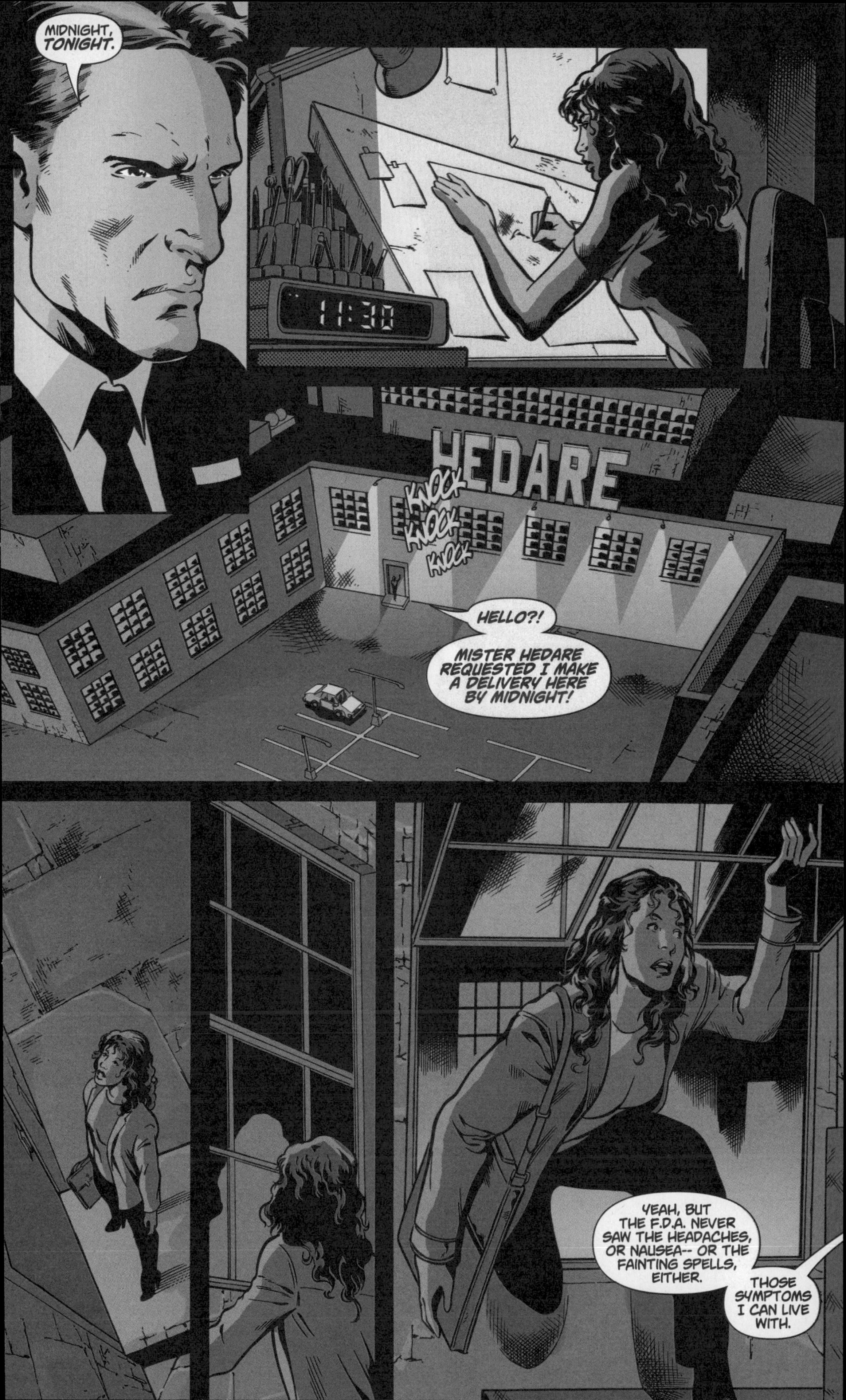
MIDNIGHT, TONIGHT.
11:30
HEDARE
KNOCK KNOCK KNOCK
HELLO?!
MISTER HEDARE REQUESTED I MAKE A DELIVERY HERE BY MIDNIGHT!
YEAH, BUT THE F.D.A. NEVER SAW THE HEADACHES, OR NAUSEA-- OR THE FAINTING SPELLS, EITHER.
THOSE SYMPTOMS I CAN LIVE WITH.

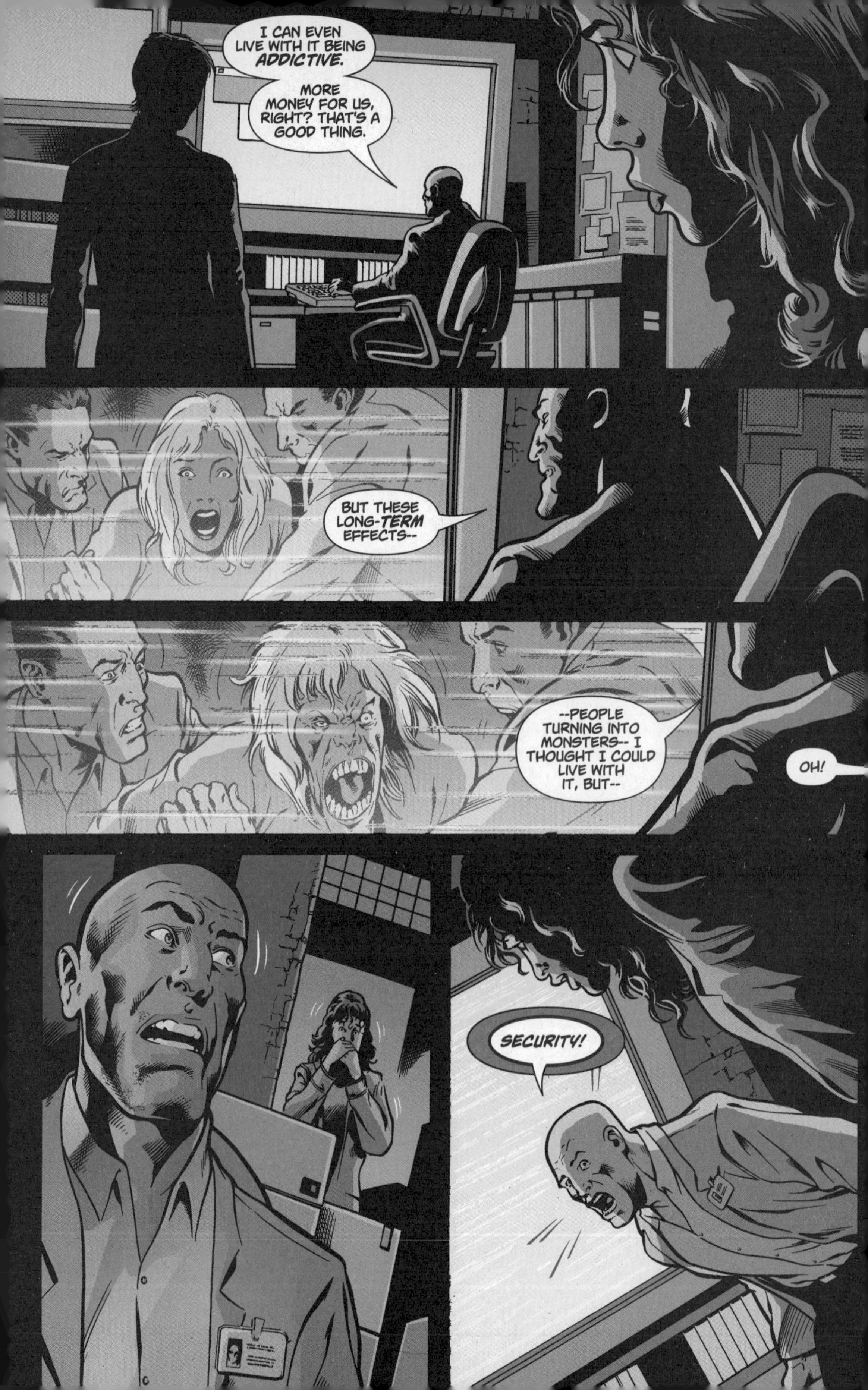
I CAN EVEN LIVE WITH IT BEING ADDICTIVE.
MORE MONEY FOR US, RIGHT? THAT'S A GOOD THING.
BUT THESE LONG-TERM EFFECTS--
--PEOPLE TURNING INTO MONSTERS-- I THOUGHT I COULD LIVE WITH IT, BUT--
OH!
SECURITY!

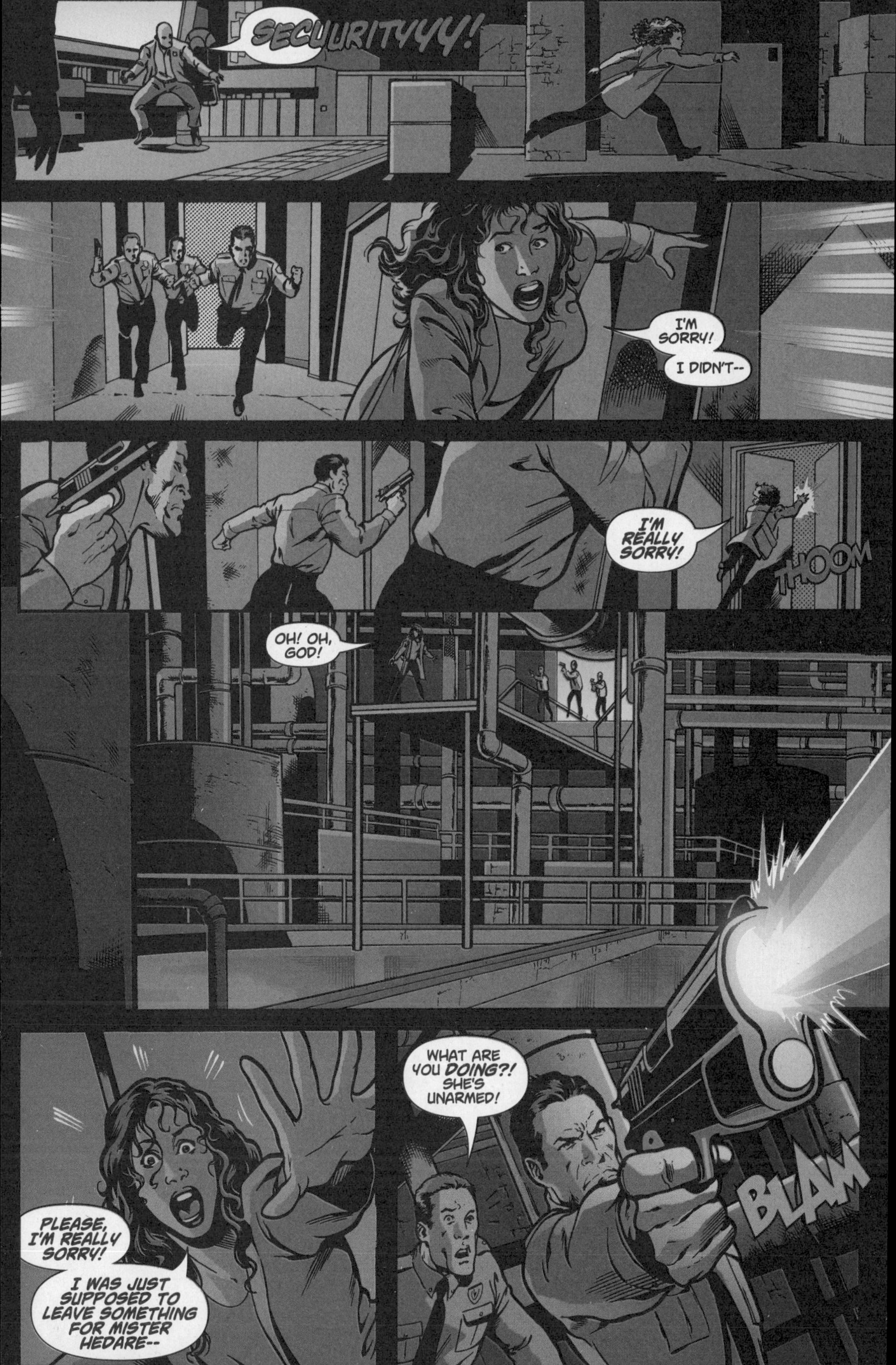
SECUUURITYYY!
I'M SORRY!
I DIDN'T--
I'M REALLY SORRY!
THOOM
OH! OH, GOD!
PLEASE, I'M REALLY SORRY!
I WAS JUST SUPPOSED TO LEAVE SOMETHING FOR MISTER HEDARE--
WHAT ARE YOU DOING?! SHE'S UNARMED!
BLAM

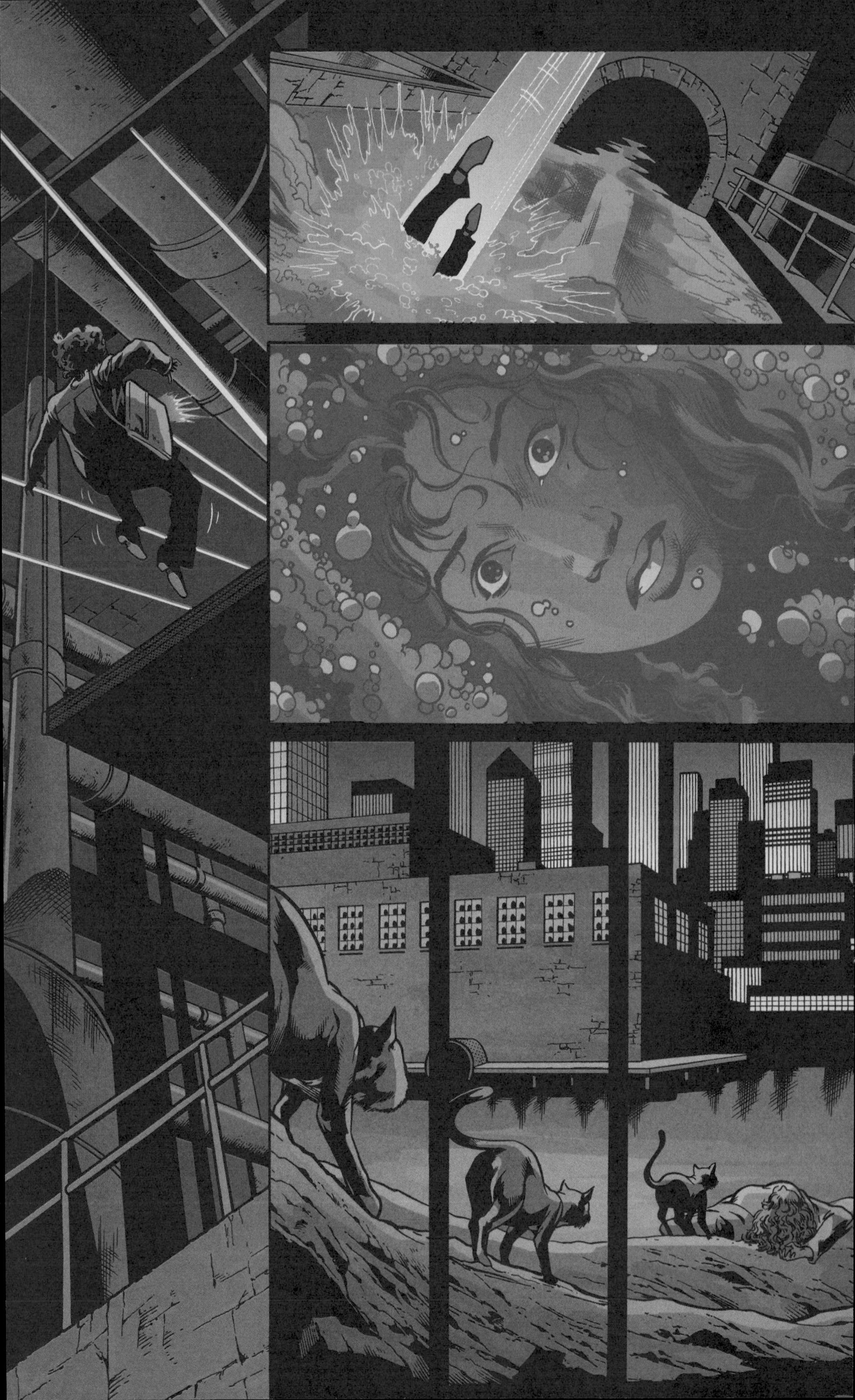

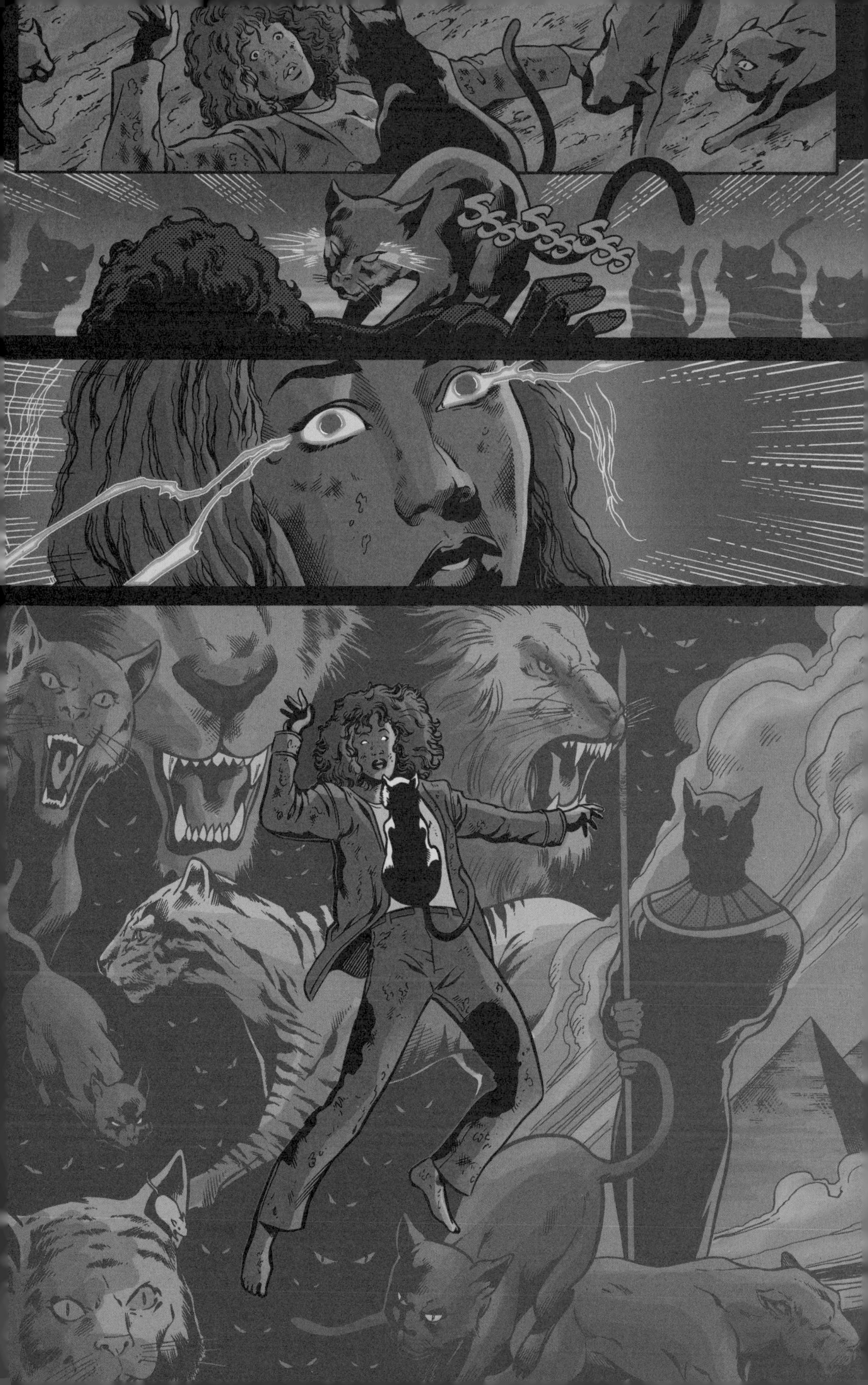
SSSSSSSS

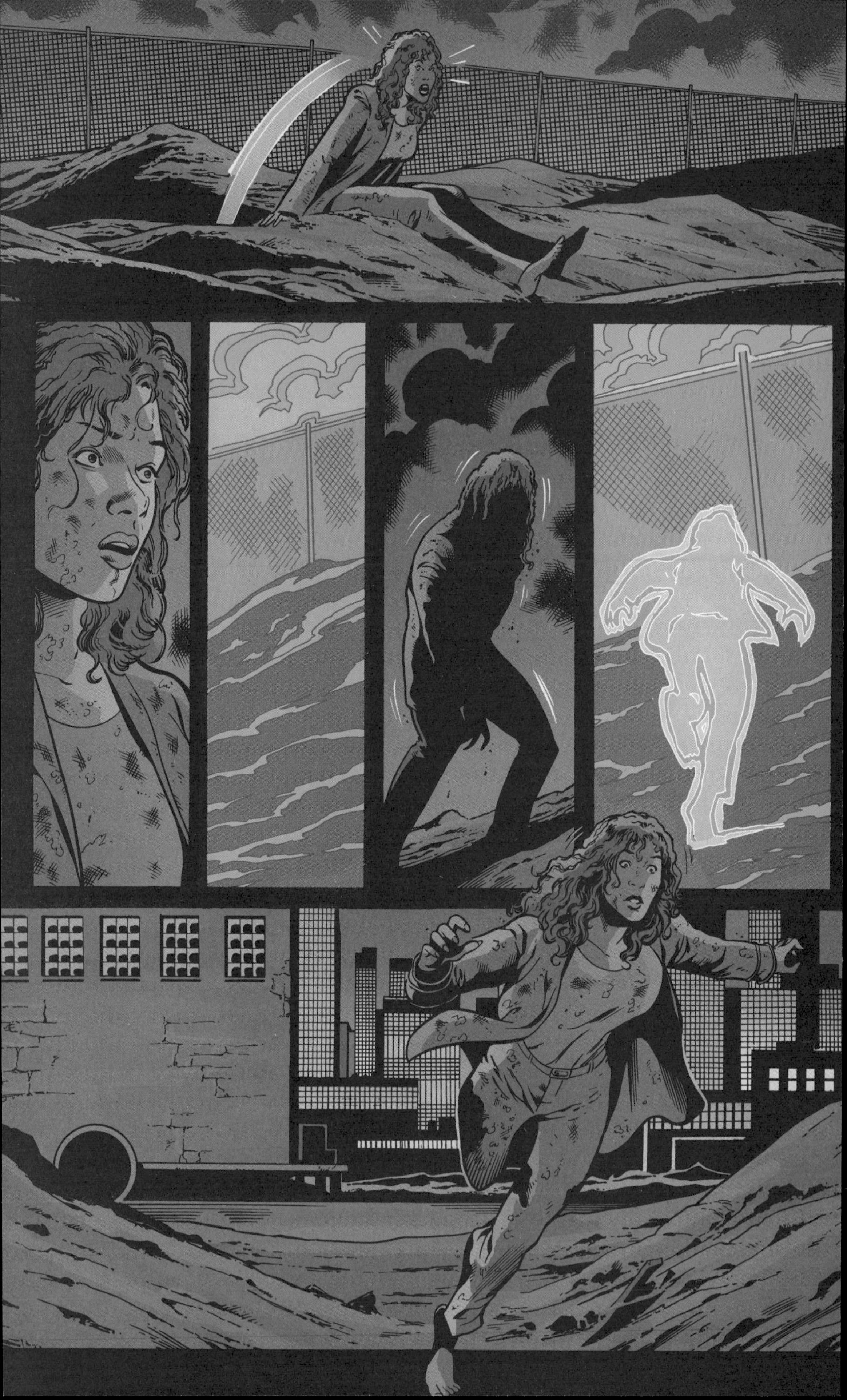

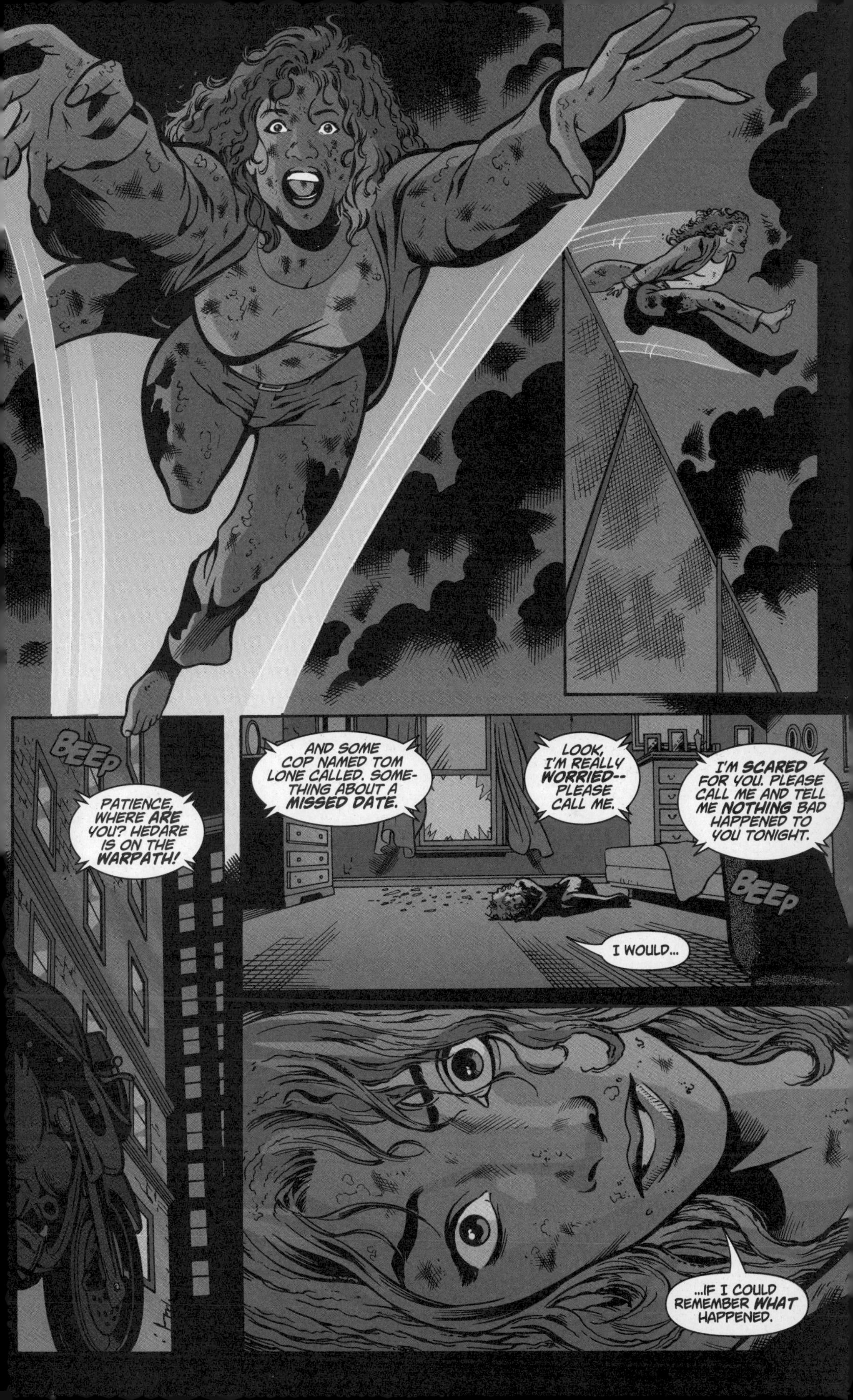
BEEP
PATIENCE, WHERE ARE YOU? HEDARE IS ON THE WARPATH!
AND SOME COP NAMED TOM LONE CALLED. SOMETHING ABOUT A MISSED DATE.
LOOK, I'M REALLY WORRIED-- PLEASE CALL ME.
I'M SCARED FOR YOU. PLEASE CALL ME AND TELL ME NOTHING BAD HAPPENED TO YOU TONIGHT.
BEEP
I WOULD...
...IF I COULD REMEMBER WHAT HAPPENED.

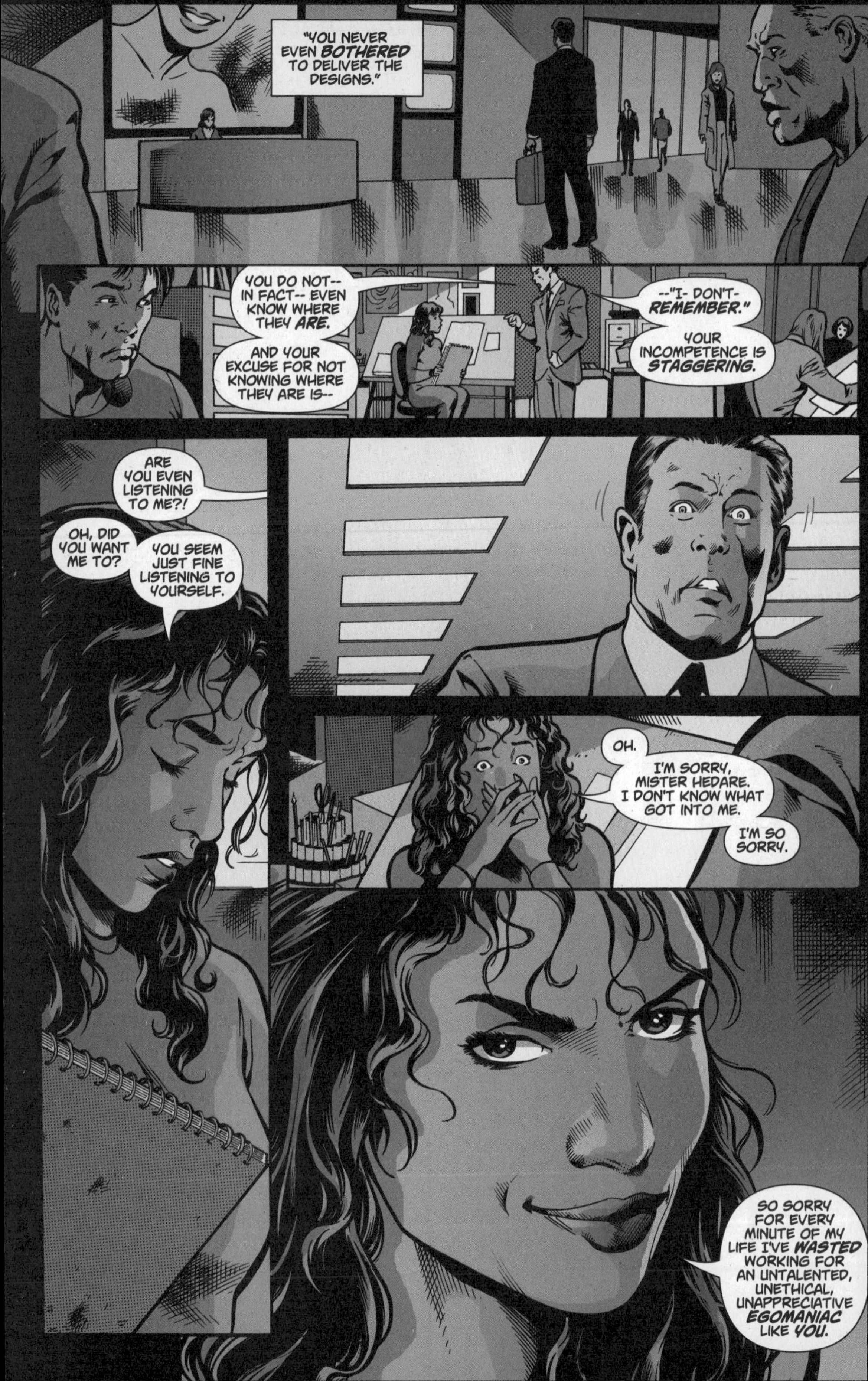
"YOU NEVER EVEN BOTHERED TO DELIVER THE DESIGNS."
YOU DO NOT-- IN FACT-- EVEN KNOW WHERE THEY ARE.
AND YOUR EXCUSE FOR NOT KNOWING WHERE THEY ARE IS--
--"I- DON'T- REMEMBER."
YOUR INCOMPETENCE IS STAGGERING.
ARE YOU EVEN LISTENING TO ME?!
OH, DID YOU WANT ME TO?
YOU SEEM JUST FINE LISTENING TO YOURSELF.
OH.
I'M SORRY, MISTER HEDARE. I DON'T KNOW WHAT GOT INTO ME.
I'M SO SORRY.
SO SORRY FOR EVERY MINUTE OF MY LIFE I'VE WASTED WORKING FOR AN UNTALENTED, UNETHICAL, UNAPPRECIATIVE EGOMANIAC LIKE YOU.

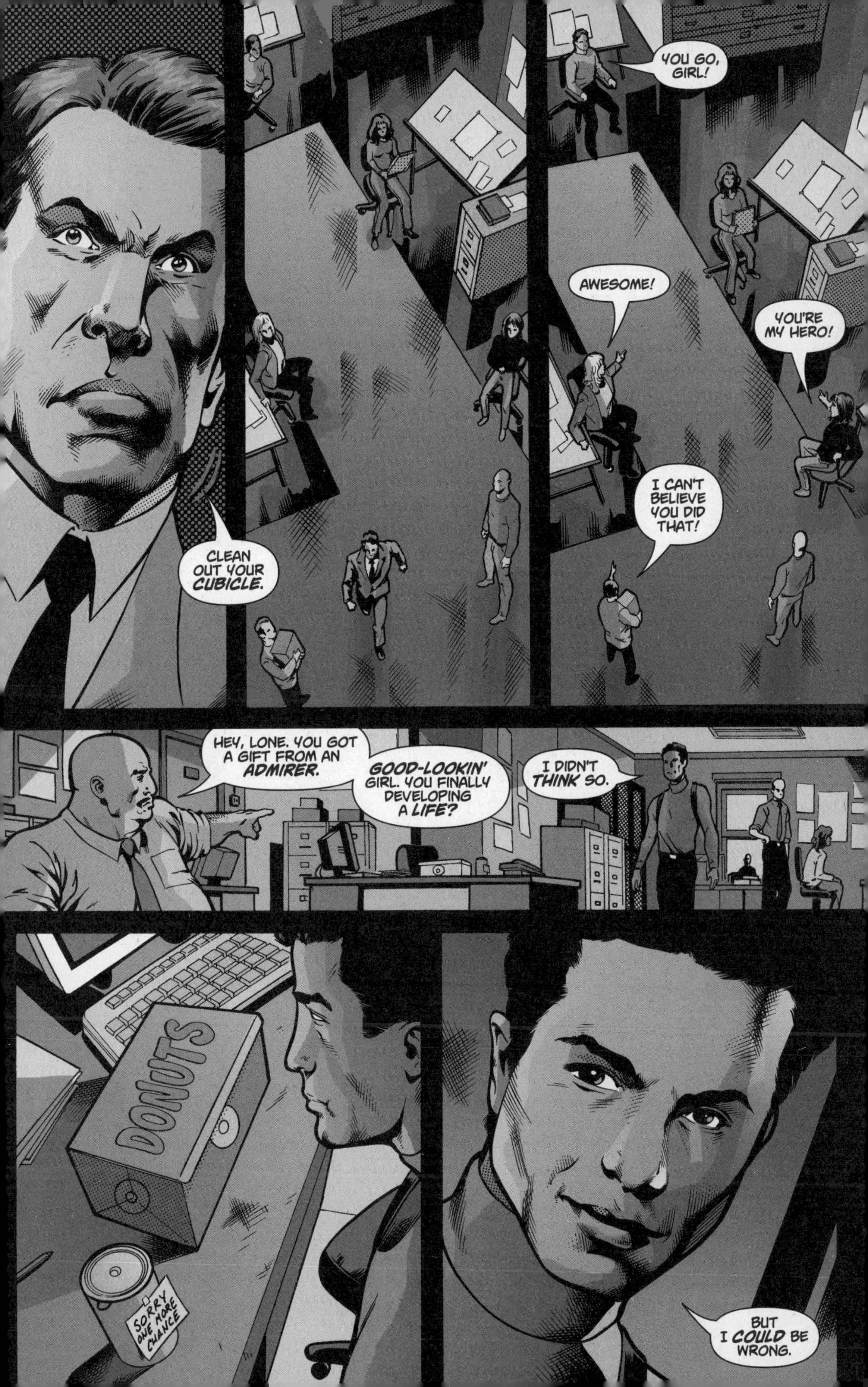
CLEAN OUT YOUR CUBICLE.
YOU GO, GIRL!
AWESOME!
YOU'RE MY HERO!
I CAN'T BELIEVE YOU DID THAT!
HEY, LONE. YOU GOT A GIFT FROM AN ADMIRER.
GOOD-LOOKIN' GIRL. YOU FINALLY DEVELOPING A LIFE?
I DIDN'T THINK SO.
DONUTS
SORRY ONE MORE CHANCE
BUT I COULD BE WRONG.

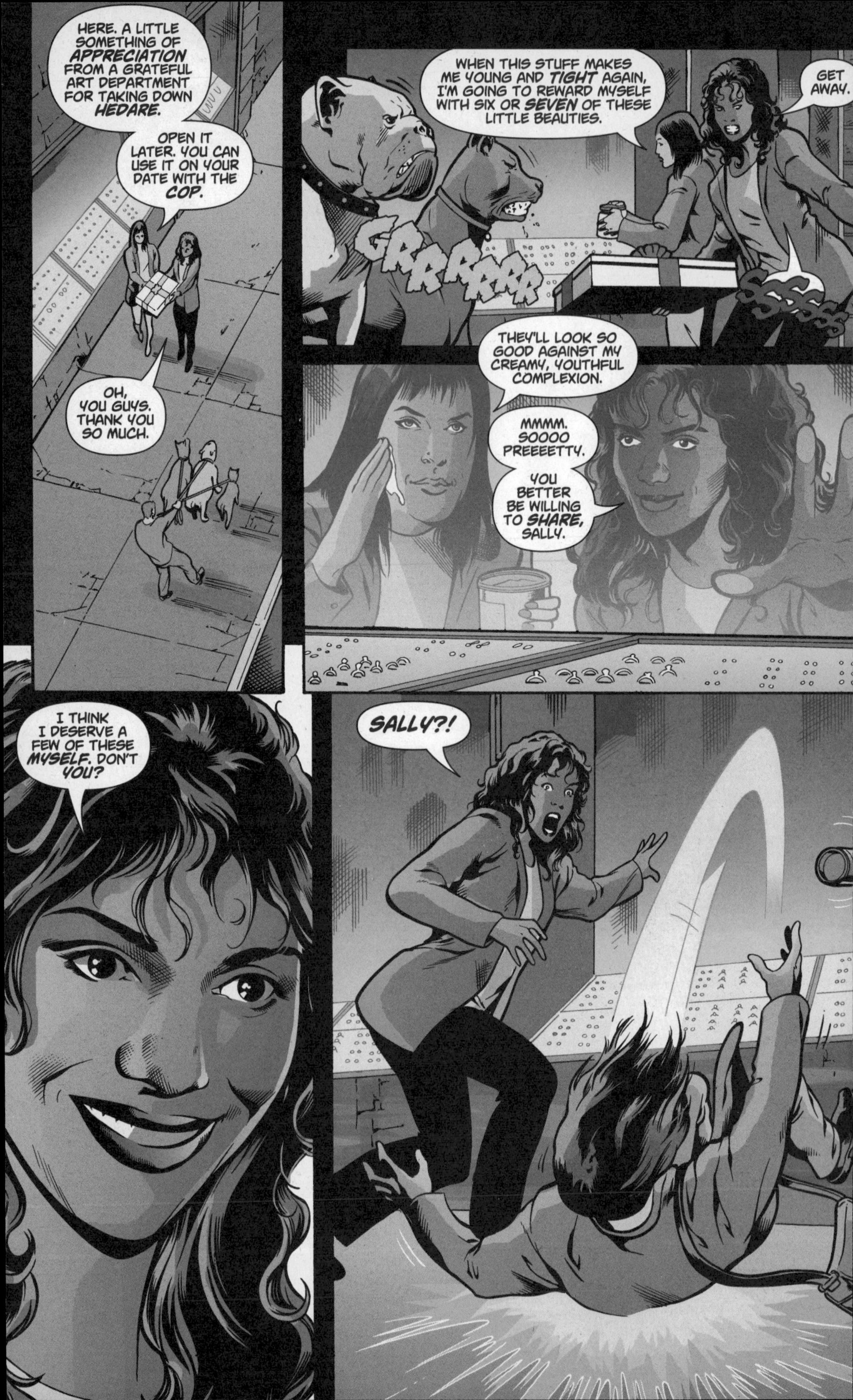
HERE. A LITTLE SOMETHING OF APPRECIATION FROM A GRATEFUL ART DEPARTMENT FOR TAKING DOWN HEDARE.
OPEN IT LATER. YOU CAN USE IT ON YOUR DATE WITH THE COP.
OH, YOU GUYS. THANK YOU SO MUCH.
WHEN THIS STUFF MAKES ME YOUNG AND TIGHT AGAIN, I'M GOING TO REWARD MYSELF WITH SIX OR SEVEN OF THESE LITTLE BEAUTIES.
GET AWAY.
GRRRRRR
SSSSSS
THEY'LL LOOK SO GOOD AGAINST MY CREAMY, YOUTHFUL COMPLEXION.
MMMM. SOOOO PREEEETTY.
YOU BETTER BE WILLING TO SHARE, SALLY.
I THINK I DESERVE A FEW OF THESE MYSELF. DON'T YOU?
SALLY?!

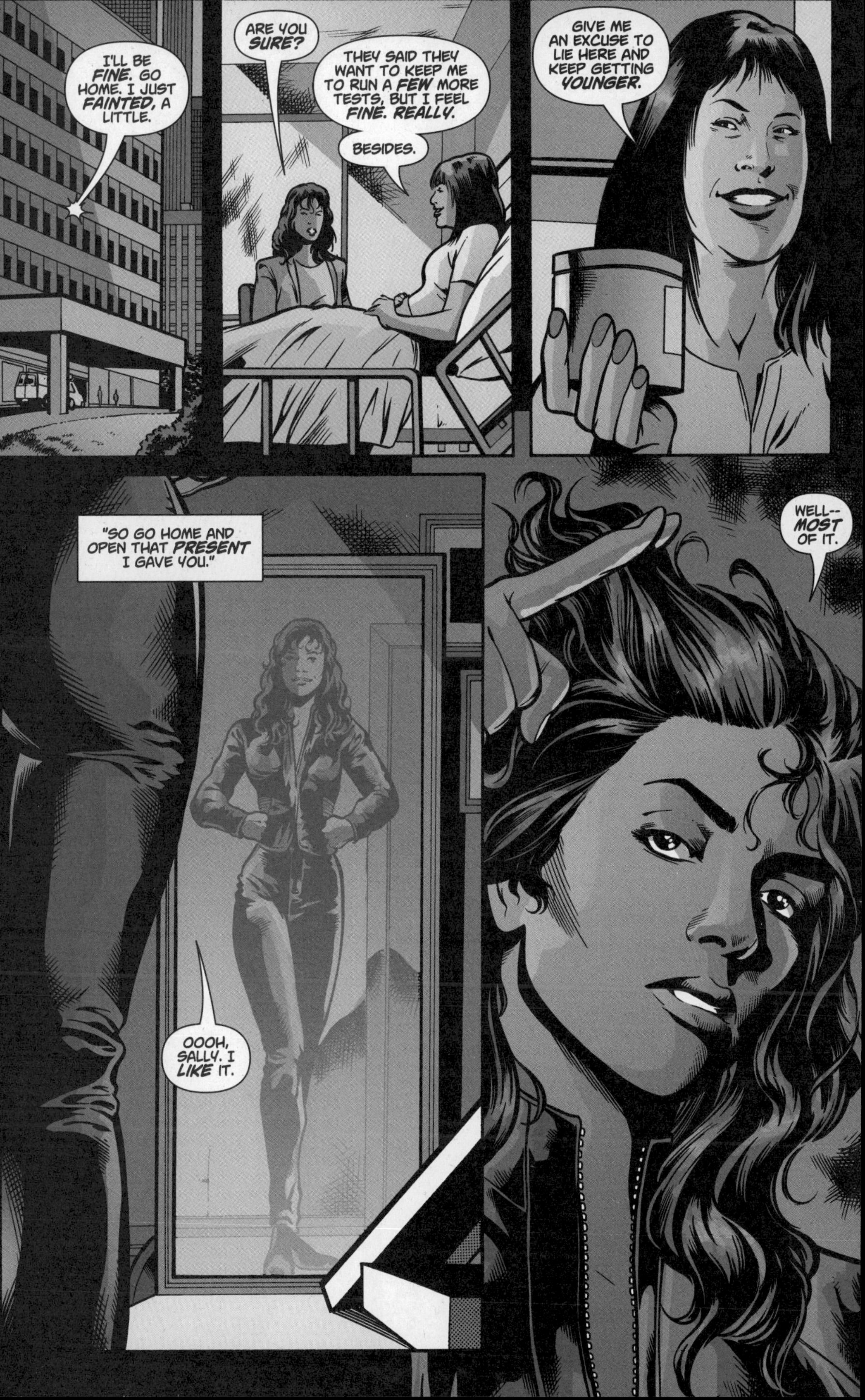
I'LL BE FINE. GO HOME. I JUST FAINTED, A LITTLE.
ARE YOU SURE?
THEY SAID THEY WANT TO KEEP ME TO RUN A FEW MORE TESTS, BUT I FEEL FINE. REALLY.
BESIDES.
GIVE ME AN EXCUSE TO LIE HERE AND KEEP GETTING YOUNGER.
"SO GO HOME AND OPEN THAT PRESENT I GAVE YOU."
OOOH, SALLY. I LIKE IT.
WELL-- MOST OF IT.

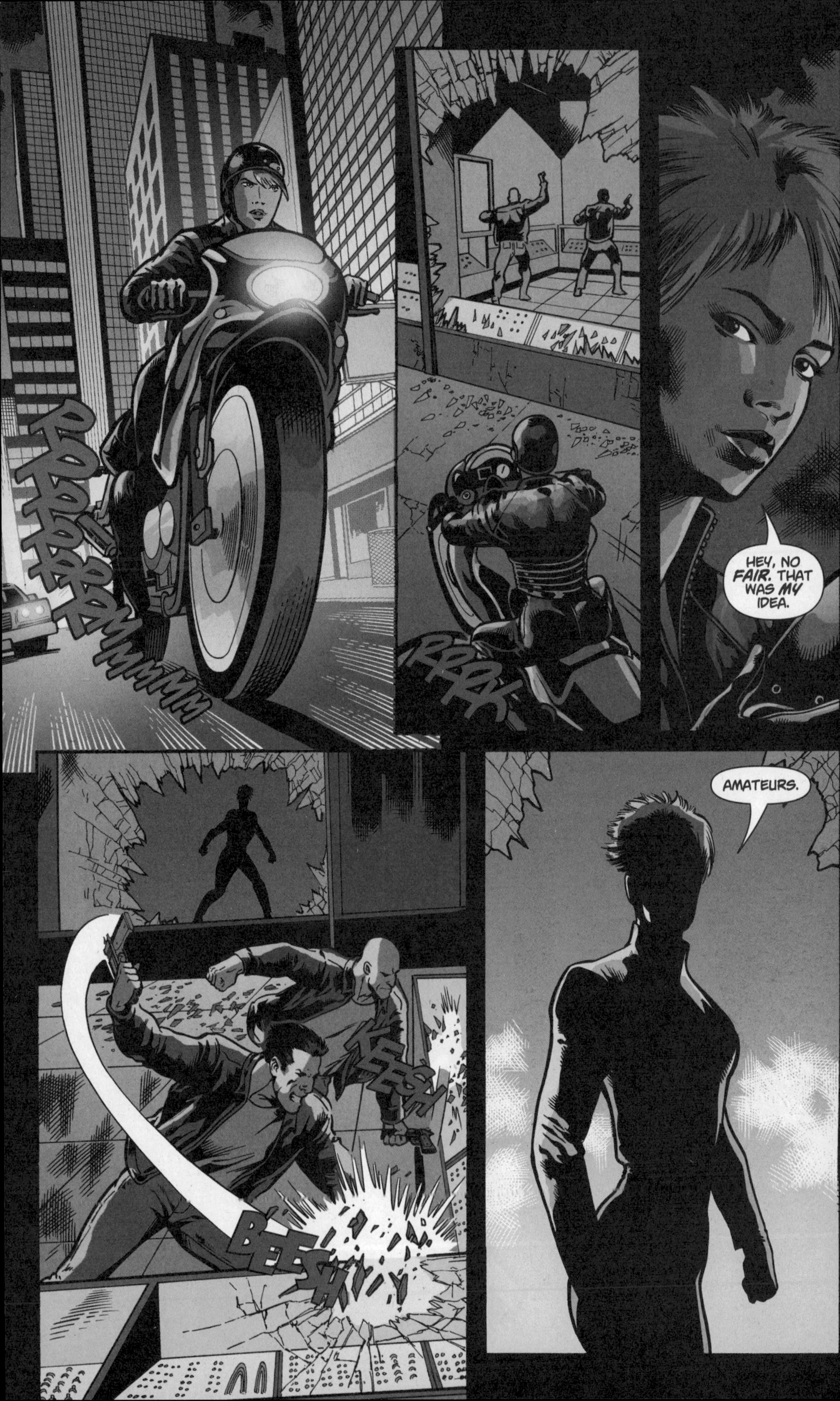
RRRRRRRMMMMMM
RRRK
HEY, NO FAIR. THAT WAS MY IDEA.
KEESH
BEESH
AMATEURS.

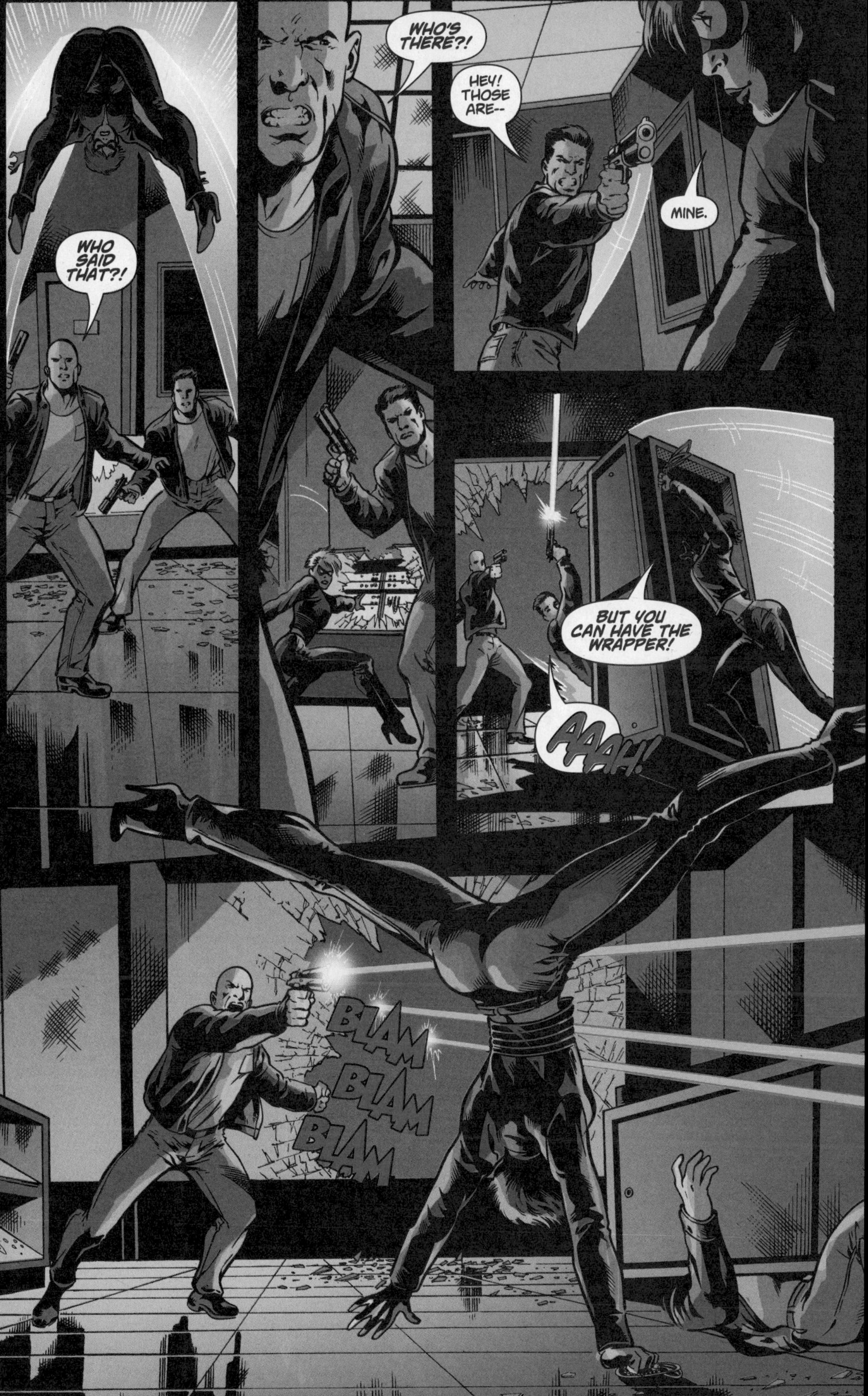
WHO SAID THAT?!
WHO'S THERE?!
HEY! THOSE ARE--
MINE.
BUT YOU CAN HAVE THE WRAPPER!
AAAH!
BLAM
BLAM
BLAM

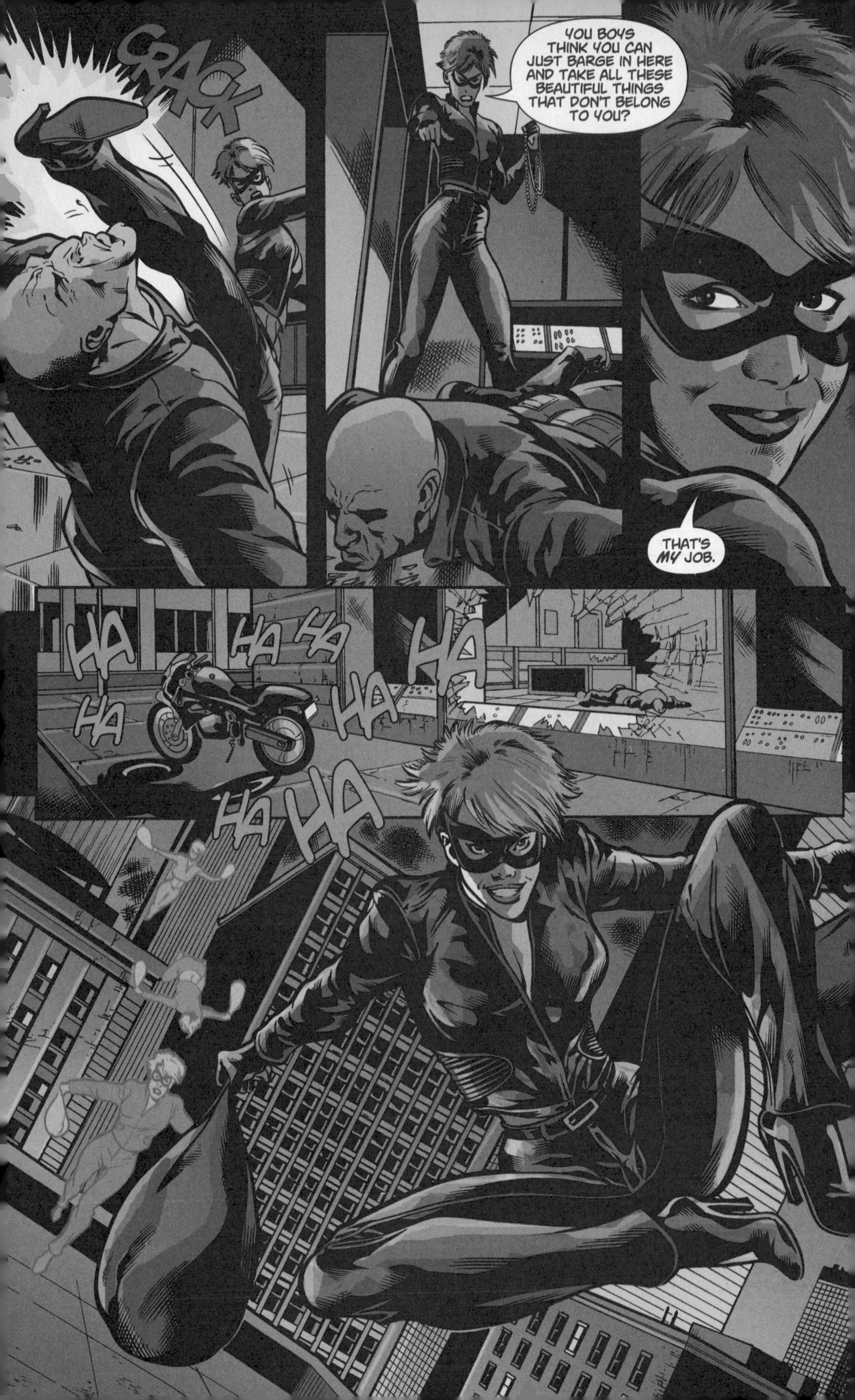
CRACK
YOU BOYS THINK YOU CAN JUST BARGE IN HERE AND TAKE ALL THESE BEAUTIFUL THINGS THAT DON'T BELONG TO YOU?
THAT'S MY JOB.
HA HA HA HA HA HA HA HA HA HA

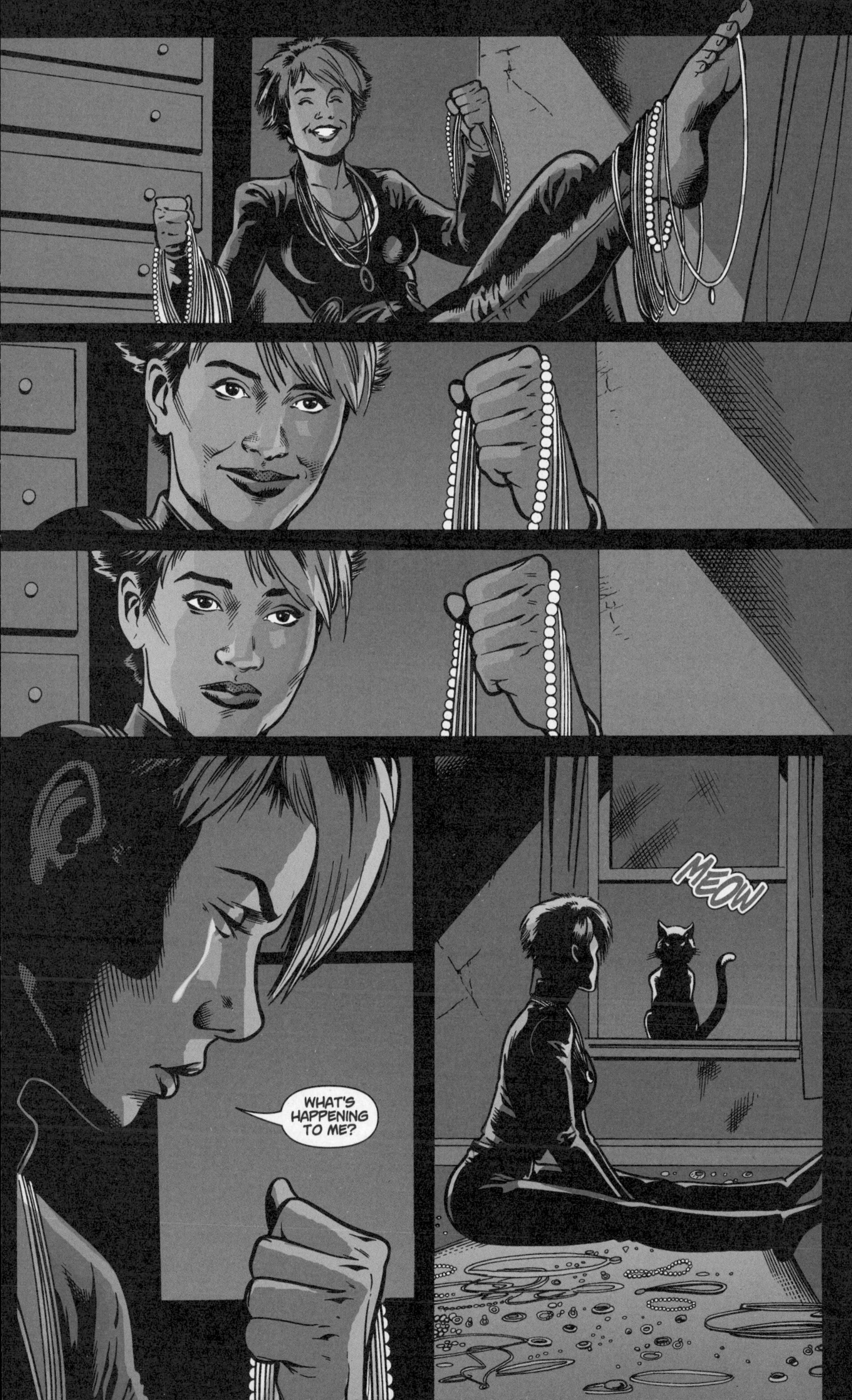
WHAT'S HAPPENING TO ME?
MEOW

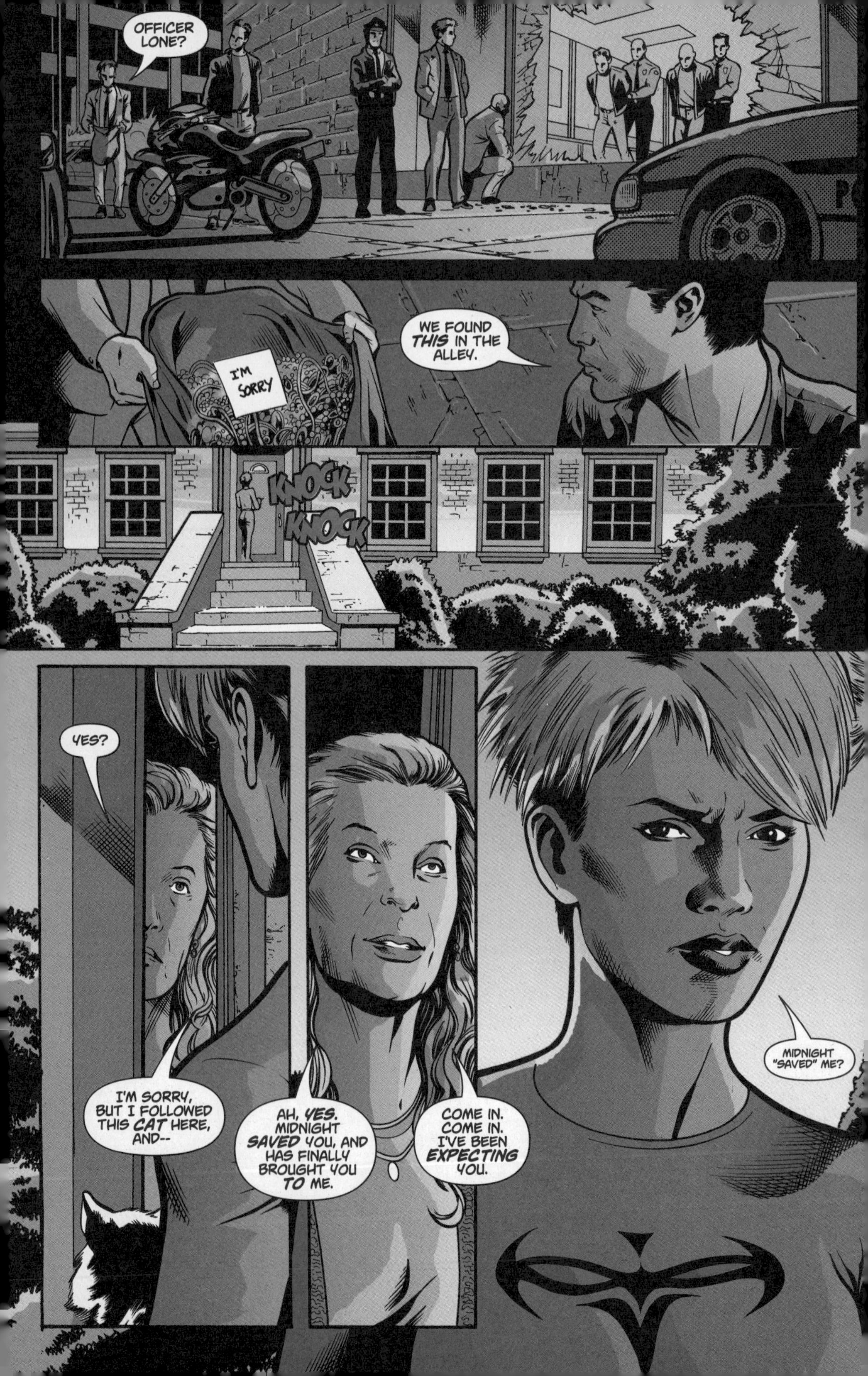
OFFICER LONE?
WE FOUND THIS IN THE ALLEY.
I'M SORRY
KNOCK KNOCK
YES?
I'M SORRY, BUT I FOLLOWED THIS CAT HERE, AND--
AH, YES. MIDNIGHT SAVED YOU, AND HAS FINALLY BROUGHT YOU TO ME.
COME IN. COME IN. I'VE BEEN EXPECTING YOU.
MIDNIGHT "SAVED" ME?

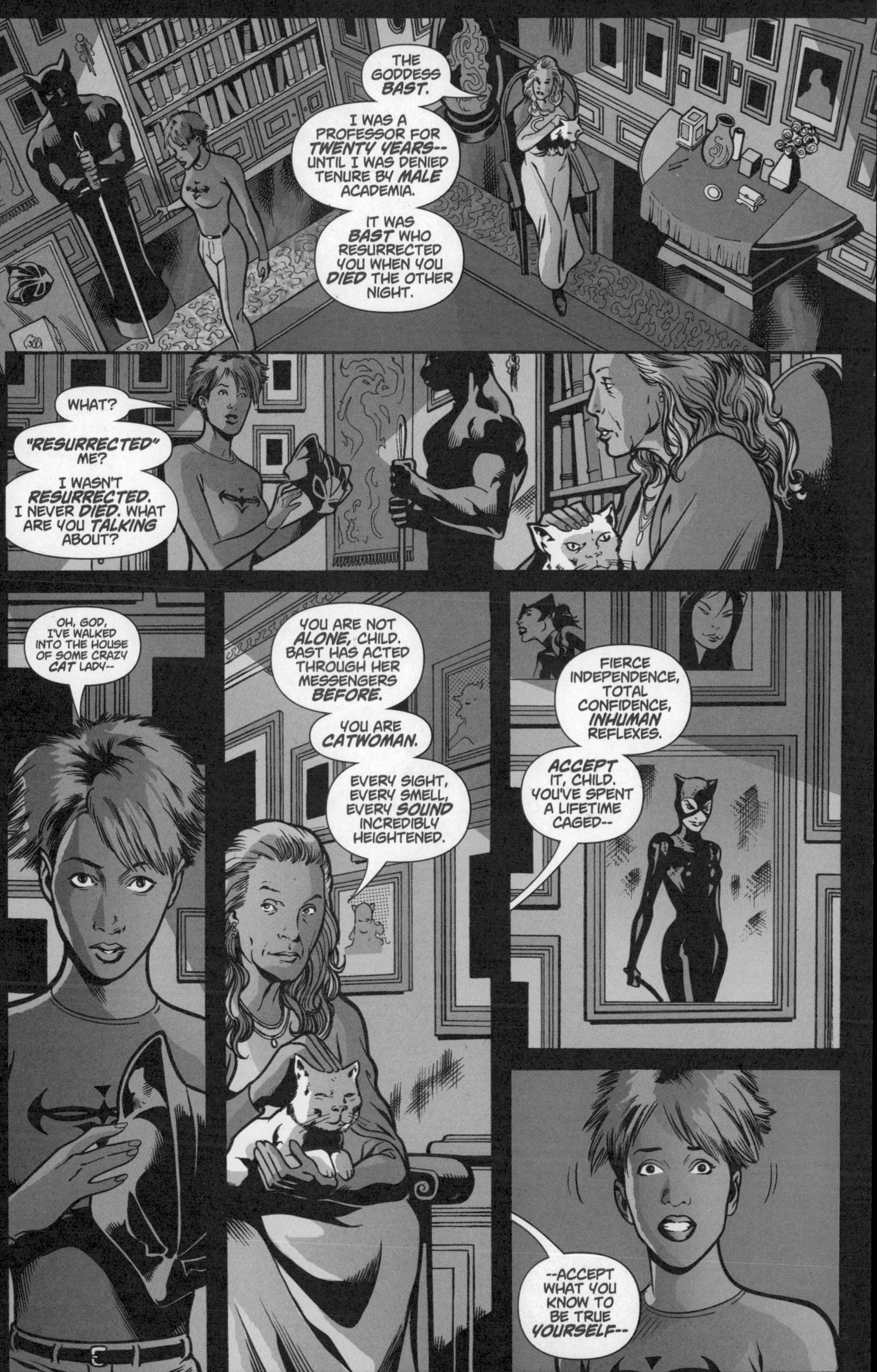
THE GODDESS BAST.
I WAS A PROFESSOR FOR TWENTY YEARS-- UNTIL I WAS DENIED TENURE BY MALE ACADEMIA.
IT WAS BAST WHO RESURRECTED YOU WHEN YOU DIED THE OTHER NIGHT.
WHAT?
"RESURRECTED" ME?
I WASN'T RESURRECTED. I NEVER DIED. WHAT ARE YOU TALKING ABOUT?
OH, GOD, I'VE WALKED INTO THE HOUSE OF SOME CRAZY CAT LADY--
YOU ARE NOT ALONE, CHILD. BAST HAS ACTED THROUGH HER MESSENGERS BEFORE.
YOU ARE CATWOMAN.
EVERY SIGHT, EVERY SMELL, EVERY SOUND INCREDIBLY HEIGHTENED.
FIERCE INDEPENDENCE, TOTAL CONFIDENCE, INHUMAN REFLEXES.
ACCEPT IT, CHILD. YOU'VE SPENT A LIFETIME CAGED--
--ACCEPT WHAT YOU KNOW TO BE TRUE YOURSELF--

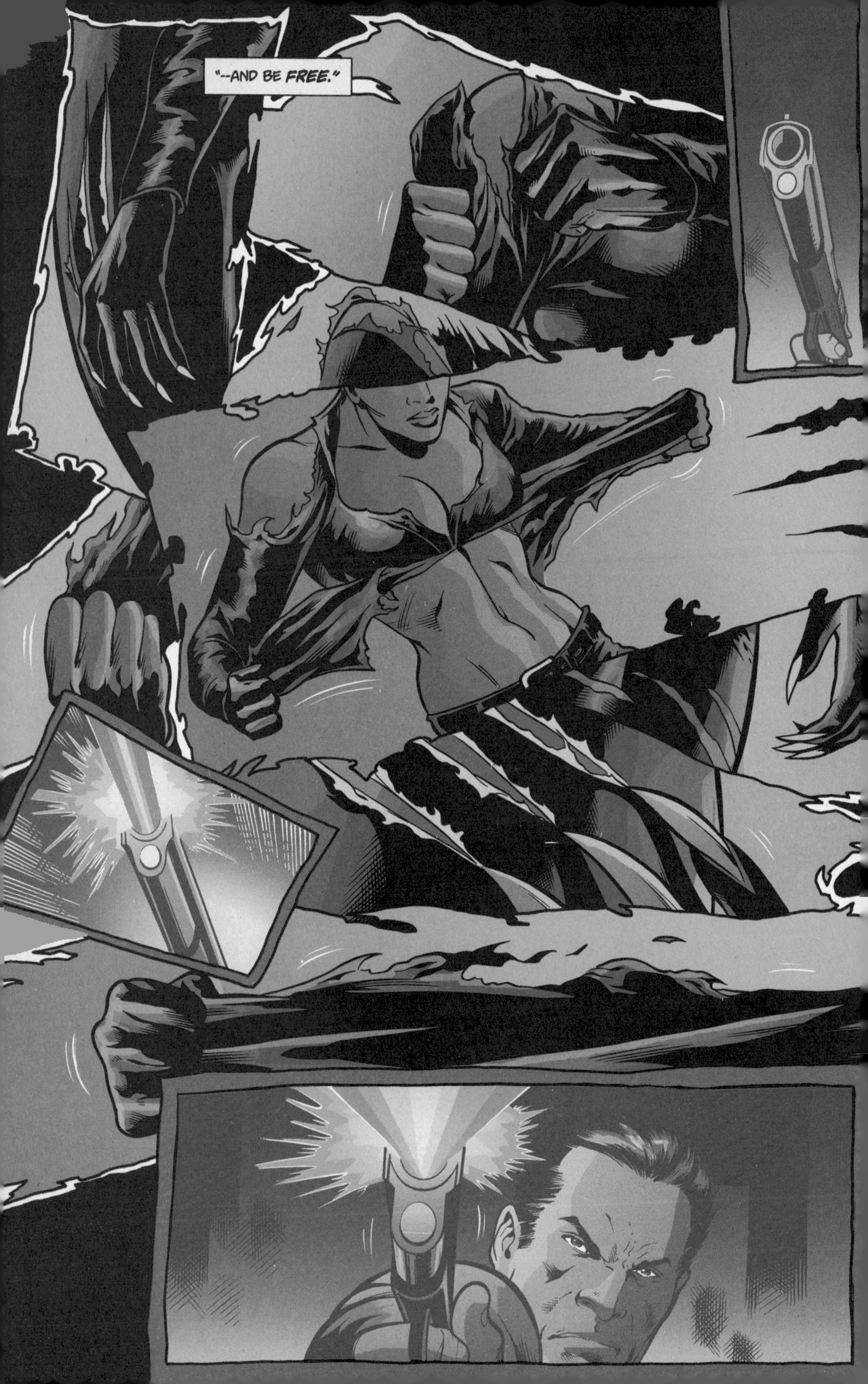
"--AND BE FREE."

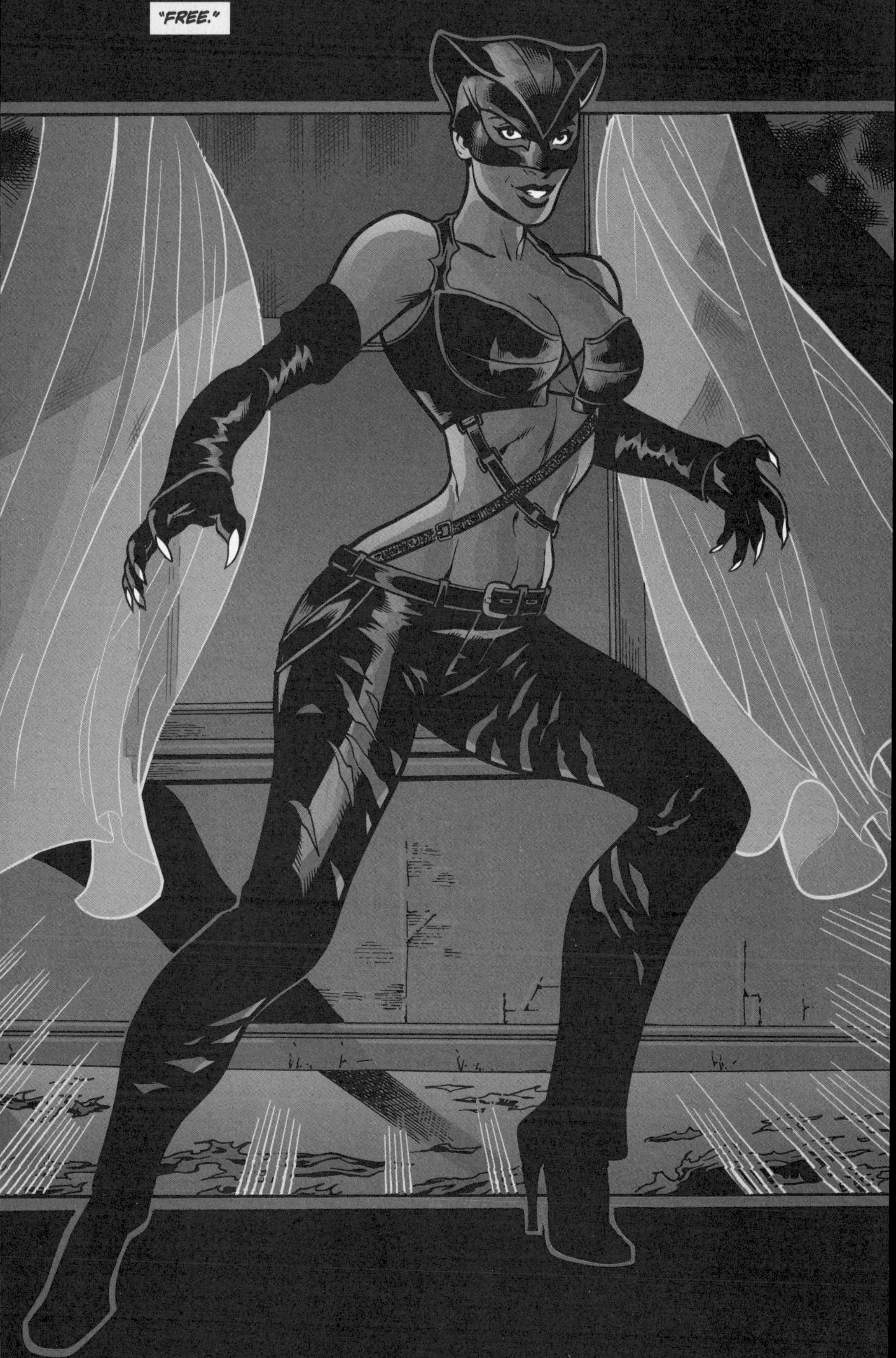
"FREE."

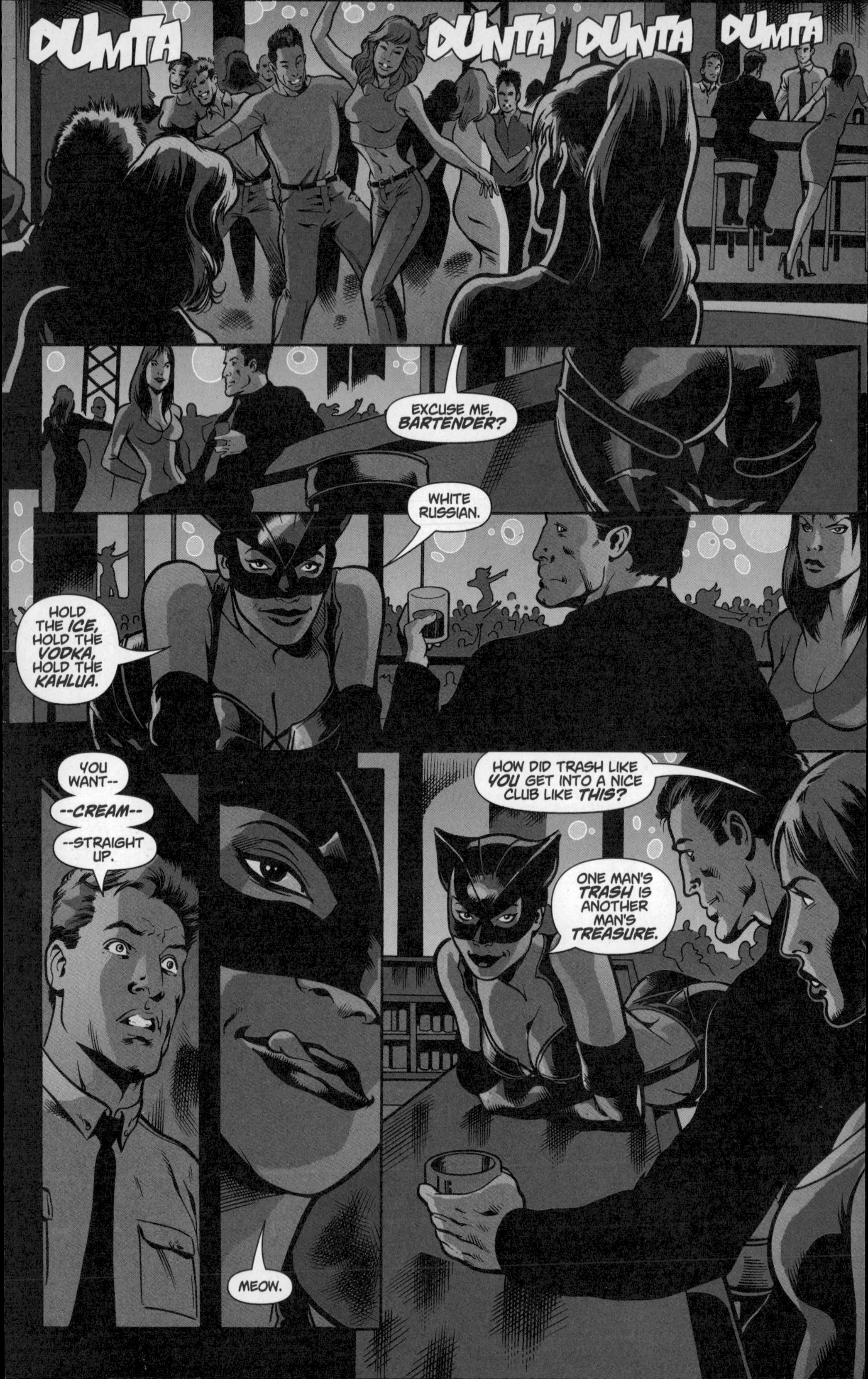
DUMTA DUNTA DUNTA DUMTA
EXCUSE ME, BARTENDER?
WHITE RUSSIAN.
HOLD THE ICE, HOLD THE VODKA, HOLD THE KAHLUA.
YOU WANT--
--CREAM--
--STRAIGHT UP.
MEOW.
HOW DID TRASH LIKE YOU GET INTO A NICE CLUB LIKE THIS?
ONE MAN'S TRASH IS ANOTHER MAN'S TREASURE.

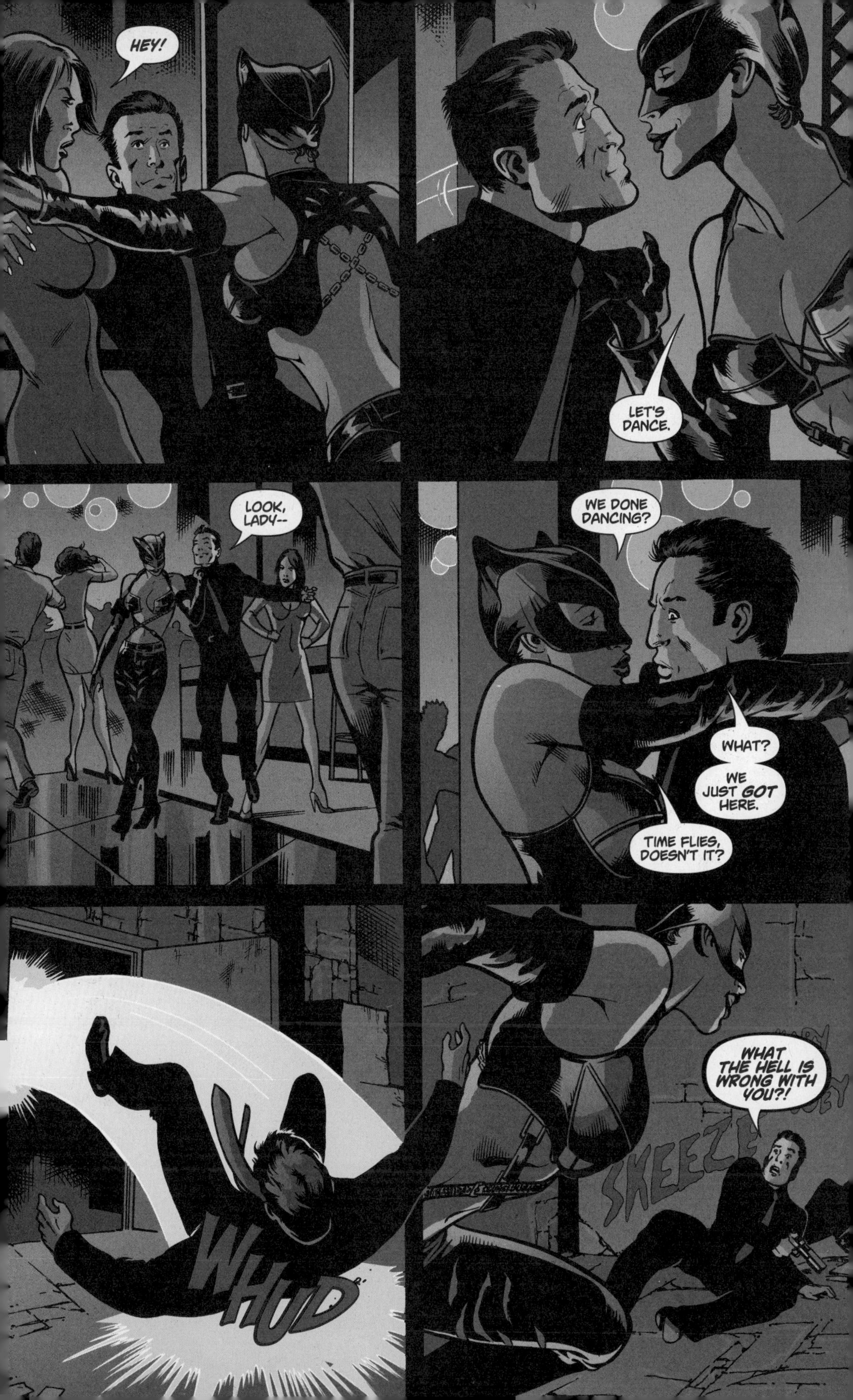
HEY!
LET'S DANCE.
LOOK, LADY--
WE DONE DANCING?
WHAT?
WE JUST GOT HERE.
TIME FLIES, DOESN'T IT?
WHUD
SKEEZE
WHAT THE HELL IS WRONG WITH YOU?!

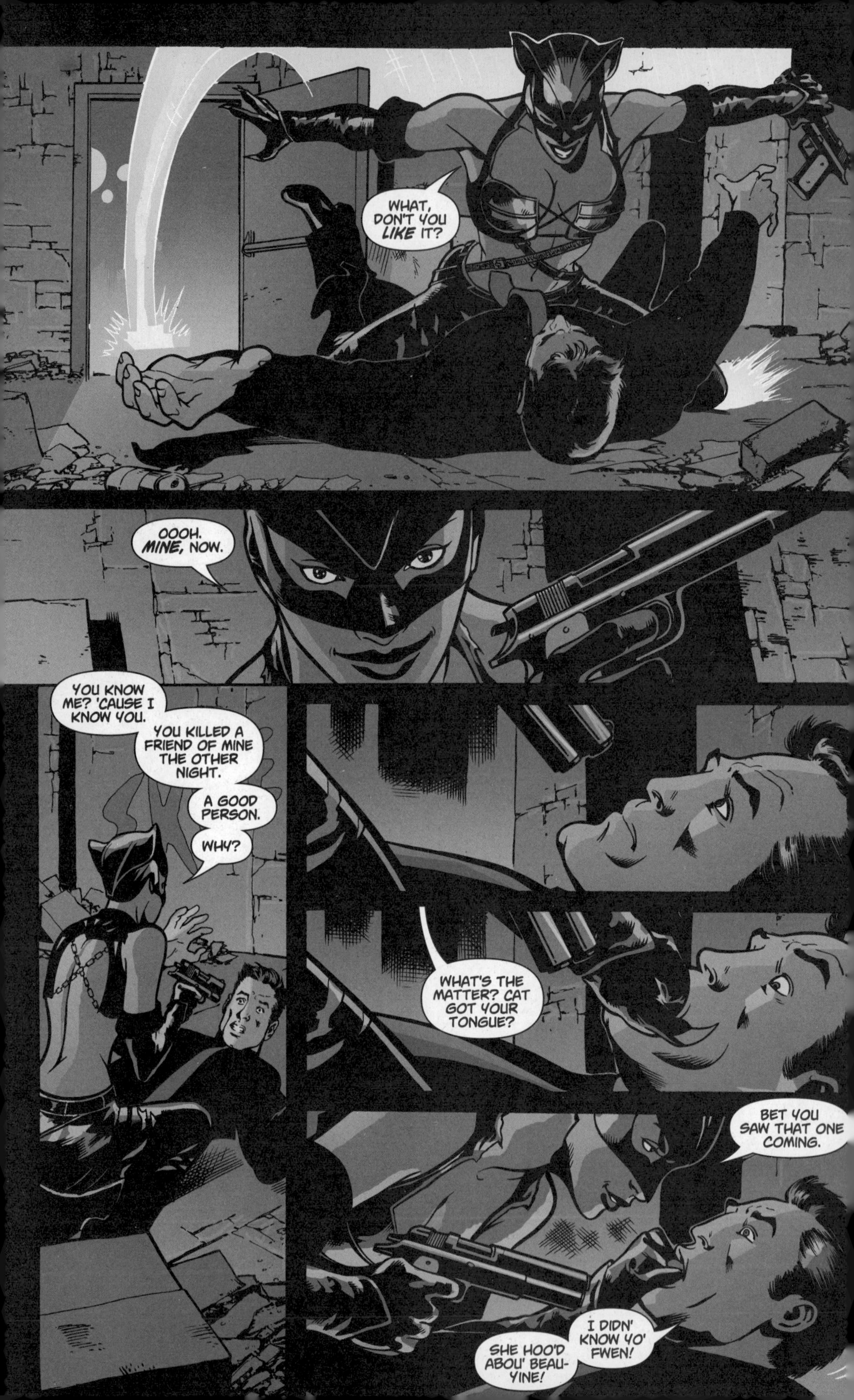
WHAT, DON'T YOU *LIKE* IT?
OOOH. *MINE,* NOW.
YOU KNOW ME? 'CAUSE I KNOW YOU.
YOU KILLED A FRIEND OF MINE THE OTHER NIGHT.
A GOOD PERSON.
WHY?
WHAT'S THE MATTER? CAT GOT YOUR TONGUE?
BET YOU SAW THAT ONE COMING.
I DIDN' KNOW YO' FWEN!
SHE HOO'D ABOU' BEAU-YINE!

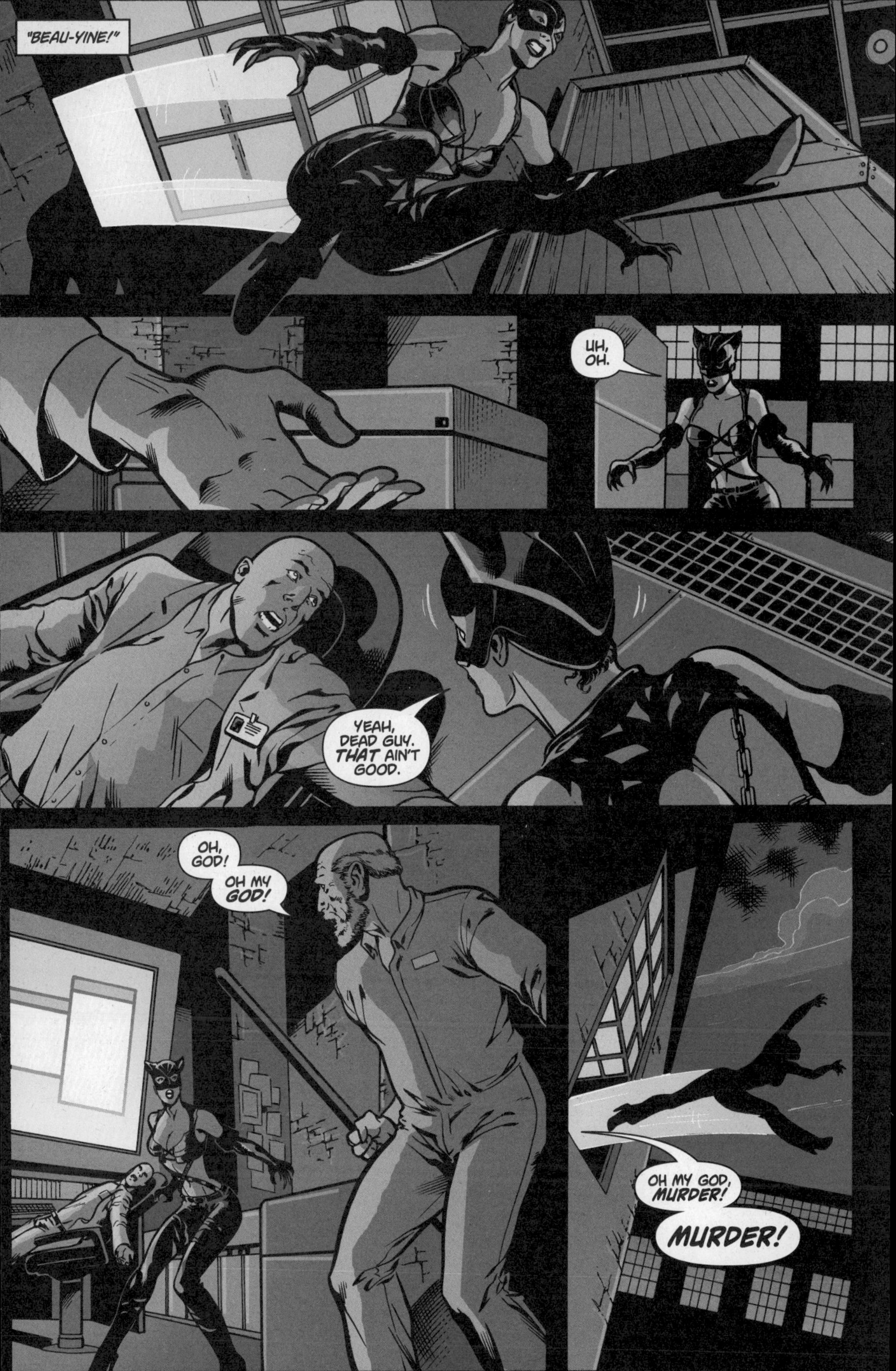

"BEAU-YINE!"
UH, OH.
YEAH, DEAD GUY. THAT AIN'T GOOD.
OH, GOD!
OH MY GOD!
OH MY GOD, MURDER!
MURDER!

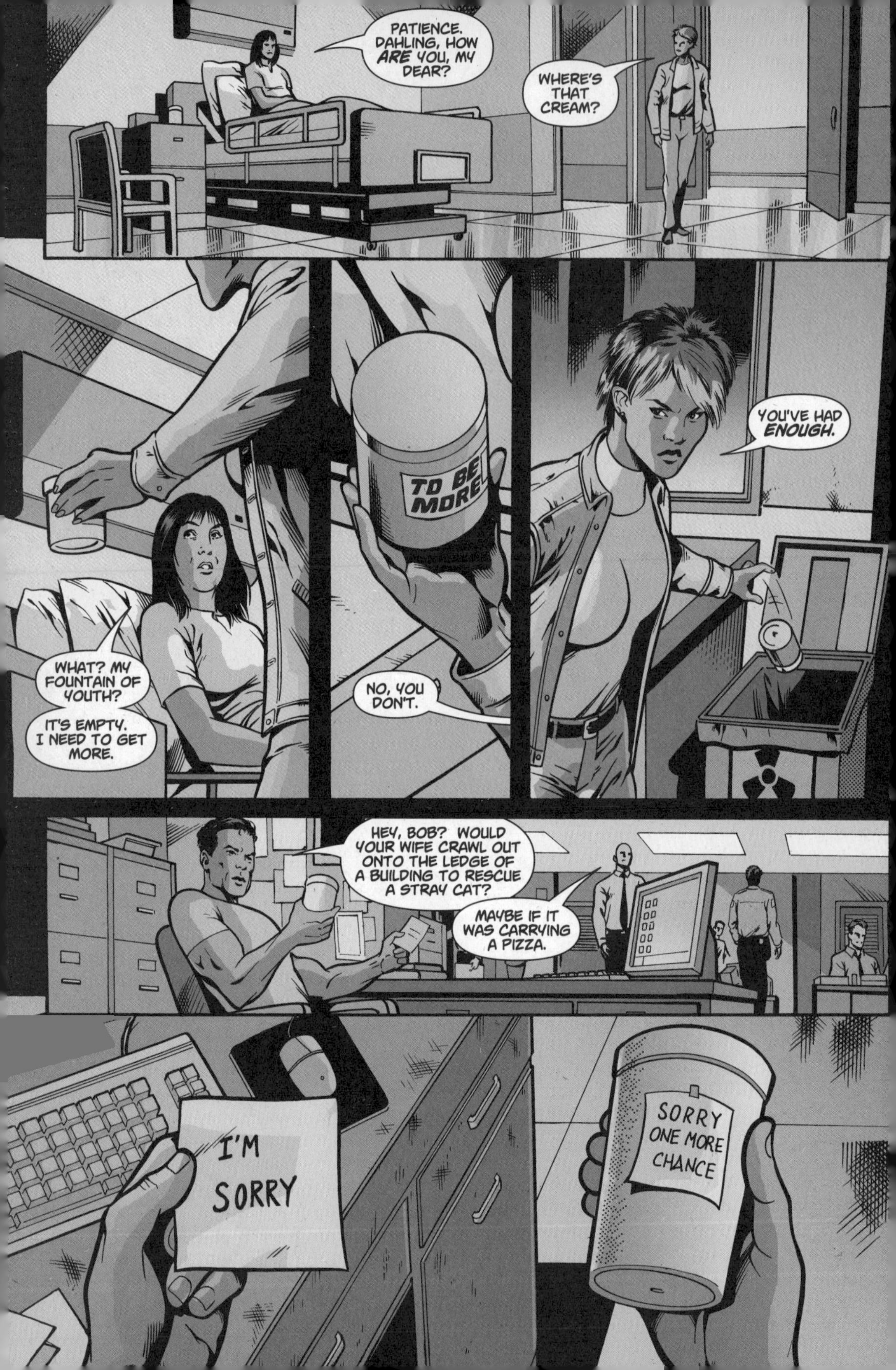
PATIENCE. DAHLING, HOW ARE YOU, MY DEAR?
WHERE'S THAT CREAM?
WHAT? MY FOUNTAIN OF YOUTH?
IT'S EMPTY. I NEED TO GET MORE.
TO BE MORE
NO, YOU DON'T.
YOU'VE HAD ENOUGH.
HEY, BOB? WOULD YOUR WIFE CRAWL OUT ONTO THE LEDGE OF A BUILDING TO RESCUE A STRAY CAT?
MAYBE IF IT WAS CARRYING A PIZZA.
I'M SORRY
SORRY ONE MORE CHANCE

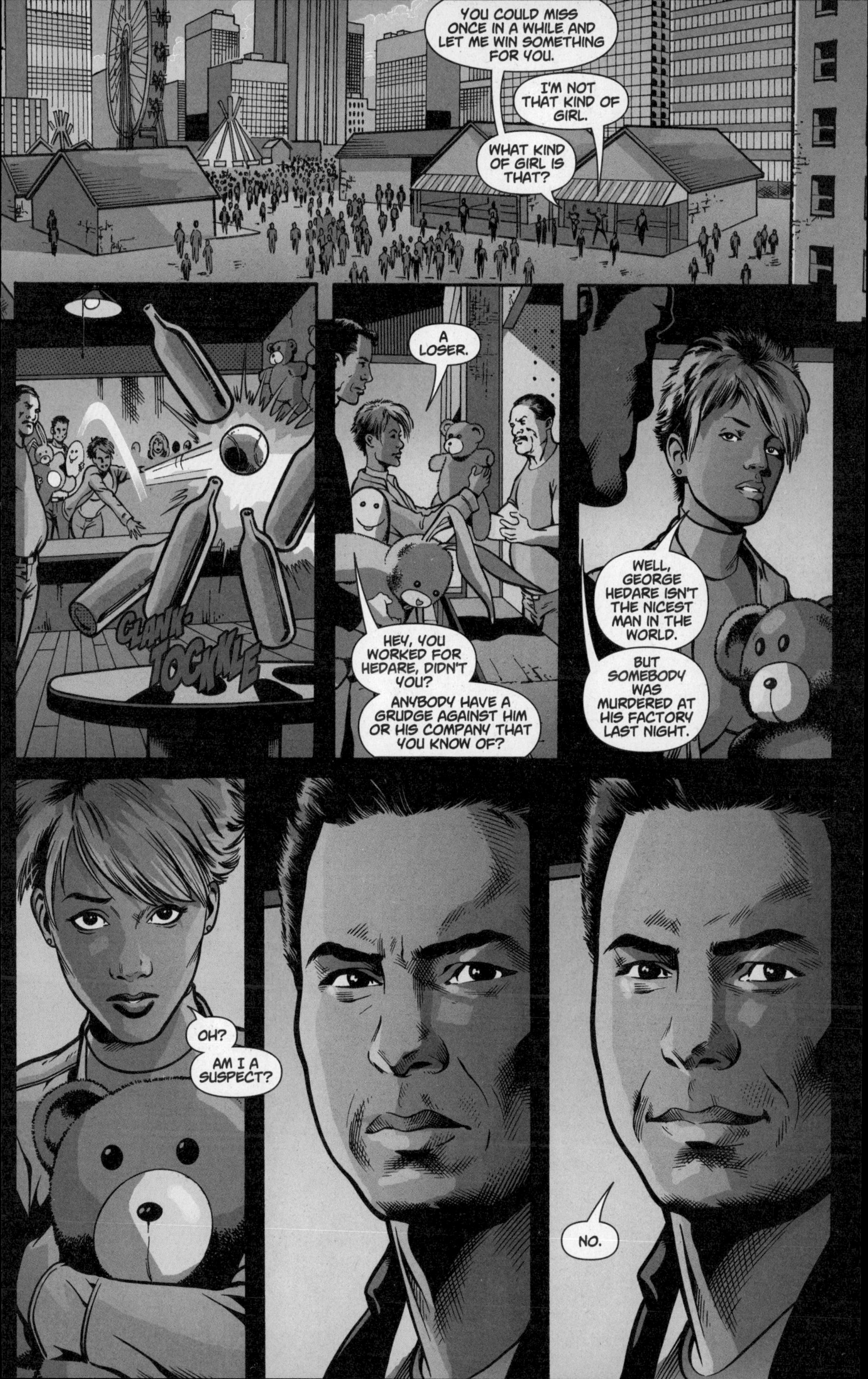
YOU COULD MISS ONCE IN A WHILE AND LET ME WIN SOMETHING FOR YOU.
I'M NOT THAT KIND OF GIRL.
WHAT KIND OF GIRL IS THAT?
CLANK-TOCKKLE
A LOSER.
HEY, YOU WORKED FOR HEDARE, DIDN'T YOU?
ANYBODY HAVE A GRUDGE AGAINST HIM OR HIS COMPANY THAT YOU KNOW OF?
WELL, GEORGE HEDARE ISN'T THE NICEST MAN IN THE WORLD.
BUT SOMEBODY WAS MURDERED AT HIS FACTORY LAST NIGHT.
OH?
AM I A SUSPECT?
NO.

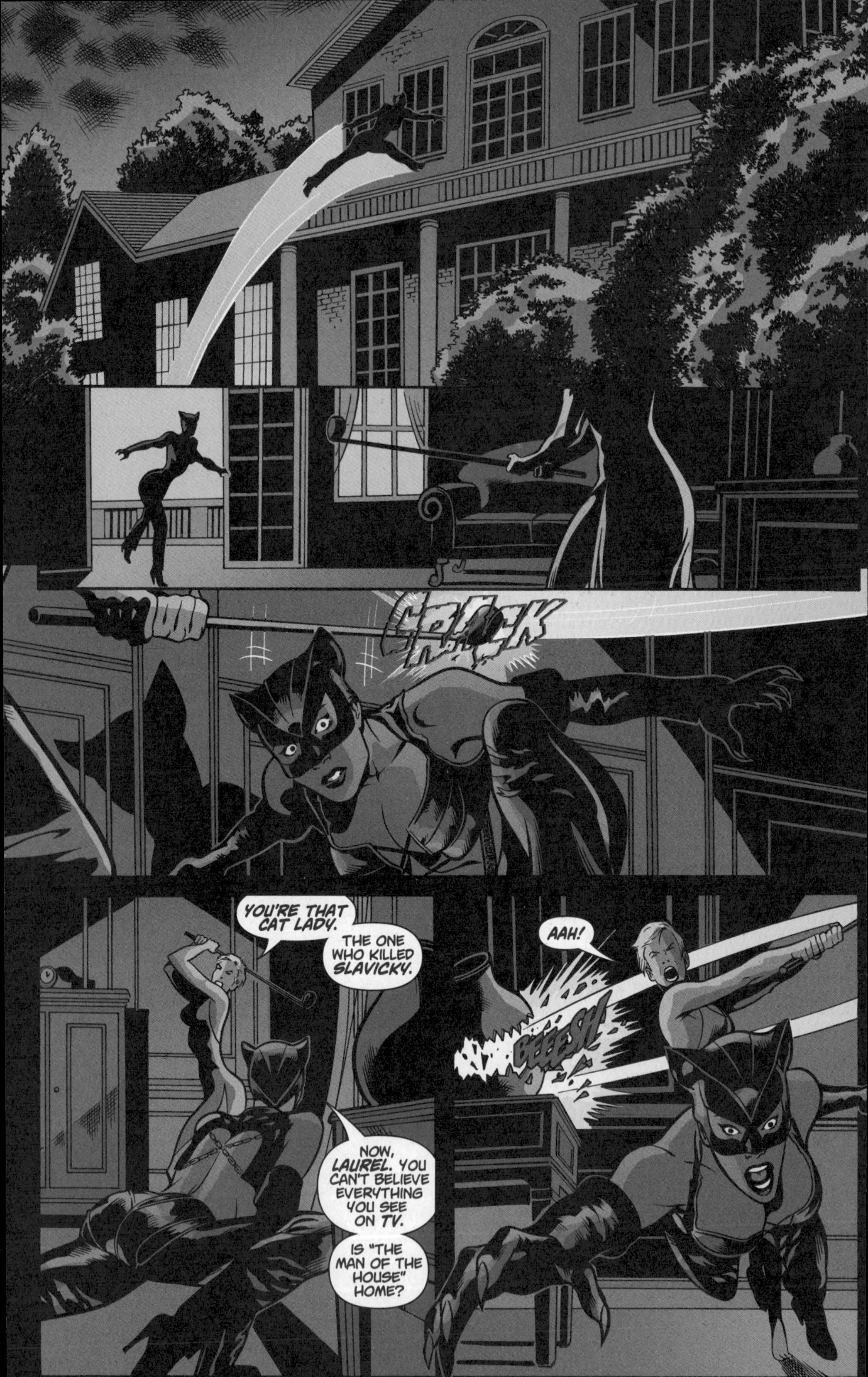
CRACK
YOU'RE THAT CAT LADY.
THE ONE WHO KILLED SLAVICKY.
NOW, LAUREL. YOU CAN'T BELIEVE EVERYTHING YOU SEE ON TV.
IS "THE MAN OF THE HOUSE" HOME?
AAH!
BEEESH!

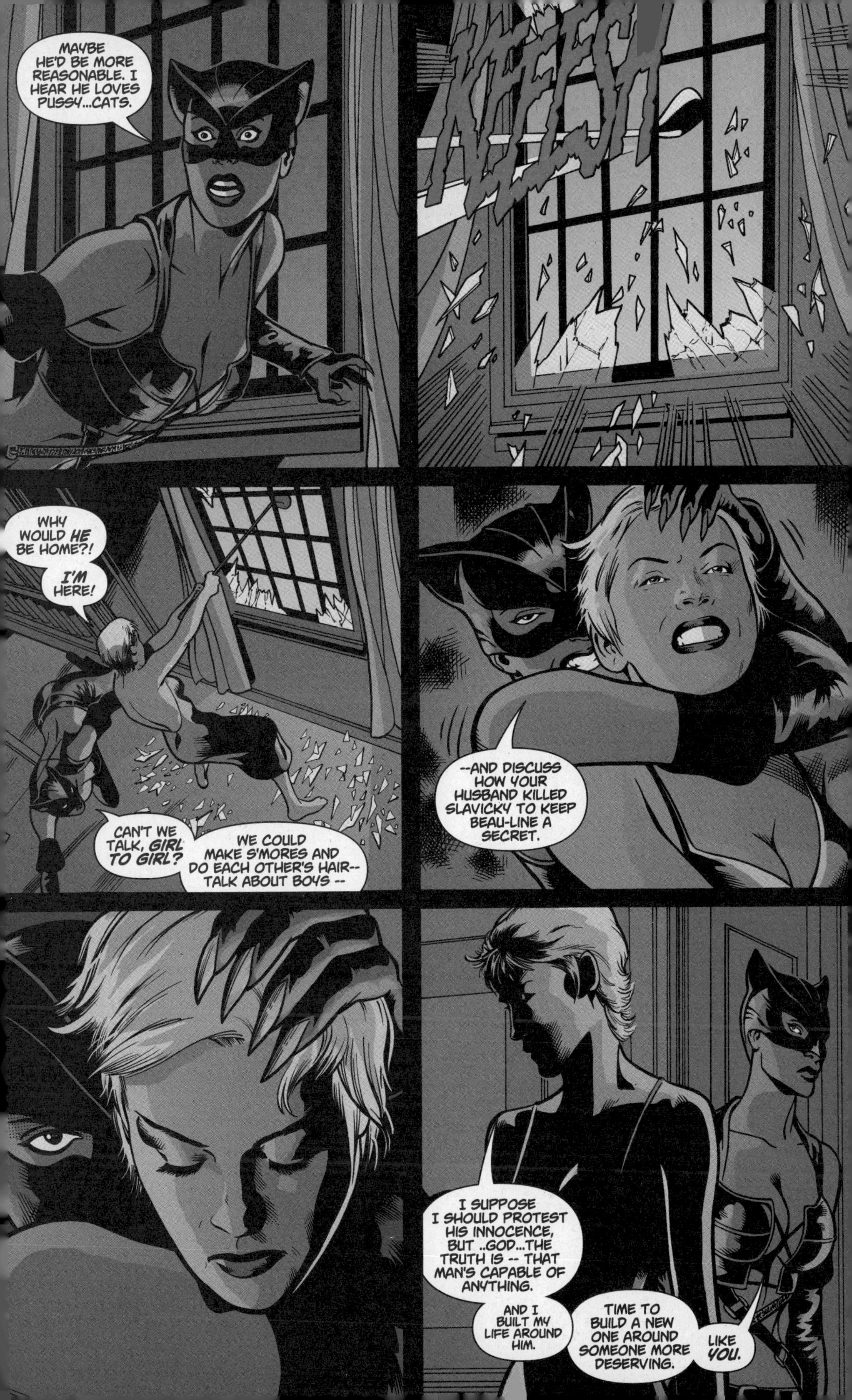

MAYBE HE'D BE MORE REASONABLE. I HEAR HE LOVES PUSSY...CATS.
WHY WOULD HE BE HOME?!
I'M HERE!
CAN'T WE TALK, GIRL TO GIRL?
WE COULD MAKE S'MORES AND DO EACH OTHER'S HAIR-- TALK ABOUT BOYS --
--AND DISCUSS HOW YOUR HUSBAND KILLED SLAVICKY TO KEEP BEAU-LINE A SECRET.
I SUPPOSE I SHOULD PROTEST HIS INNOCENCE, BUT ..GOD...THE TRUTH IS -- THAT MAN'S CAPABLE OF ANYTHING.
AND I BUILT MY LIFE AROUND HIM.
TIME TO BUILD A NEW ONE AROUND SOMEONE MORE DESERVING.
LIKE YOU.

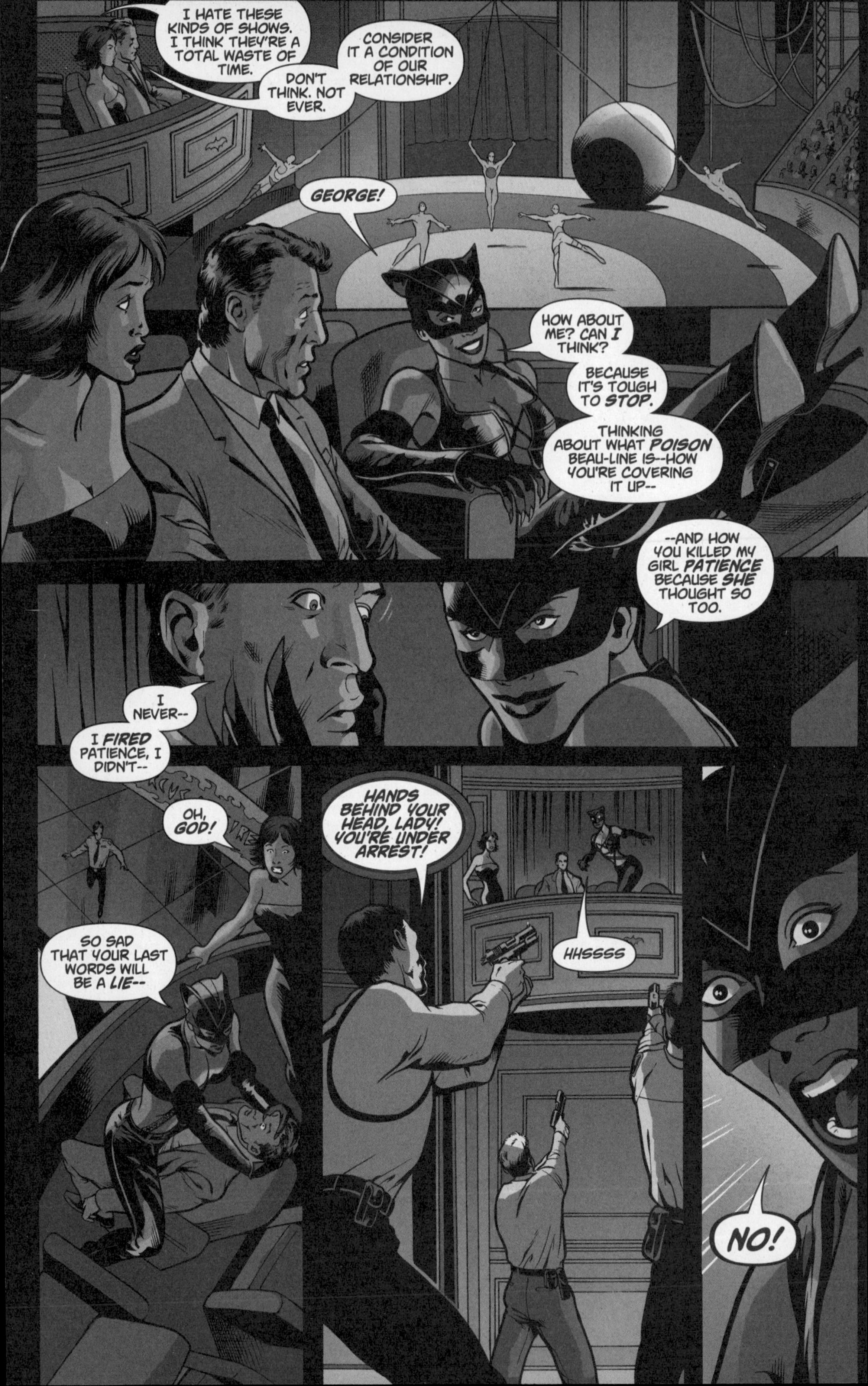
I HATE THESE KINDS OF SHOWS. I THINK THEY'RE A TOTAL WASTE OF TIME.
DON'T THINK. NOT EVER.
CONSIDER IT A CONDITION OF OUR RELATIONSHIP.
GEORGE!
HOW ABOUT ME? CAN I THINK?
BECAUSE IT'S TOUGH TO STOP.
THINKING ABOUT WHAT POISON BEAU-LINE IS--HOW YOU'RE COVERING IT UP--
--AND HOW YOU KILLED MY GIRL PATIENCE BECAUSE SHE THOUGHT SO TOO.
I NEVER--
I FIRED PATIENCE, I DIDN'T--
OH, GOD!
SO SAD THAT YOUR LAST WORDS WILL BE A LIE--
HANDS BEHIND YOUR HEAD, LADY! YOU'RE UNDER ARREST!
HHSSSS
NO!

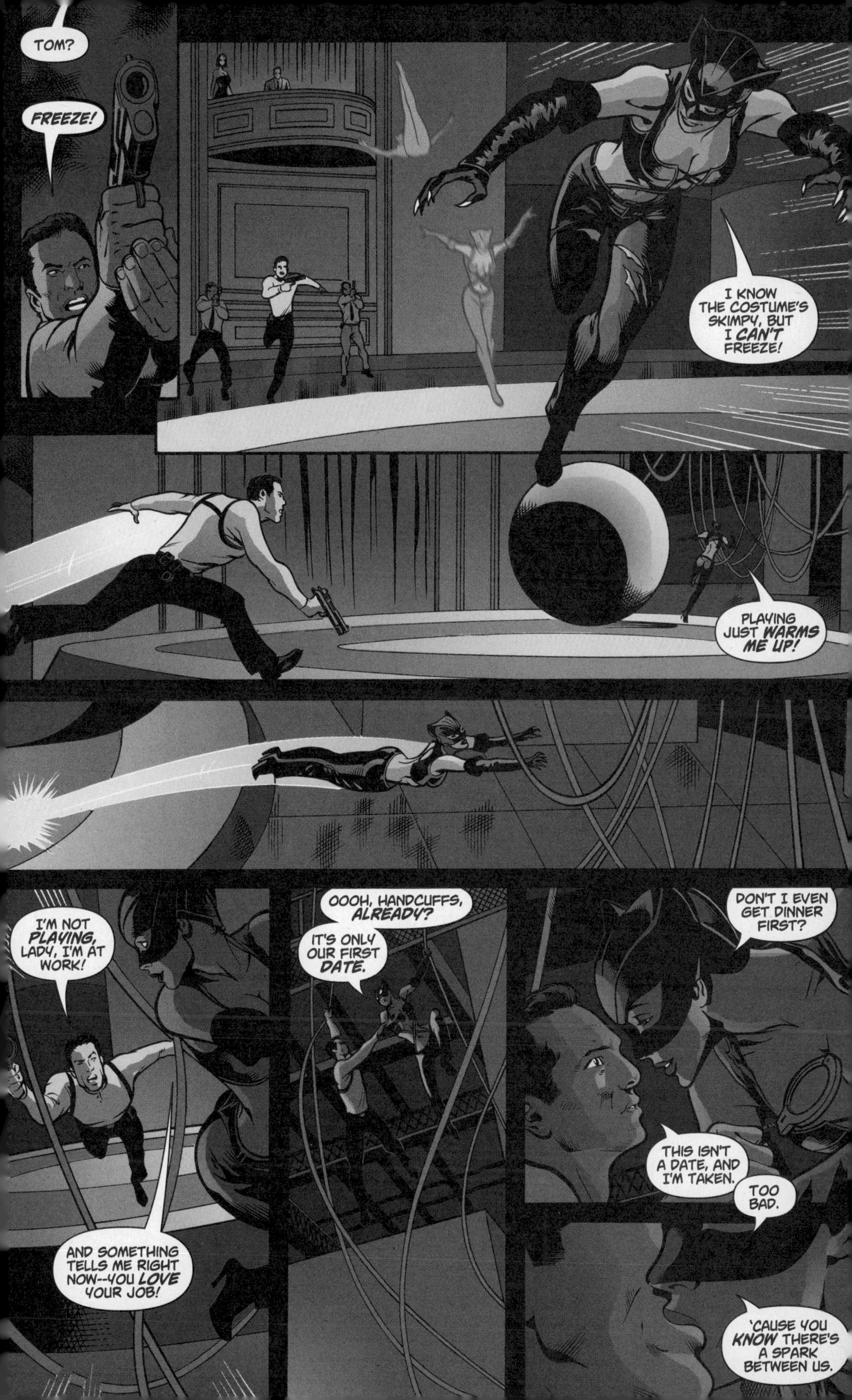
TOM?
FREEZE!
I KNOW THE COSTUME'S SKIMPY, BUT I CAN'T FREEZE!
PLAYING JUST WARMS ME UP!
I'M NOT PLAYING, LADY, I'M AT WORK!
AND SOMETHING TELLS ME RIGHT NOW--YOU LOVE YOUR JOB!
OOOH, HANDCUFFS, ALREADY?
IT'S ONLY OUR FIRST DATE.
DON'T I EVEN GET DINNER FIRST?
THIS ISN'T A DATE, AND I'M TAKEN.
TOO BAD.
'CAUSE YOU KNOW THERE'S A SPARK BETWEEN US.

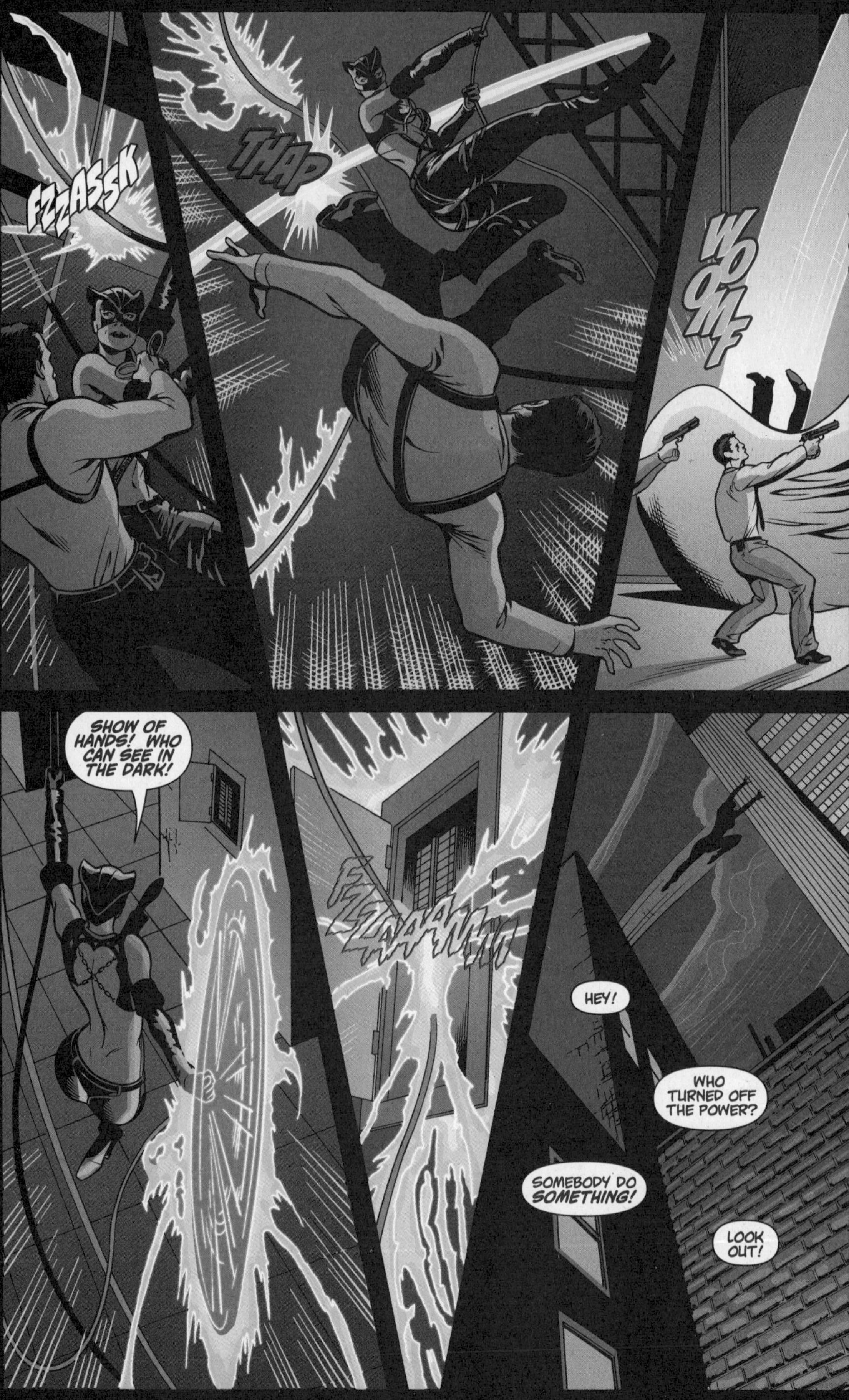
FZZASSK
THAP
WOOMF
SHOW OF HANDS! WHO CAN SEE IN THE DARK!
FZZAAAMM
HEY!
WHO TURNED OFF THE POWER?
SOMEBODY DO SOMETHING!
LOOK OUT!

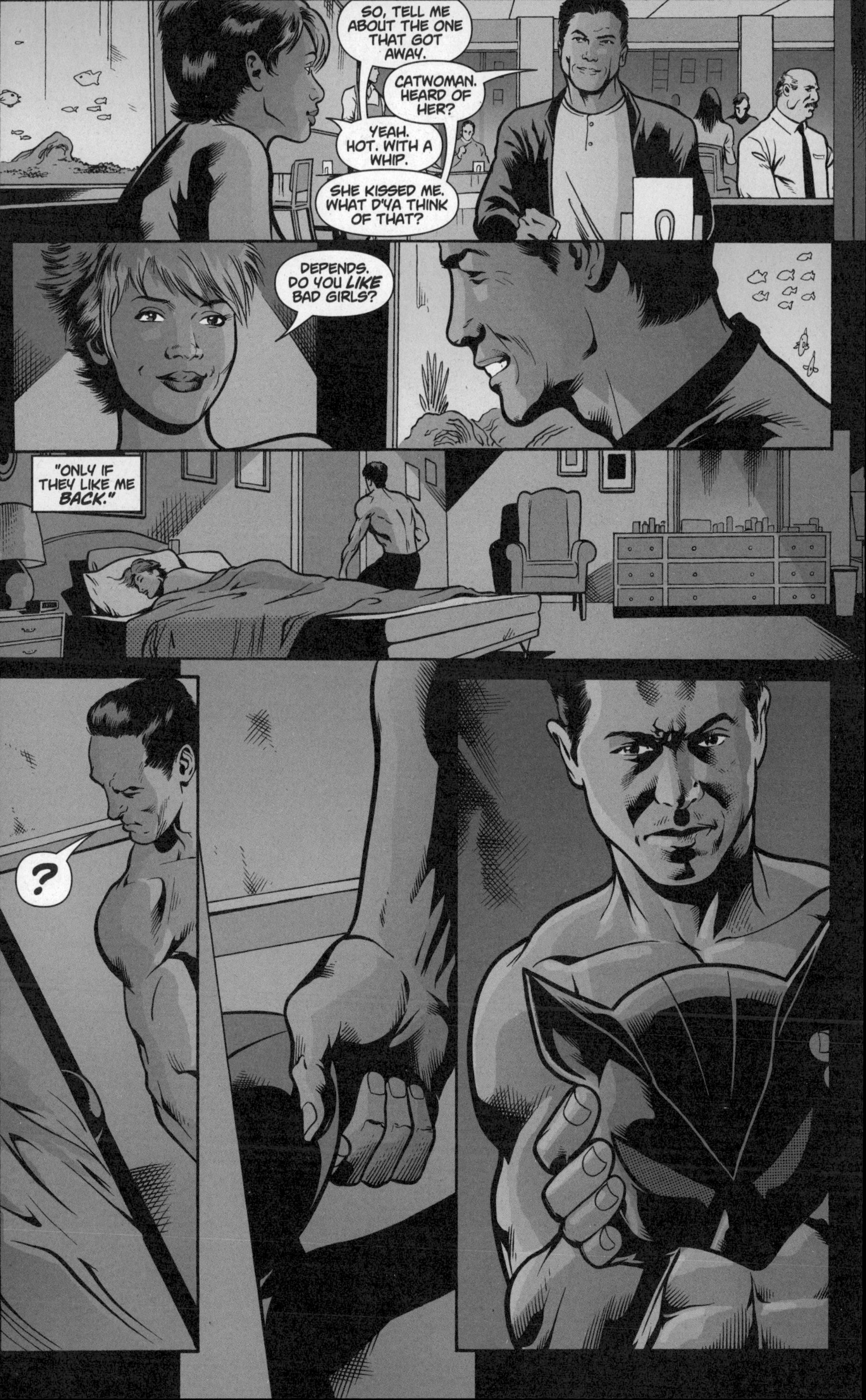
SO, TELL ME ABOUT THE ONE THAT GOT AWAY.
CATWOMAN. HEARD OF HER?
YEAH. HOT. WITH A WHIP.
SHE KISSED ME. WHAT D'YA THINK OF THAT?
DEPENDS. DO YOU LIKE BAD GIRLS?
"ONLY IF THEY LIKE ME BACK."
?

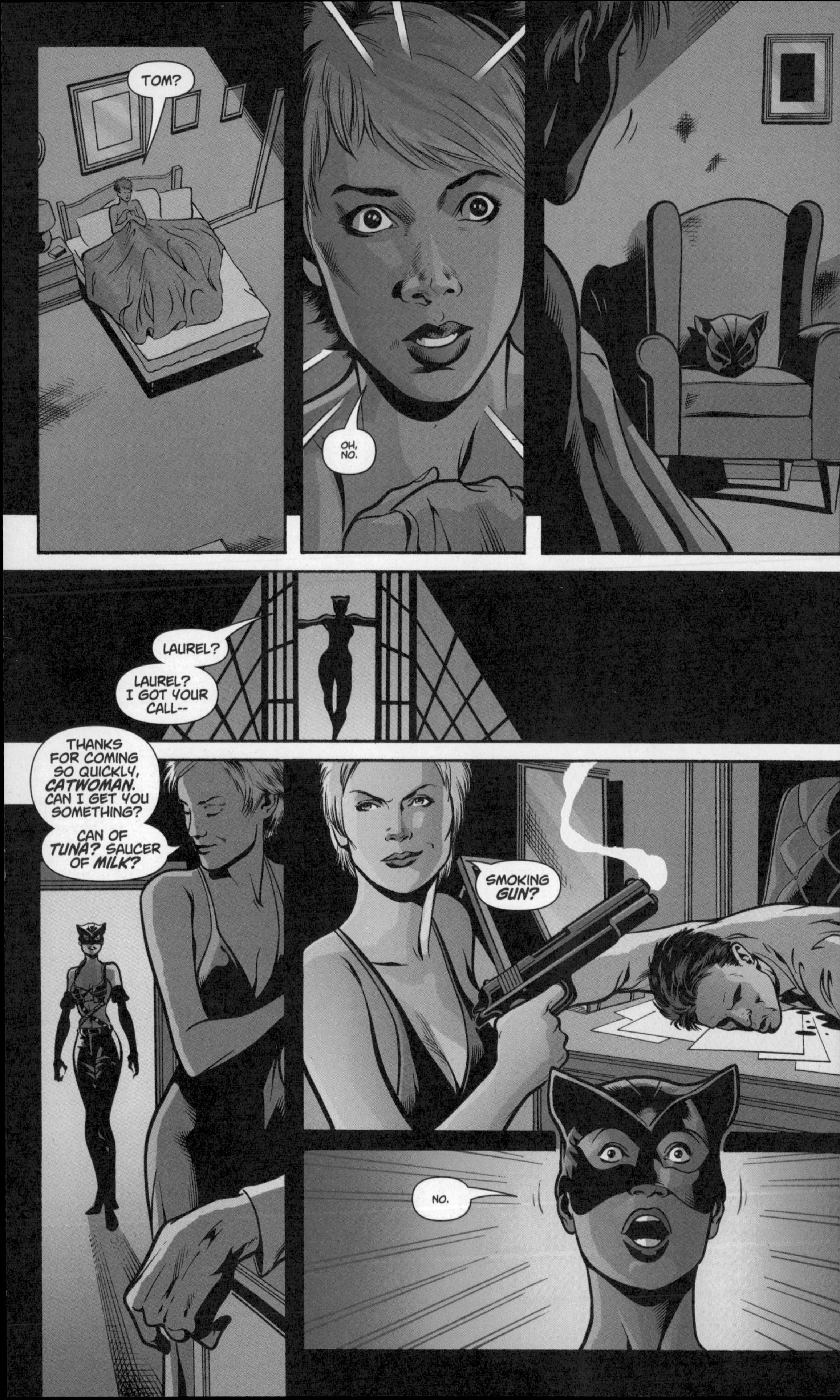
TOM?
OH, NO.
LAUREL?
LAUREL? I GOT YOUR CALL--
THANKS FOR COMING SO QUICKLY, CATWOMAN. CAN I GET YOU SOMETHING?
CAN OF TUNA? SAUCER OF MILK?
SMOKING GUN?
NO.

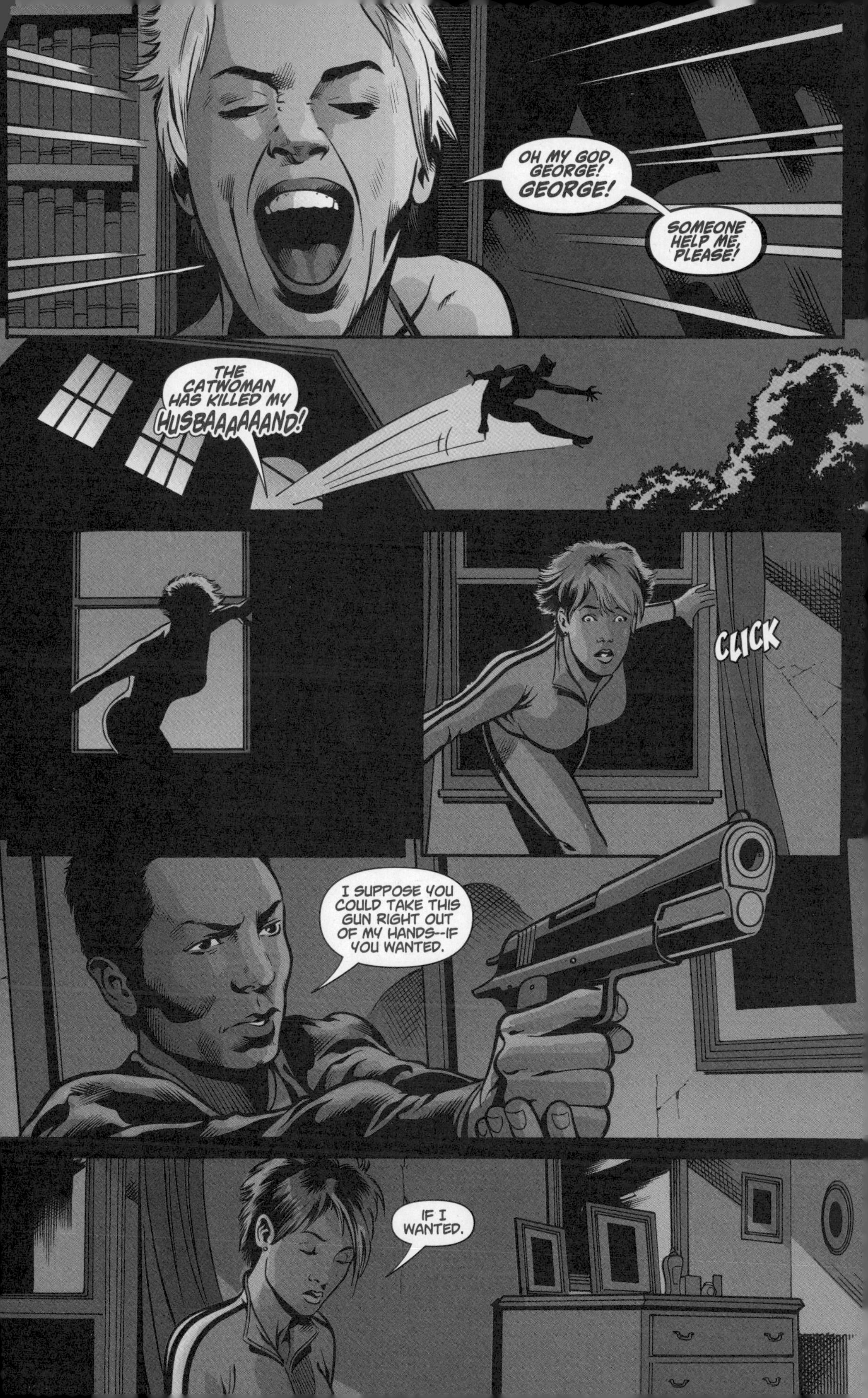
OH MY GOD, GEORGE! GEORGE!
SOMEONE HELP ME, PLEASE!
THE CATWOMAN HAS KILLED MY HUSBAAAAAAND!
CLICK
I SUPPOSE YOU COULD TAKE THIS GUN RIGHT OUT OF MY HANDS--IF YOU WANTED.
IF I WANTED.

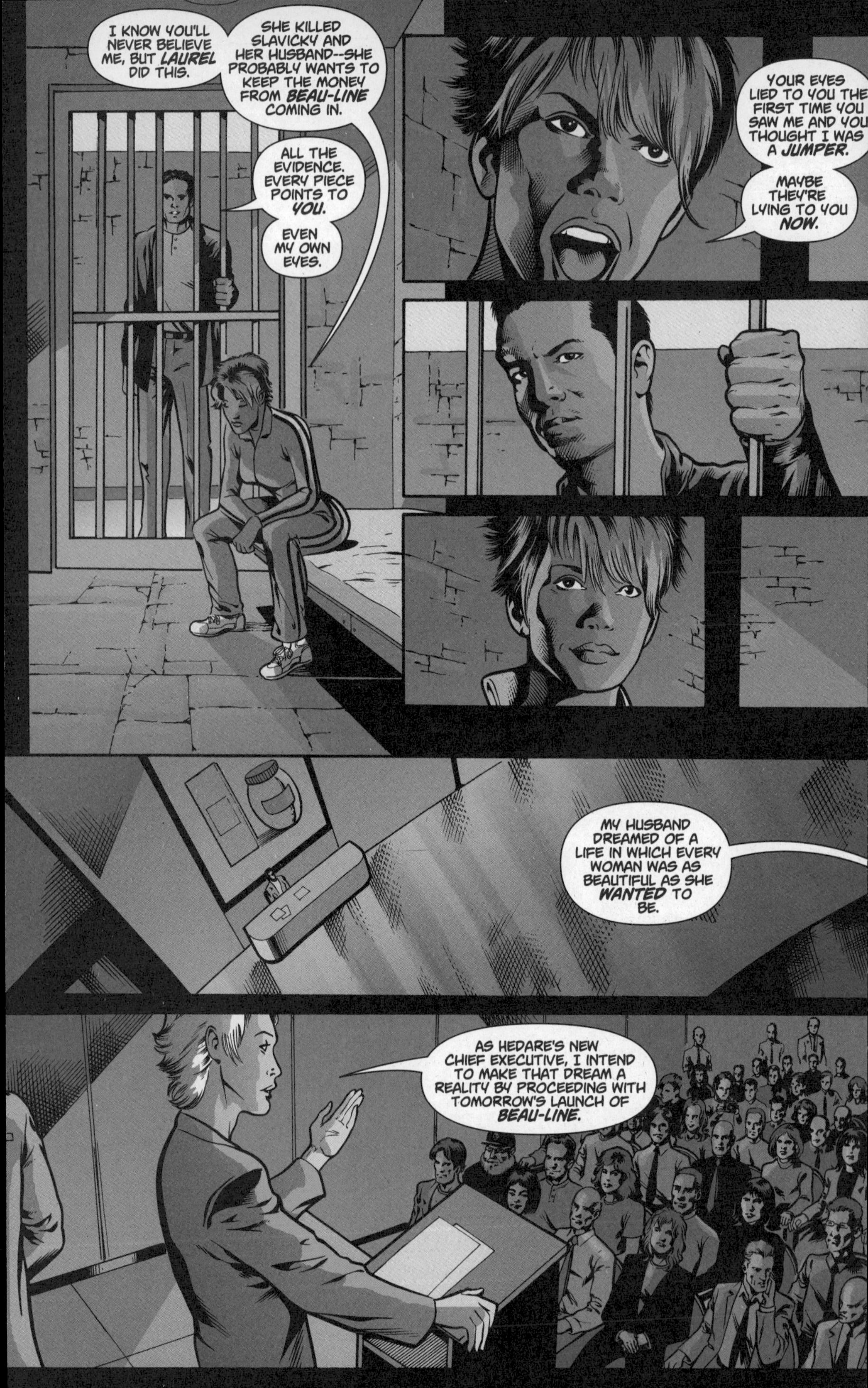
I KNOW YOU'LL NEVER BELIEVE ME, BUT LAUREL DID THIS.
SHE KILLED SLAVICKY AND HER HUSBAND--SHE PROBABLY WANTS TO KEEP THE MONEY FROM BEAU-LINE COMING IN.
ALL THE EVIDENCE. EVERY PIECE POINTS TO YOU.
EVEN MY OWN EYES.
YOUR EYES LIED TO YOU THE FIRST TIME YOU SAW ME AND YOU THOUGHT I WAS A JUMPER.
MAYBE THEY'RE LYING TO YOU NOW.
MY HUSBAND DREAMED OF A LIFE IN WHICH EVERY WOMAN WAS AS BEAUTIFUL AS SHE WANTED TO BE.
AS HEDARE'S NEW CHIEF EXECUTIVE, I INTEND TO MAKE THAT DREAM A REALITY BY PROCEEDING WITH TOMORROW'S LAUNCH OF BEAU-LINE.

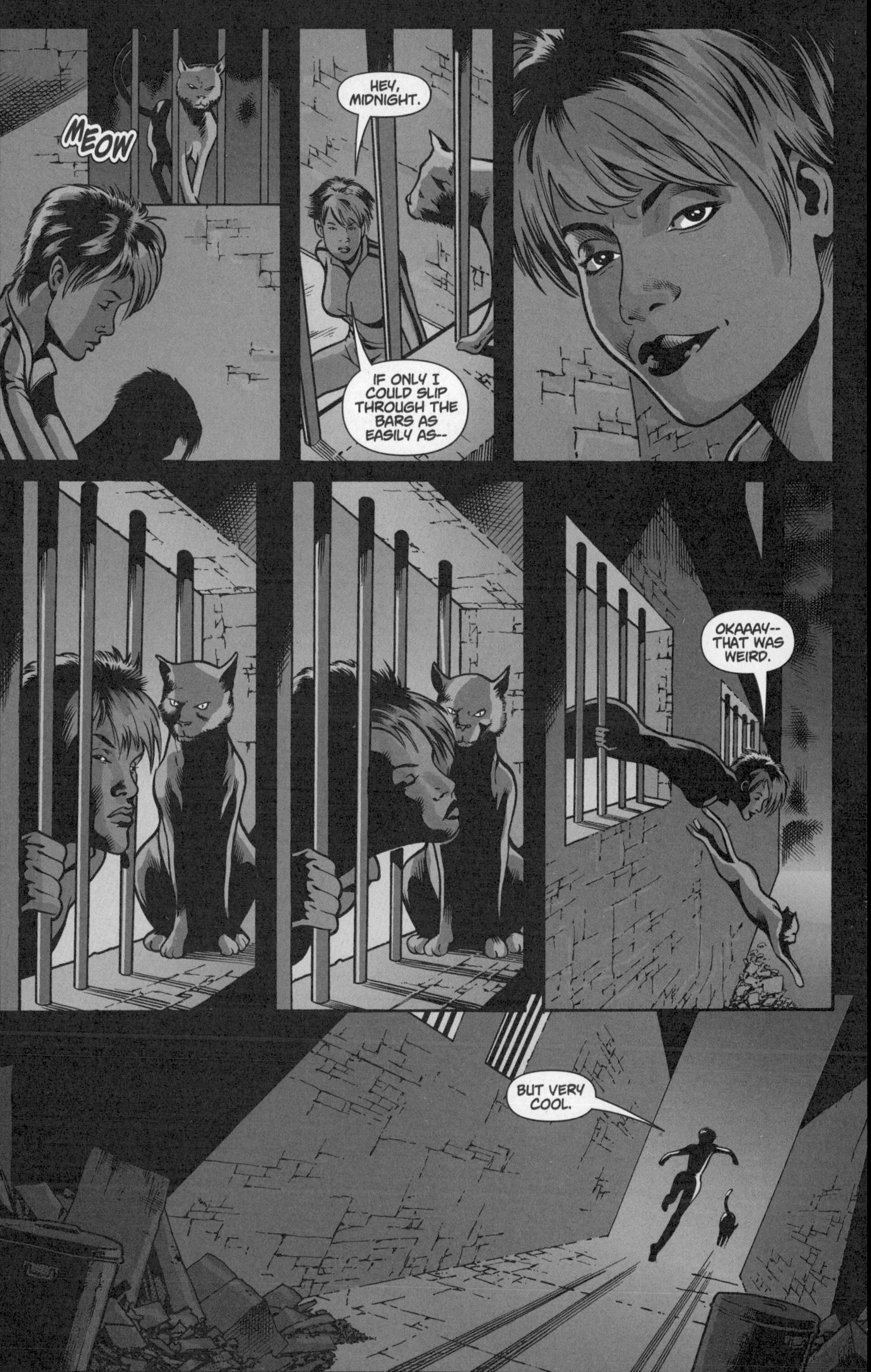
MEOW
HEY, MIDNIGHT.
IF ONLY I COULD SLIP THROUGH THE BARS AS EASILY AS--
OKAAAY-- THAT WAS WEIRD.
BUT VERY COOL.

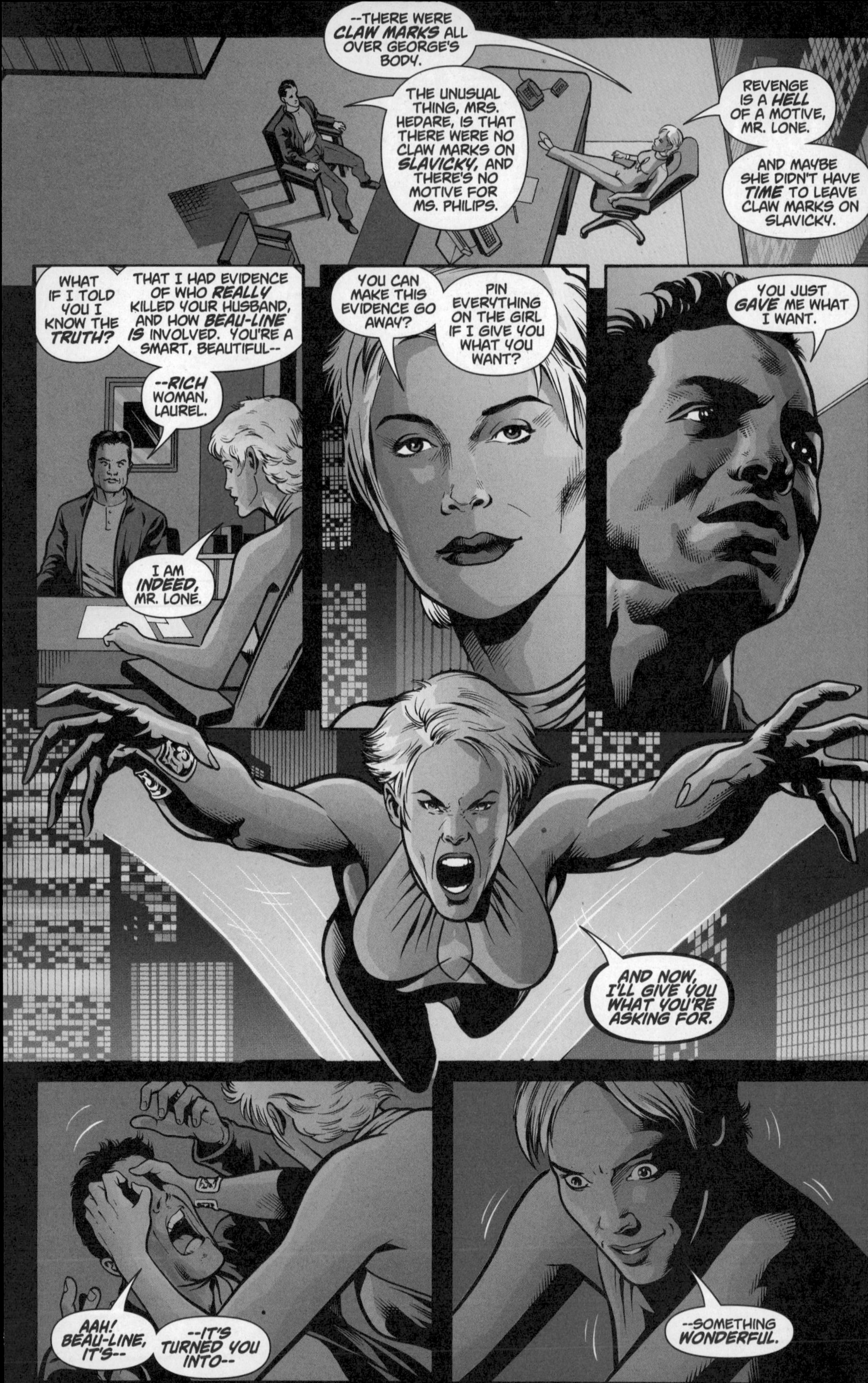
--THERE WERE CLAW MARKS ALL OVER GEORGE'S BODY.
THE UNUSUAL THING, MRS. HEDARE, IS THAT THERE WERE NO CLAW MARKS ON SLAVICKY, AND THERE'S NO MOTIVE FOR MS. PHILIPS.
REVENGE IS A HELL OF A MOTIVE, MR. LONE.
AND MAYBE SHE DIDN'T HAVE TIME TO LEAVE CLAW MARKS ON SLAVICKY.
WHAT IF I TOLD YOU I KNOW THE TRUTH?
THAT I HAD EVIDENCE OF WHO REALLY KILLED YOUR HUSBAND, AND HOW BEAU-LINE IS INVOLVED. YOU'RE A SMART, BEAUTIFUL--
--RICH WOMAN, LAUREL.
I AM INDEED, MR. LONE.
YOU CAN MAKE THIS EVIDENCE GO AWAY?
PIN EVERYTHING ON THE GIRL IF I GIVE YOU WHAT YOU WANT?
YOU JUST GAVE ME WHAT I WANT.
AND NOW, I'LL GIVE YOU WHAT YOU'RE ASKING FOR.
AAH! BEAU-LINE, IT'S--
--IT'S TURNED YOU INTO--
--SOMETHING WONDERFUL.

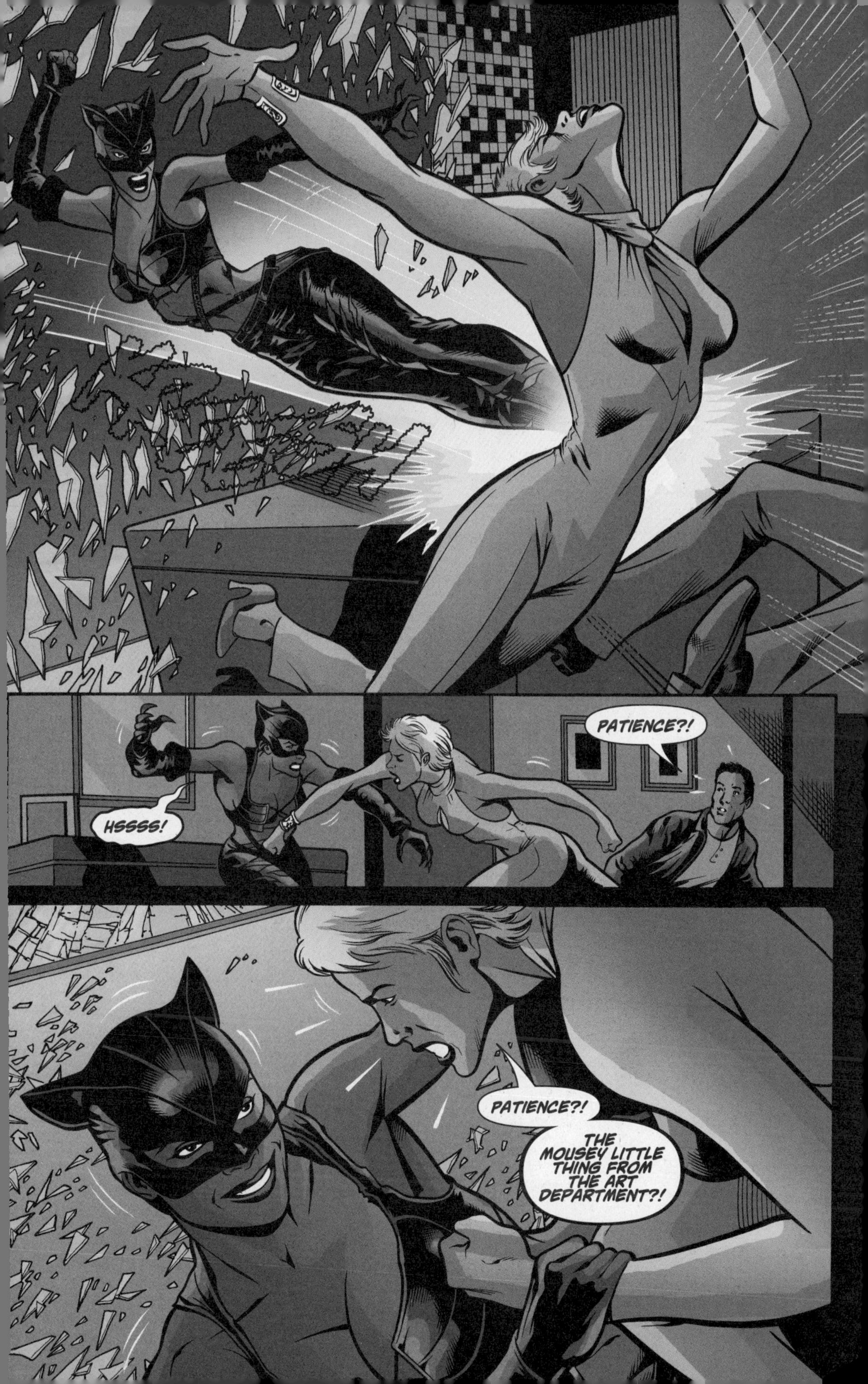

PATIENCE?!
HSSSS!
PATIENCE?!
THE MOUSEY LITTLE THING FROM THE ART DEPARTMENT?!

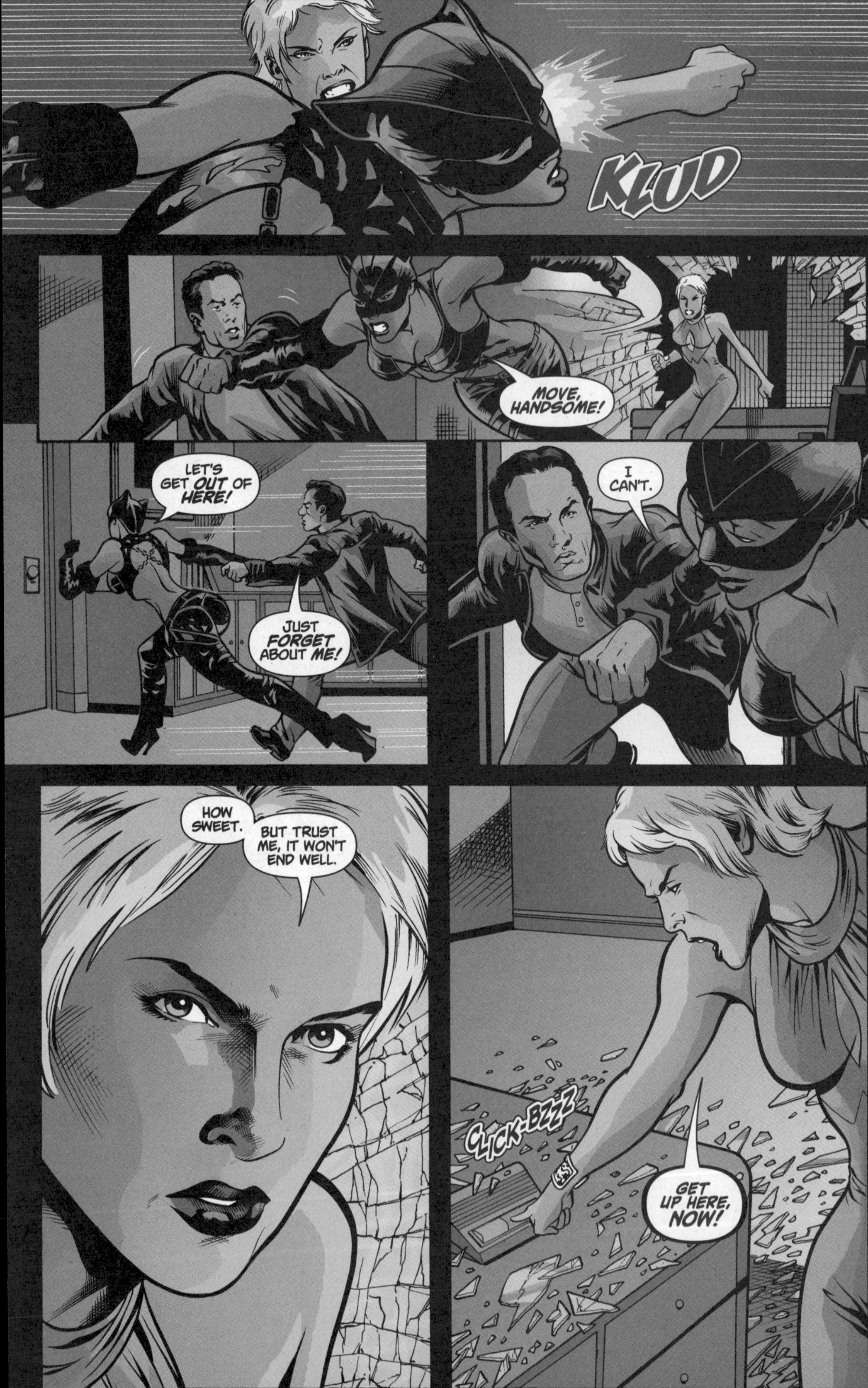
KLUD
MOVE, HANDSOME!
LET'S GET OUT OF HERE!
JUST FORGET ABOUT ME!
I CAN'T.
HOW SWEET.
BUT TRUST ME, IT WON'T END WELL.
CLICK-BZZZ
GET UP HERE, NOW!

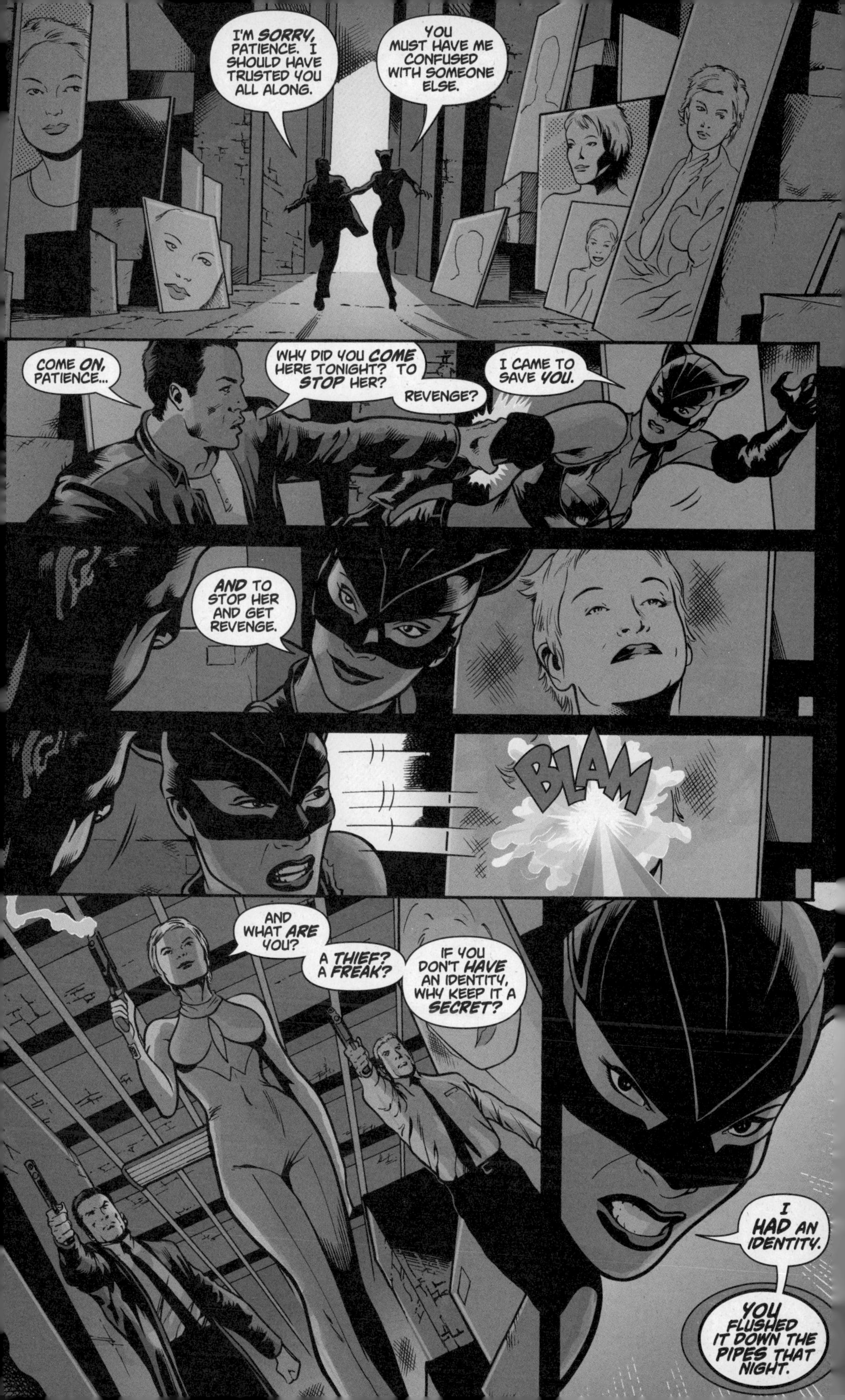
I'M SORRY, PATIENCE. I SHOULD HAVE TRUSTED YOU ALL ALONG.
YOU MUST HAVE ME CONFUSED WITH SOMEONE ELSE.
COME ON, PATIENCE...
WHY DID YOU COME HERE TONIGHT? TO STOP HER?
REVENGE?
I CAME TO SAVE YOU.
AND TO STOP HER AND GET REVENGE.
BLAM
AND WHAT ARE YOU?
A THIEF? A FREAK?
IF YOU DON'T HAVE AN IDENTITY, WHY KEEP IT A SECRET?
I HAD AN IDENTITY.
YOU FLUSHED IT DOWN THE PIPES THAT NIGHT.

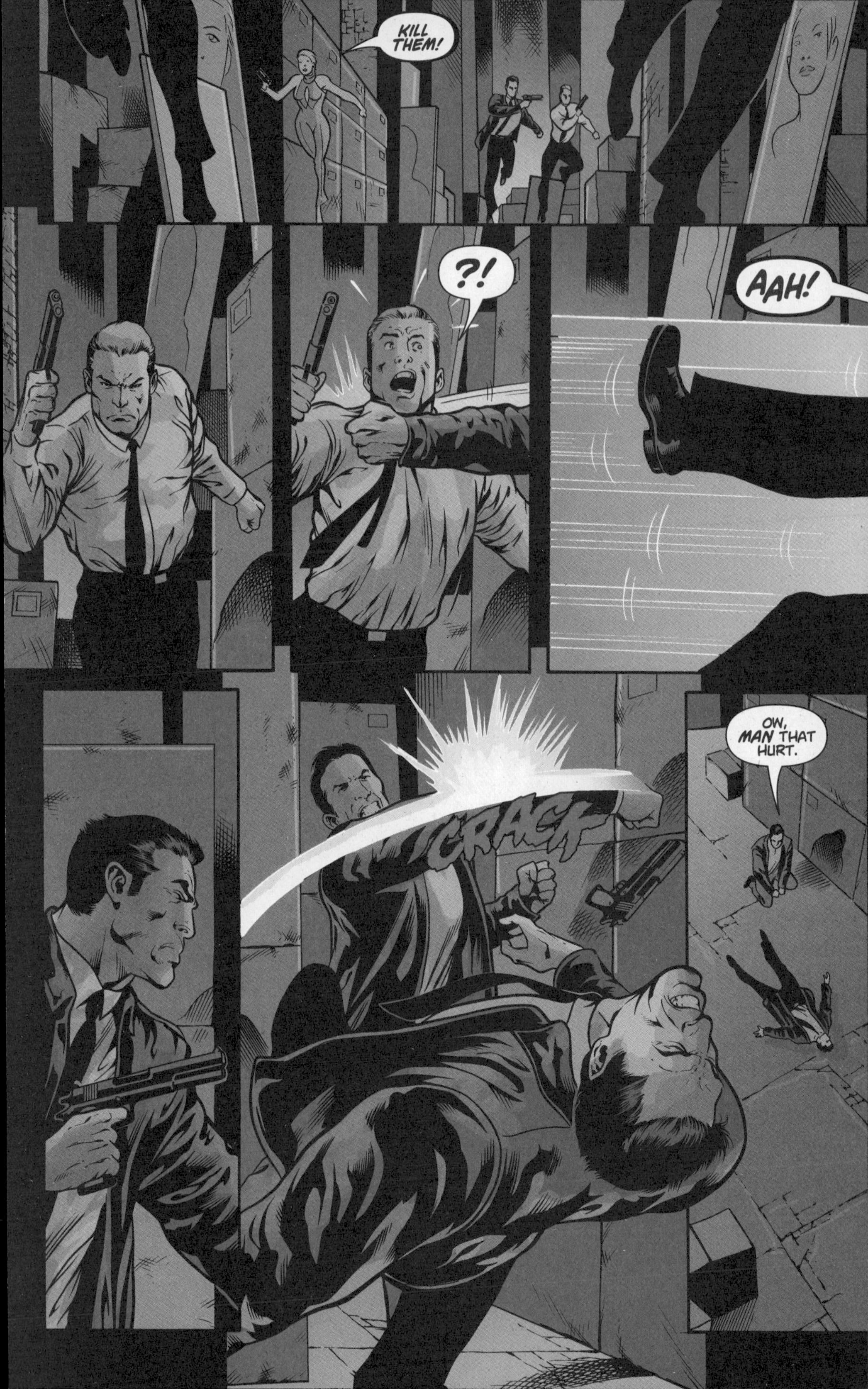
KILL THEM!
?!
AAH!
CRACK
OW, MAN THAT HURT.

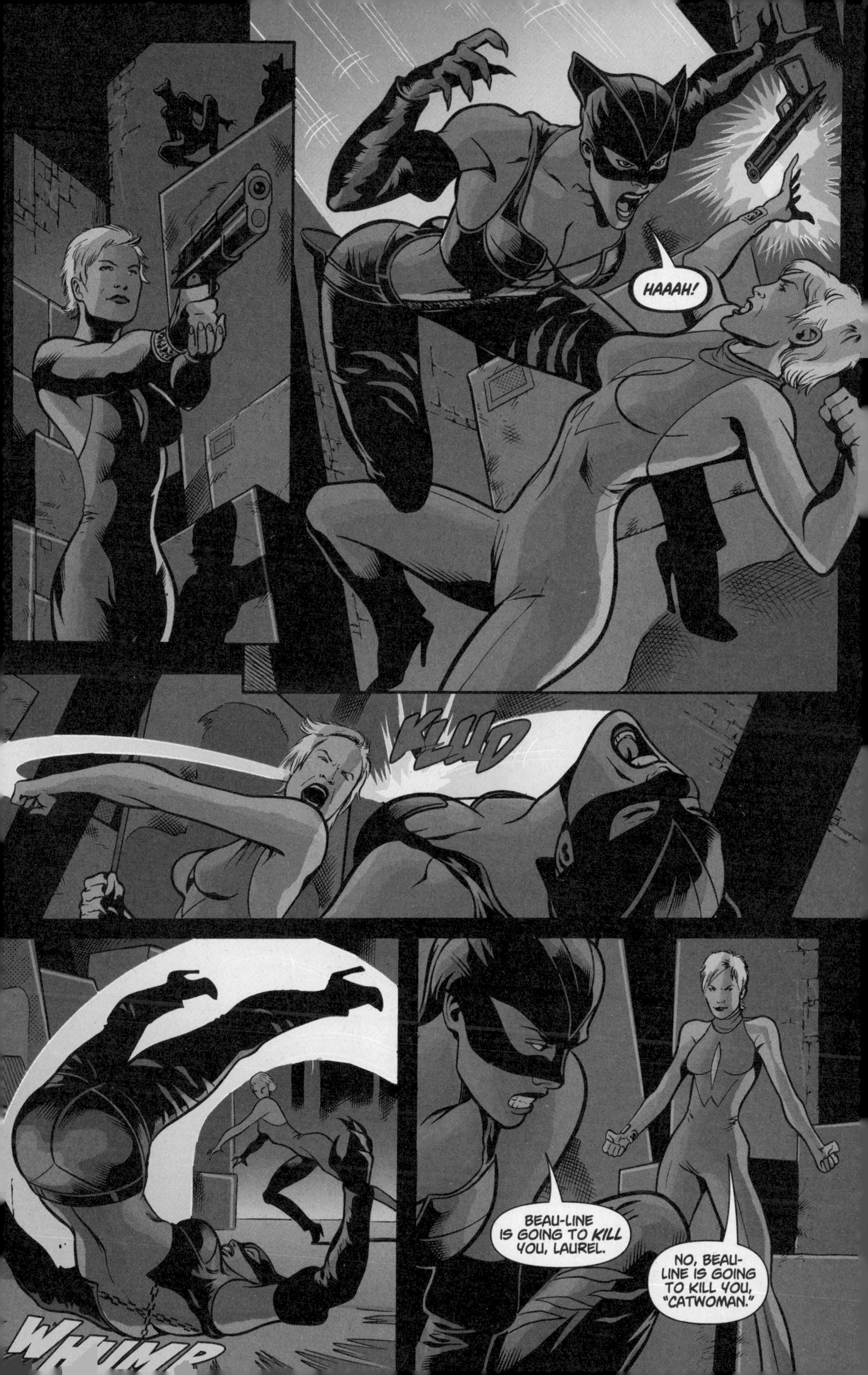
HAAAH!
KLUD
WHUMP
BEAU-LINE IS GOING TO KILL YOU, LAUREL.
NO, BEAU-LINE IS GOING TO KILL YOU, "CATWOMAN."

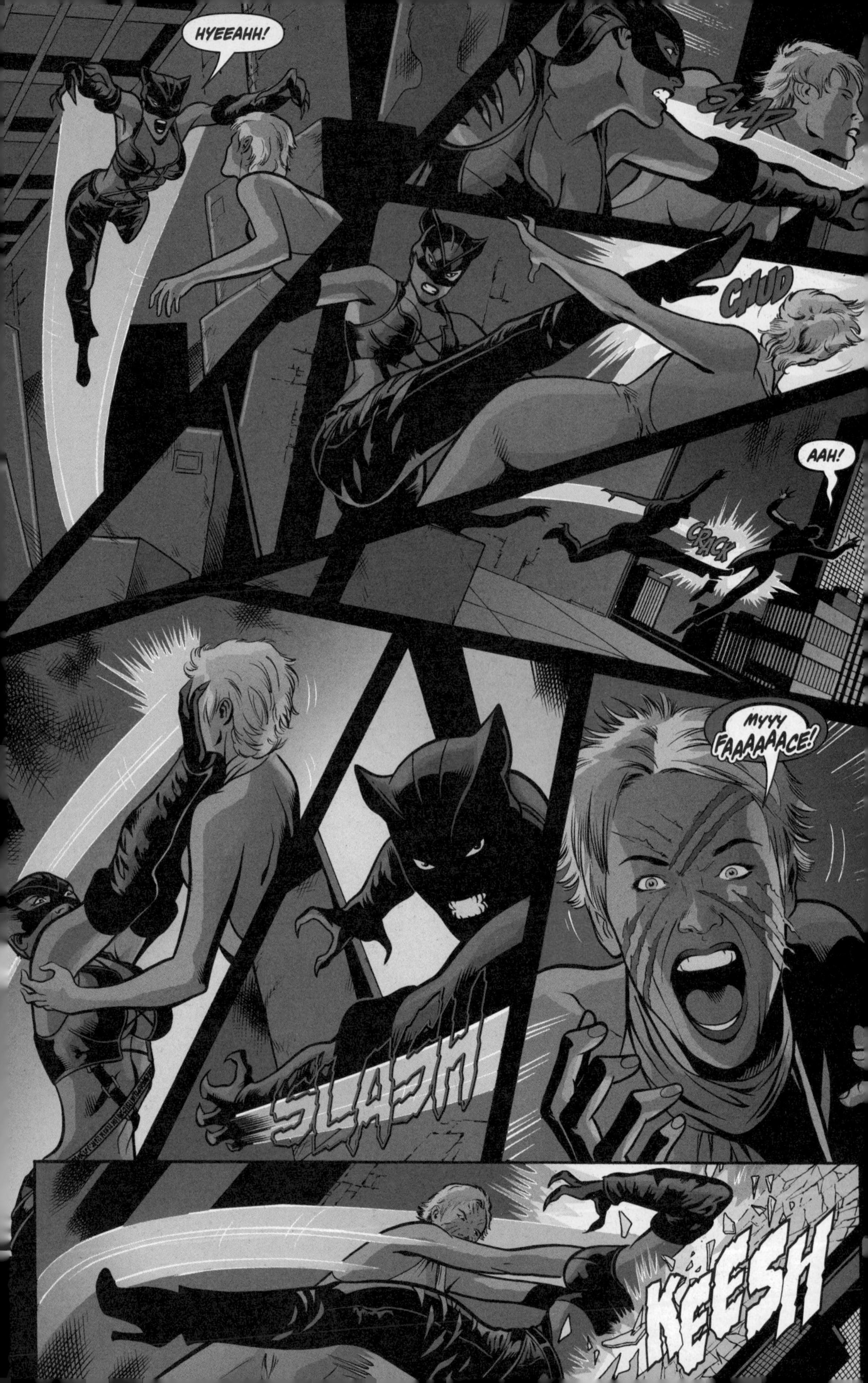
HYEEAHH!
SLAP
CHUD
AAH!
CRACK
SLASH
MYYY FAAAAAACE!
KEESH

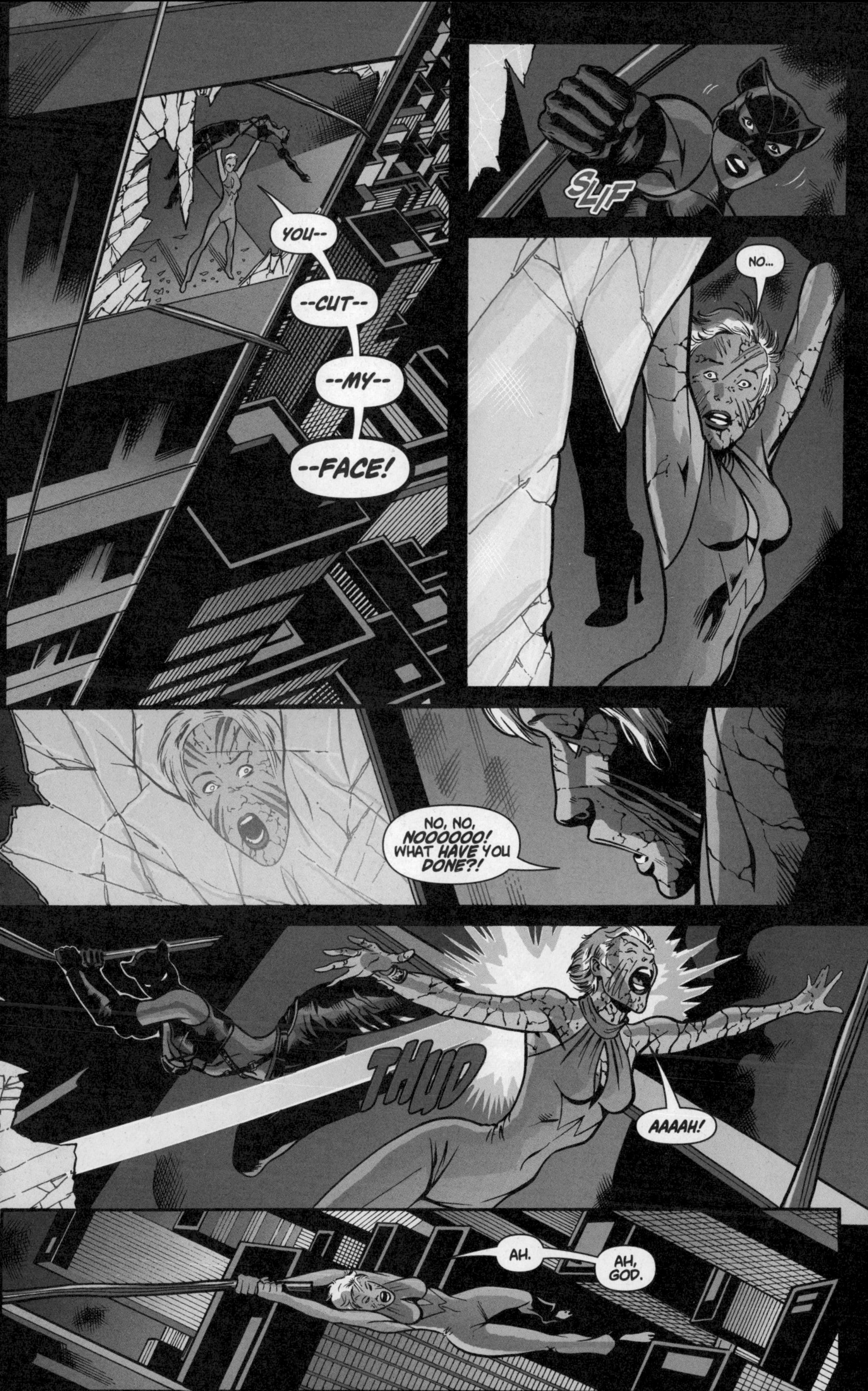
YOU--
--CUT--
--MY--
--FACE!
SLIF
NO...
NO, NO, NOOOOOO! WHAT HAVE YOU DONE?!
THUD
AAAAH!
AH.
AH, GOD.

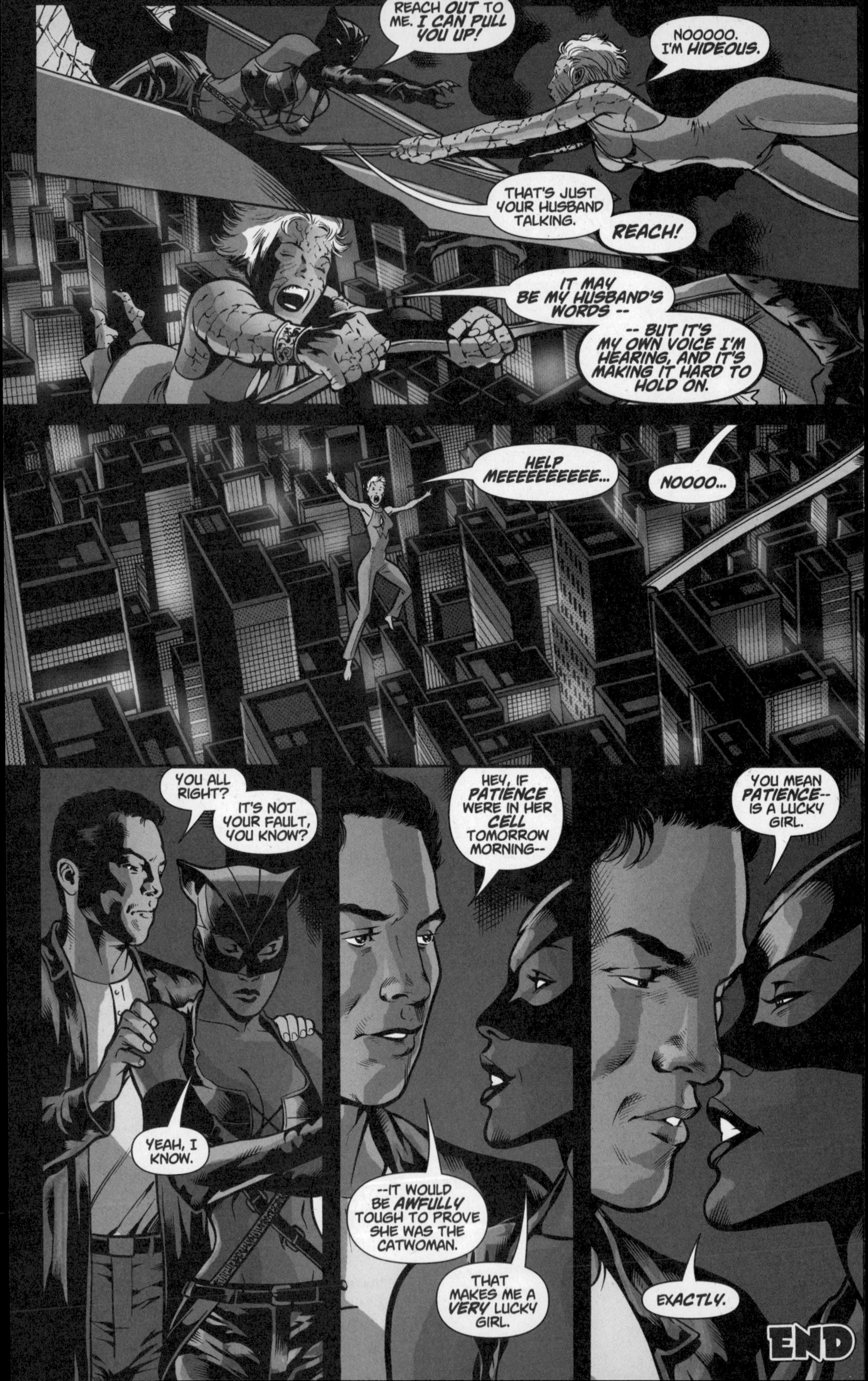
REACH OUT TO ME. I CAN PULL YOU UP!
NOOOOO. I'M HIDEOUS.
THAT'S JUST YOUR HUSBAND TALKING.
REACH!
IT MAY BE MY HUSBAND'S WORDS --
-- BUT IT'S MY OWN VOICE I'M HEARING, AND IT'S MAKING IT HARD TO HOLD ON.
HELP MEEEEEEEEEE...
NOOOO...
YOU ALL RIGHT?
IT'S NOT YOUR FAULT, YOU KNOW?
YEAH, I KNOW.
HEY, IF PATIENCE WERE IN HER CELL TOMORROW MORNING--
--IT WOULD BE AWFULLY TOUGH TO PROVE SHE WAS THE CATWOMAN.
THAT MAKES ME A VERY LUCKY GIRL.
YOU MEAN PATIENCE-- IS A LUCKY GIRL.
EXACTLY.
END

Superstar artist Jim Lee was invited to the Vancouver set of *Catwoman* and got to draw Halle Berry in costume! Some of those sketches are shown here for the first time.

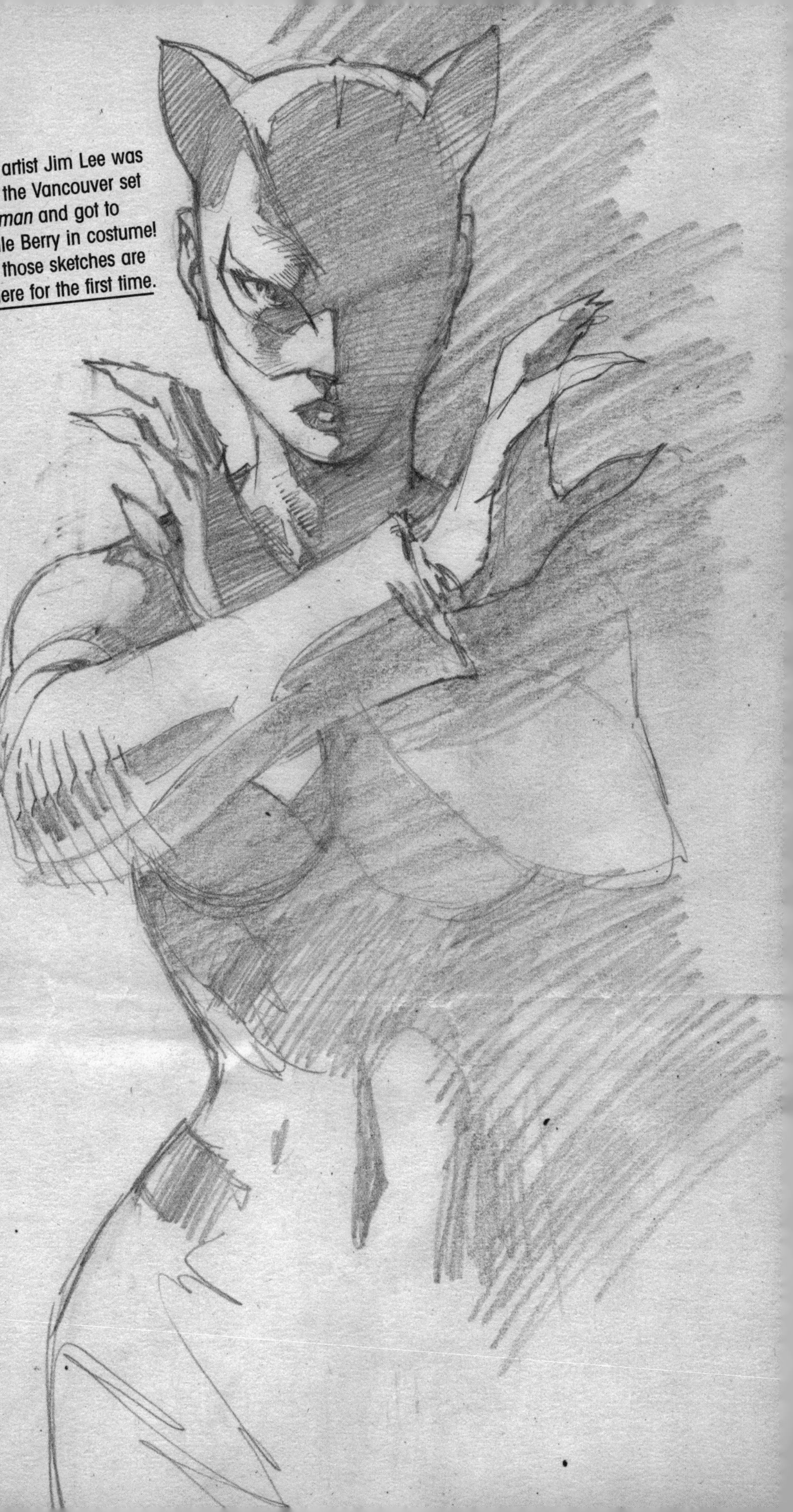

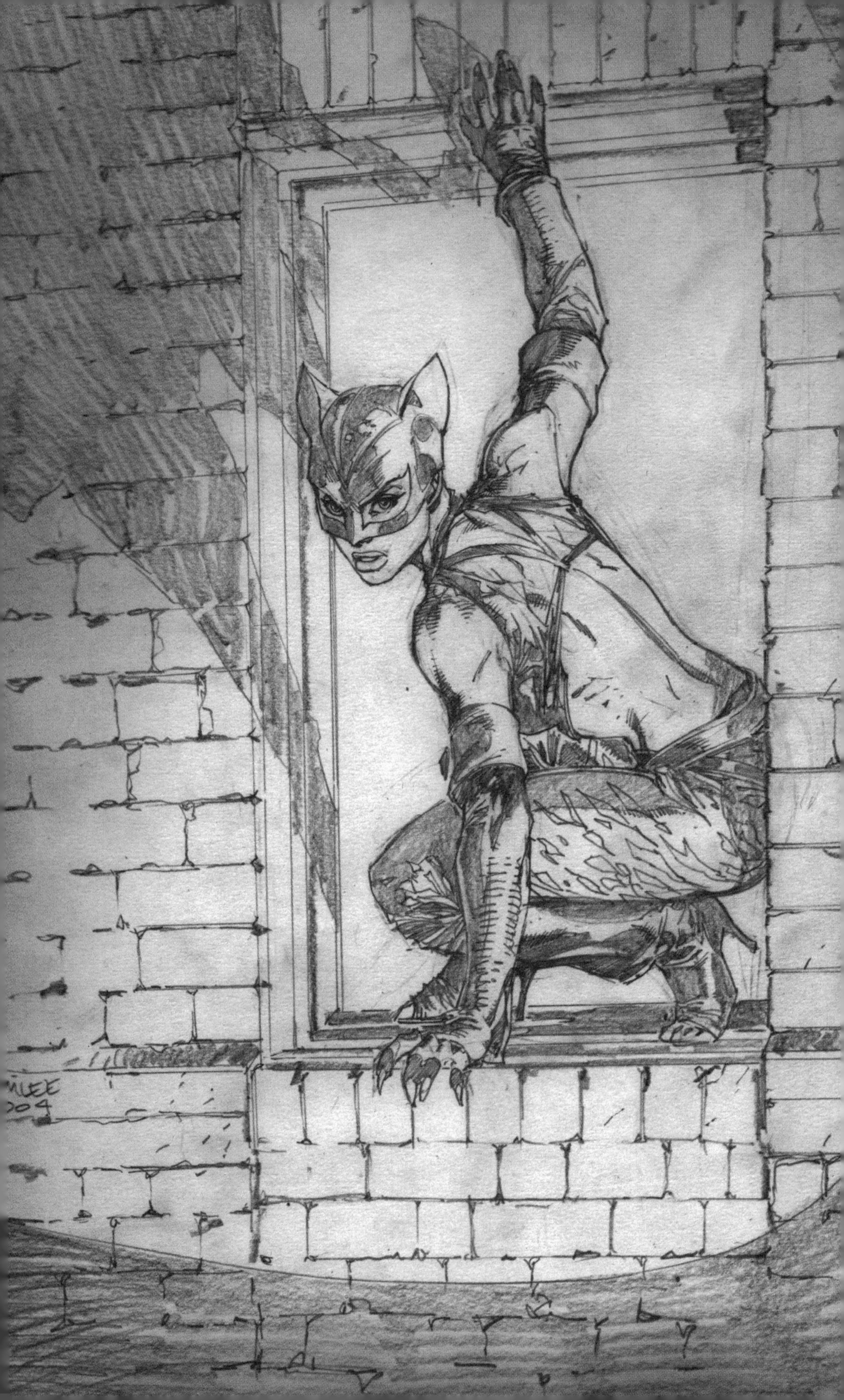

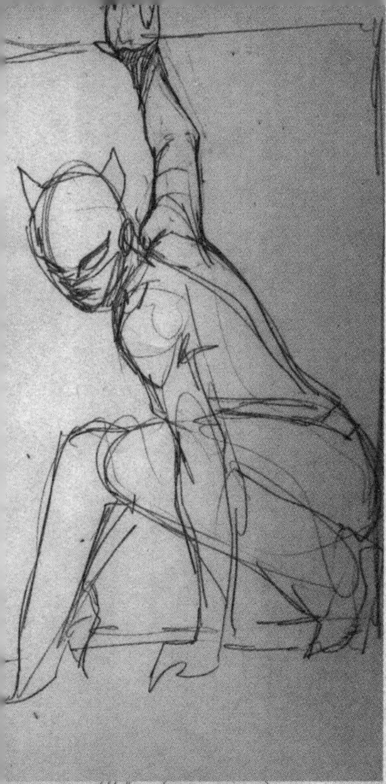

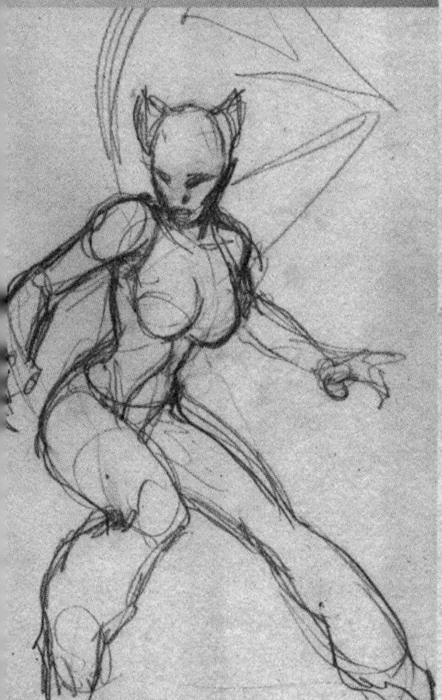

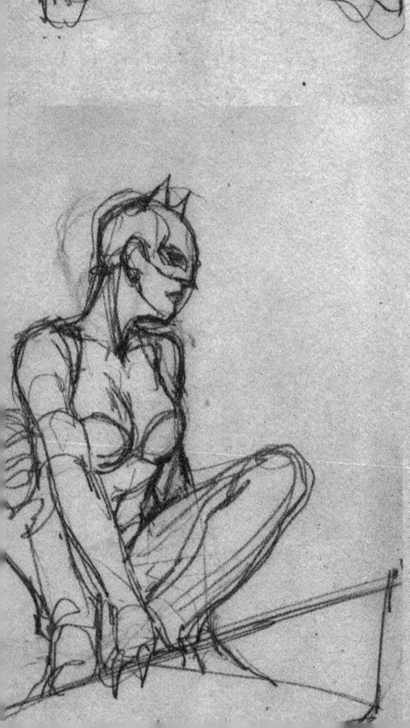

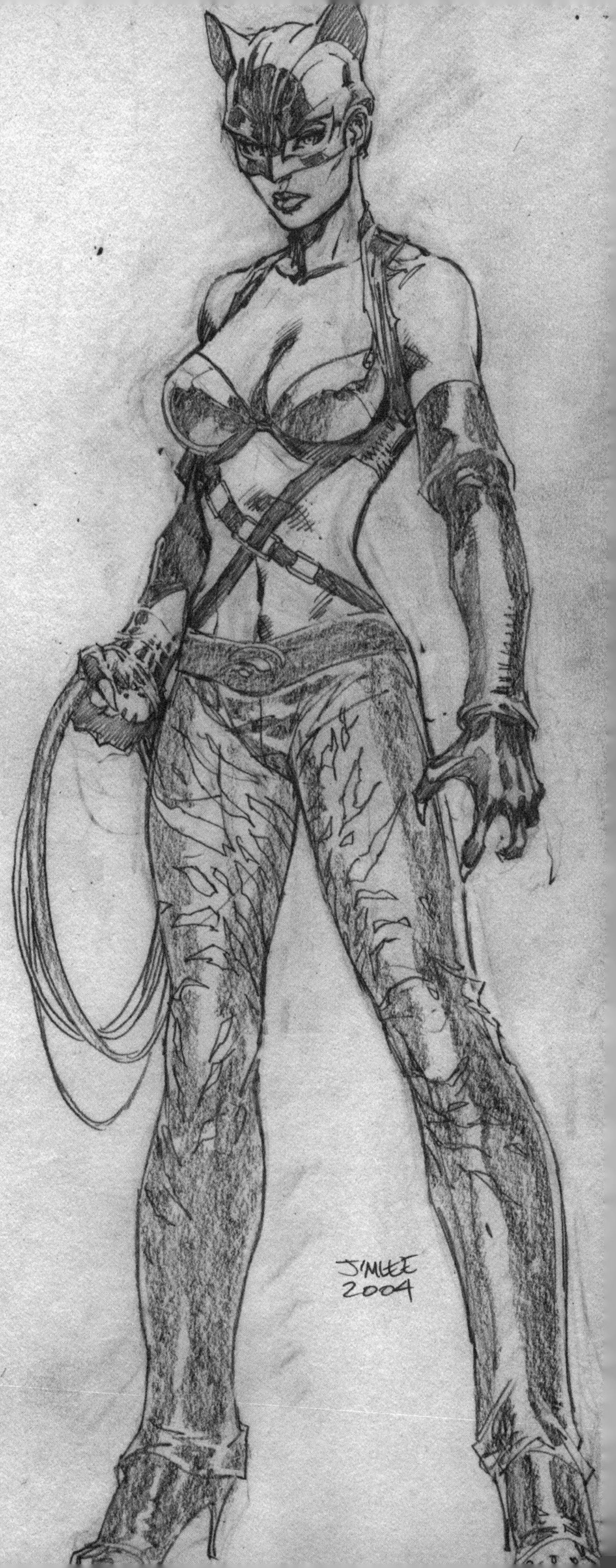
JIMLEE
2004

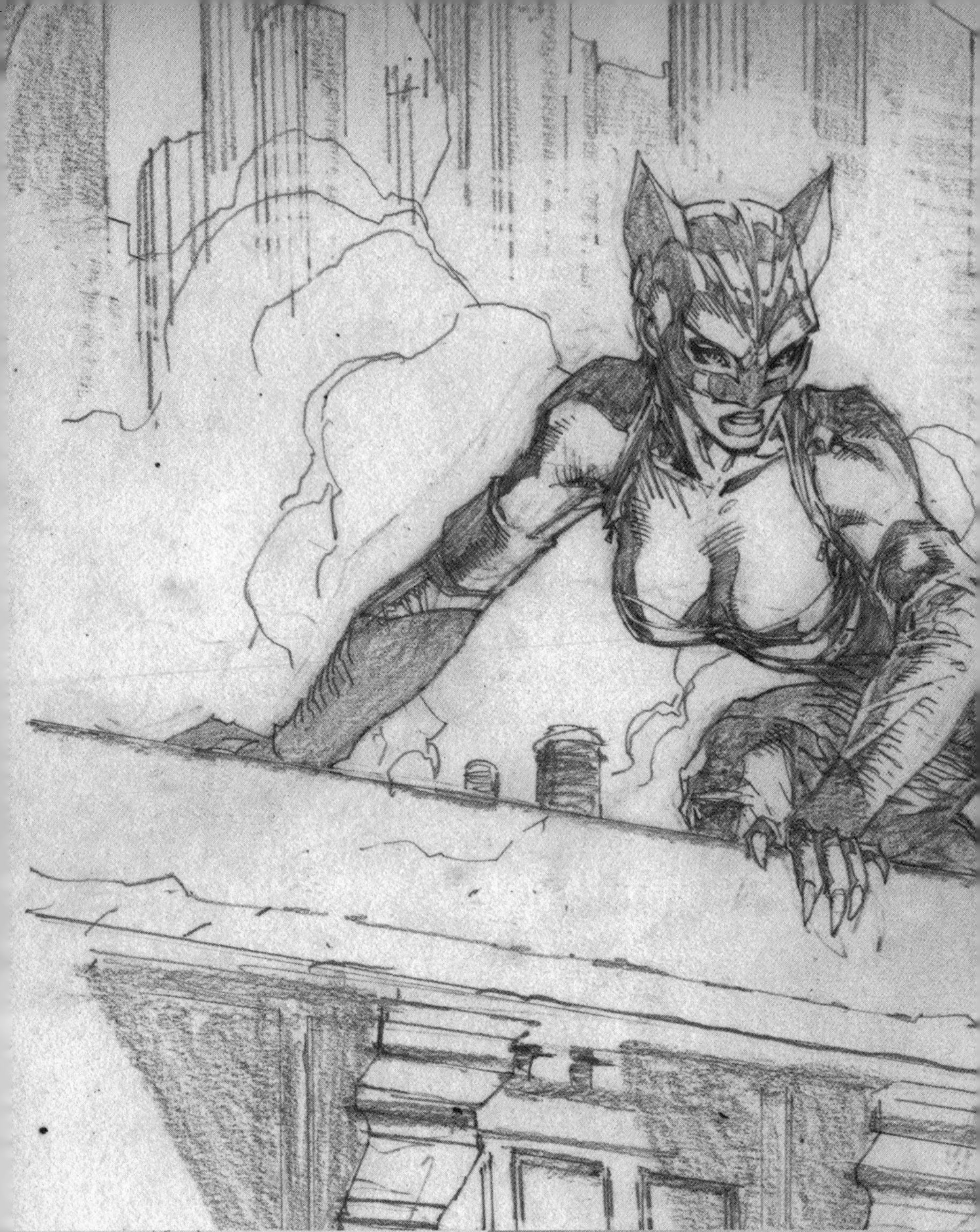

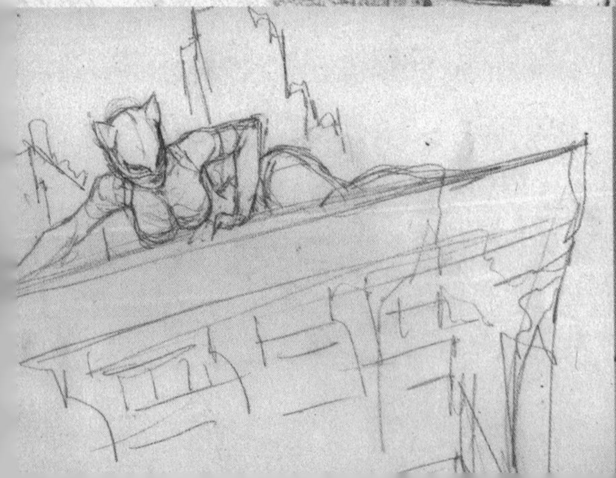

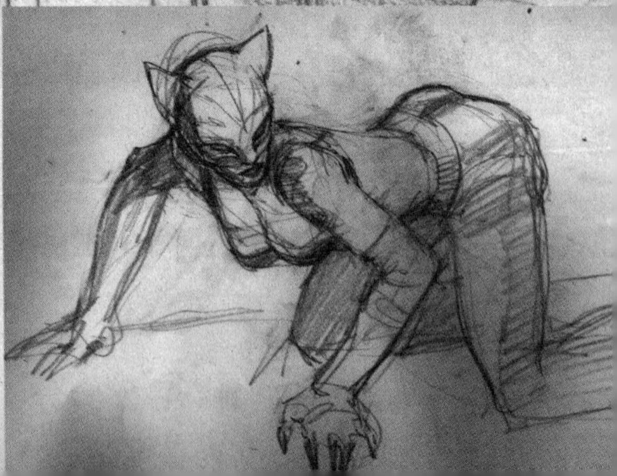

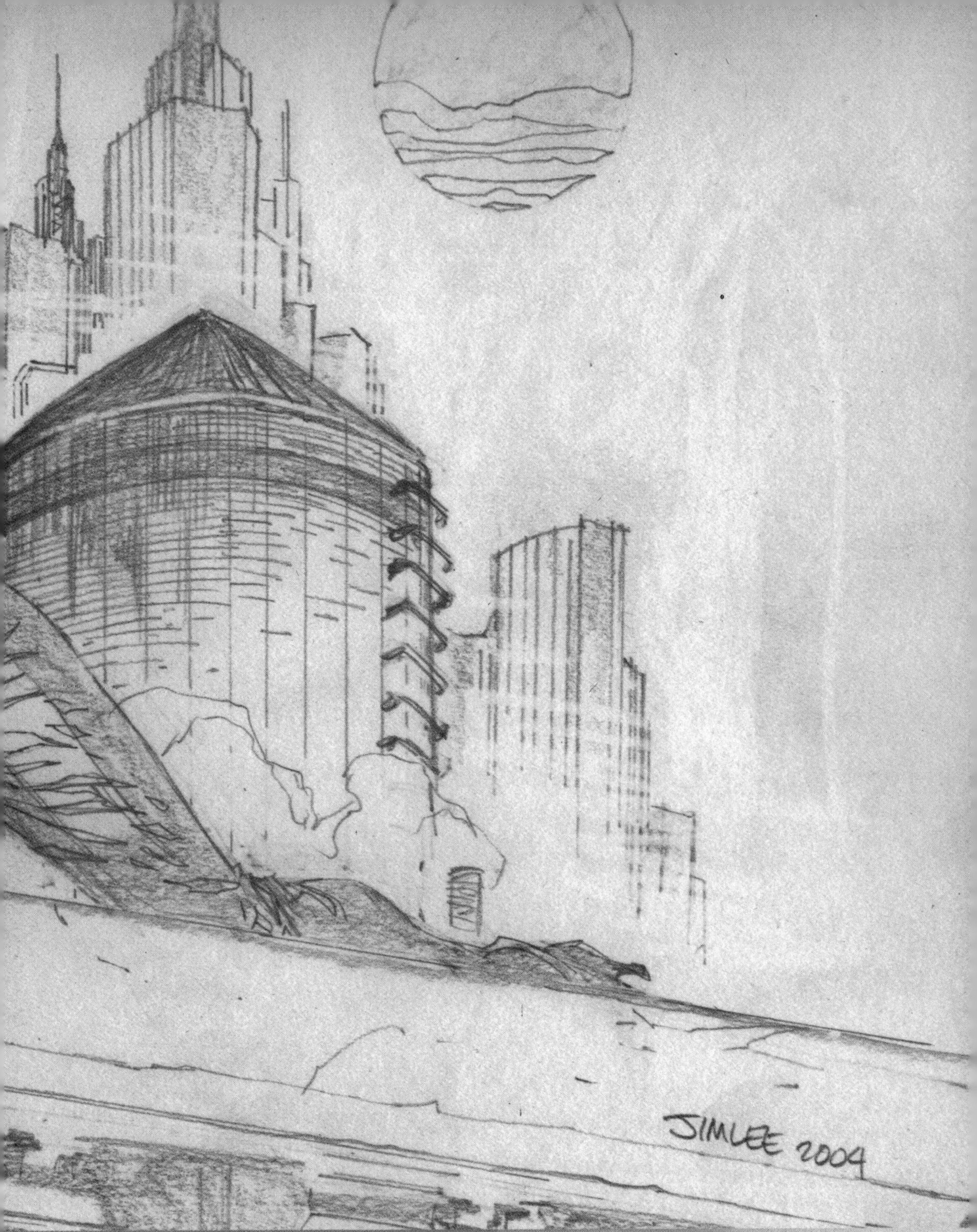
JIMLEE 2004

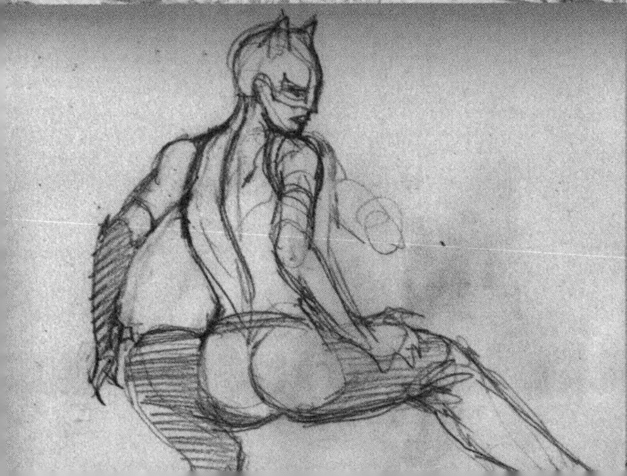

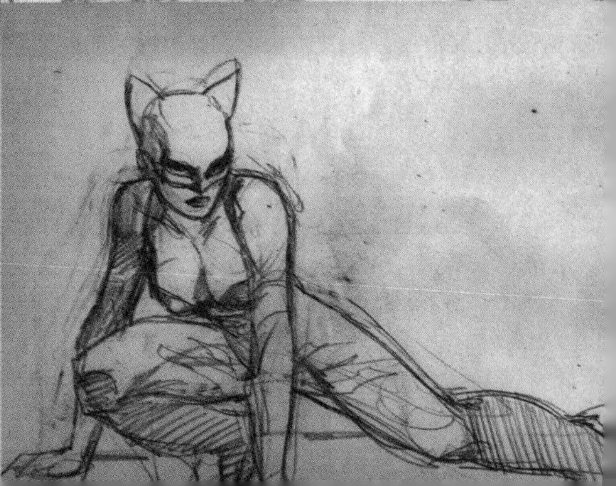

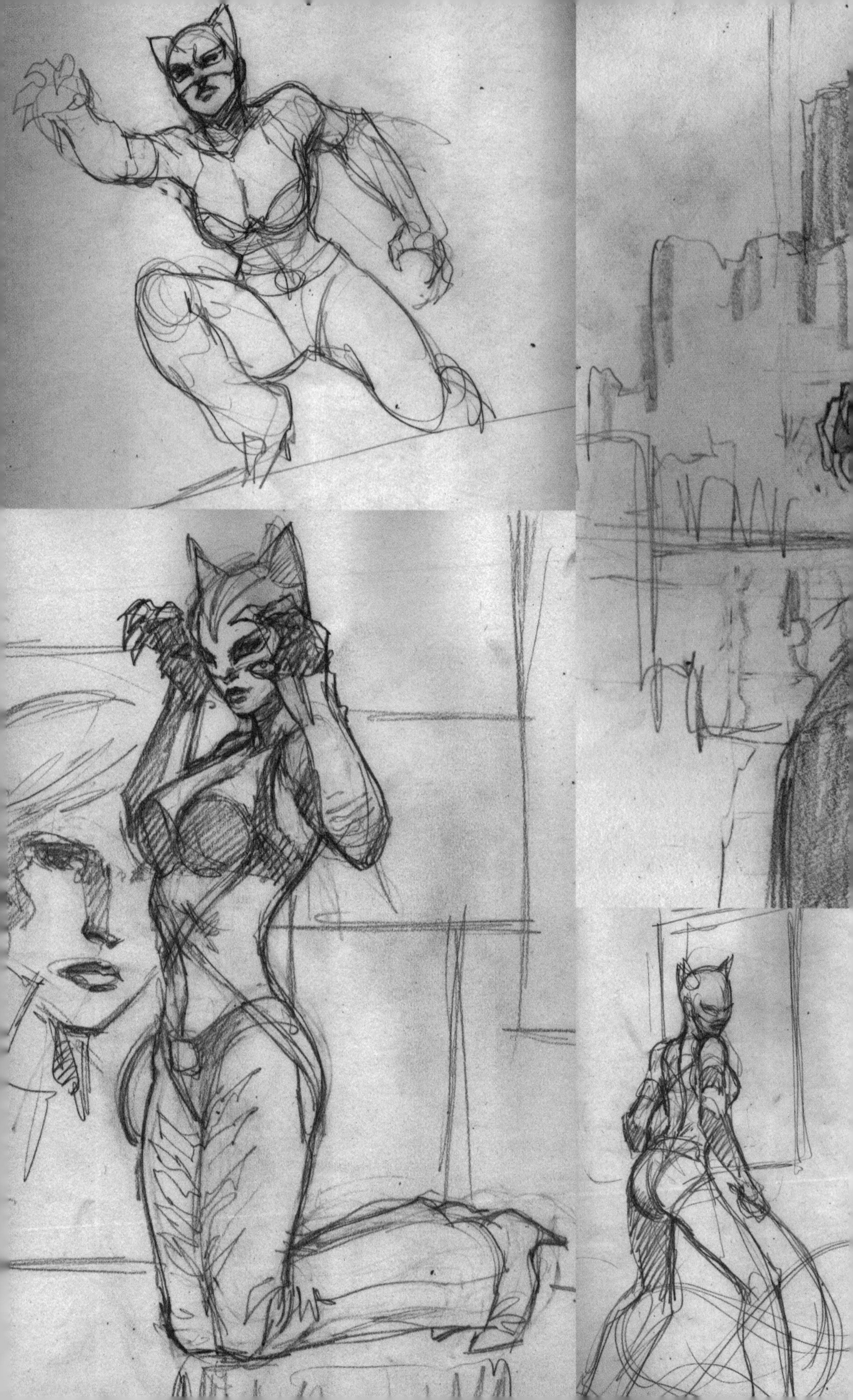

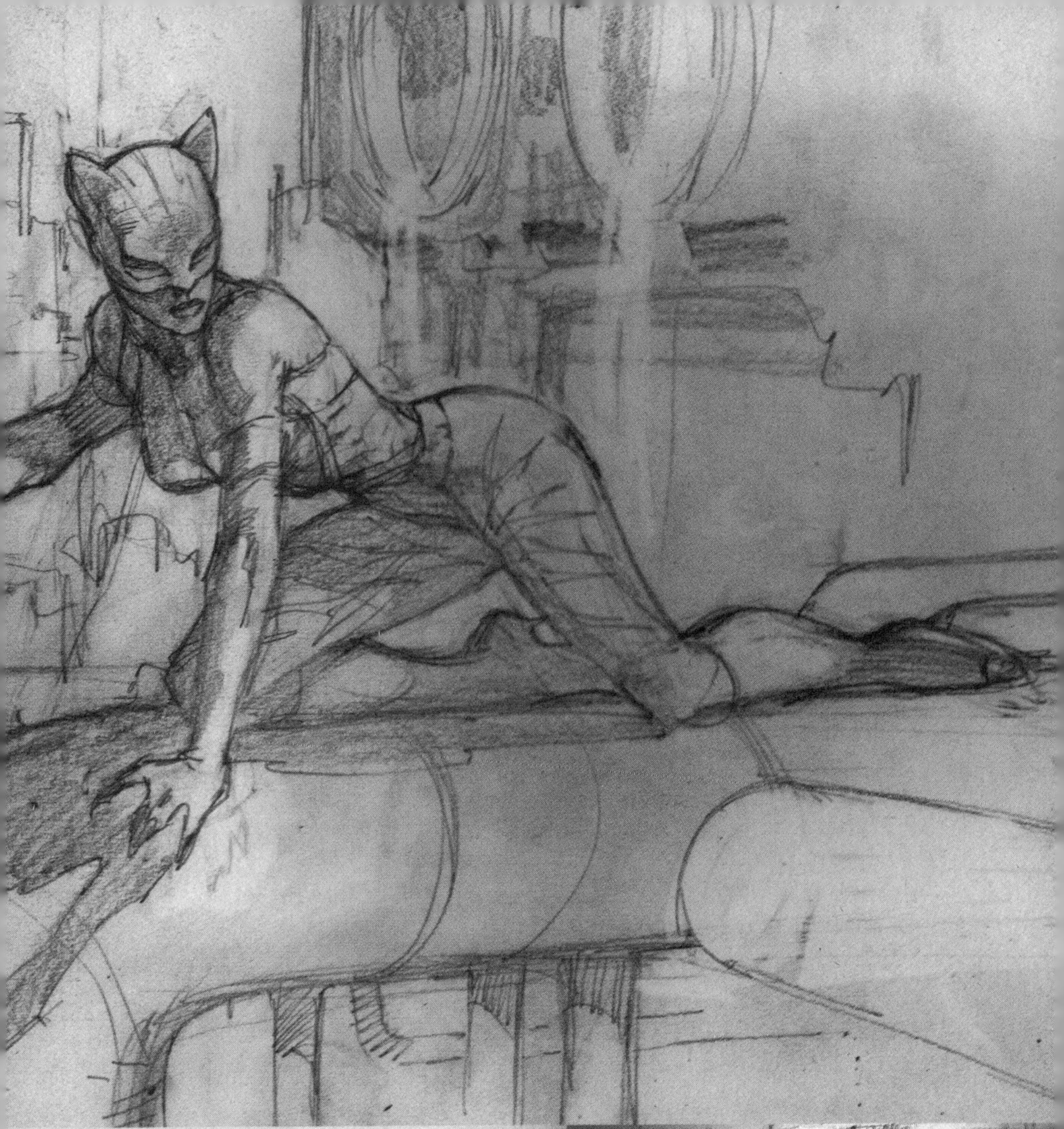

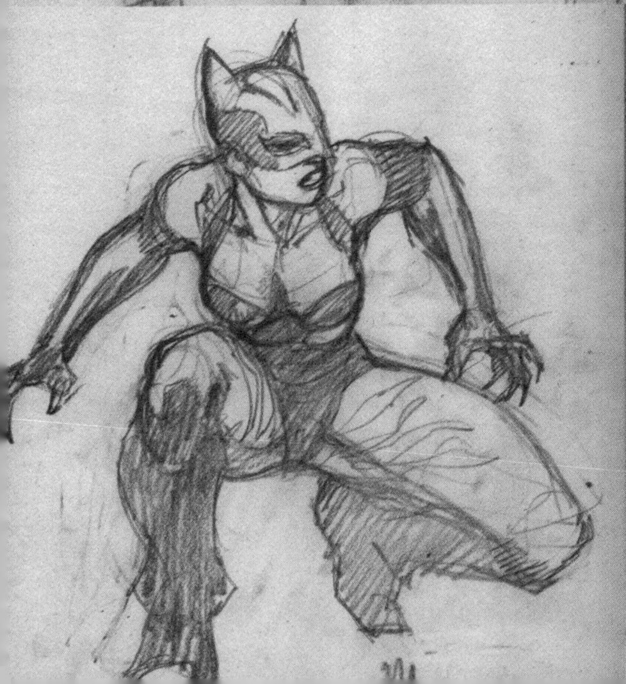

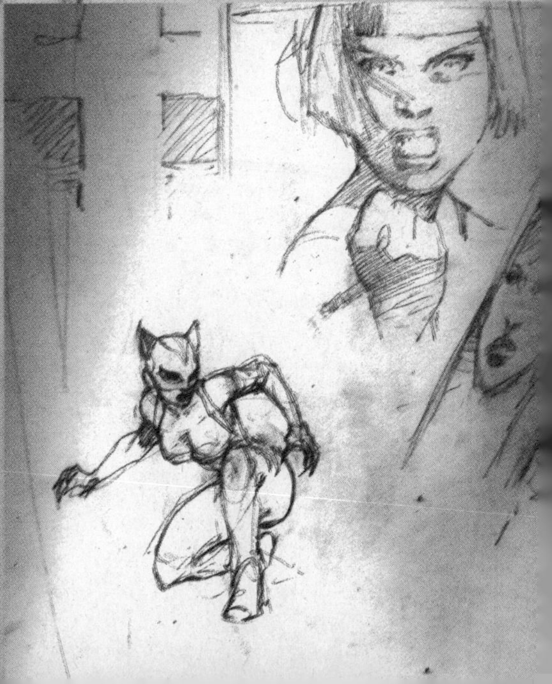

# OTHER CAT TALES

From the pages of DC Comics

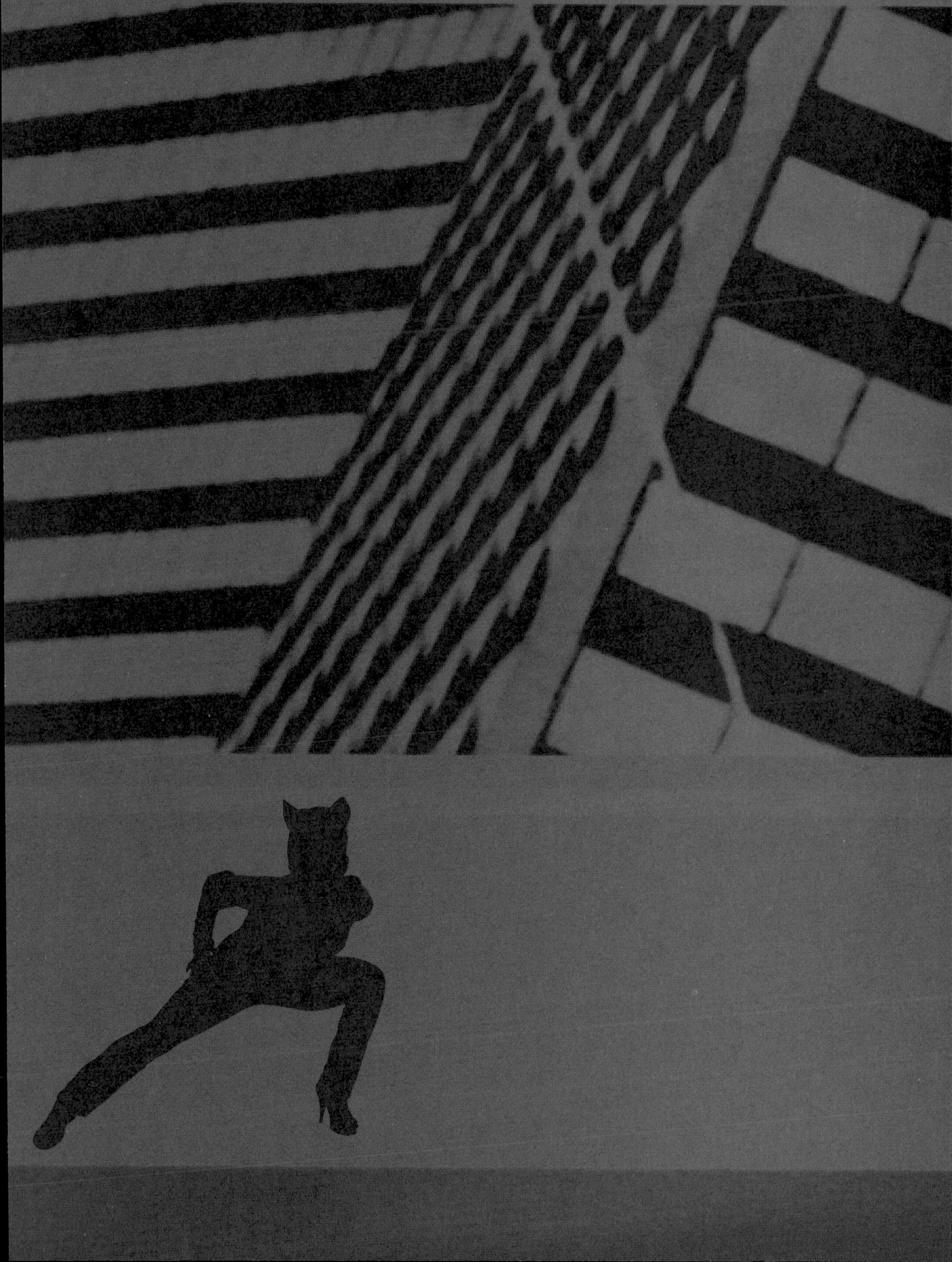

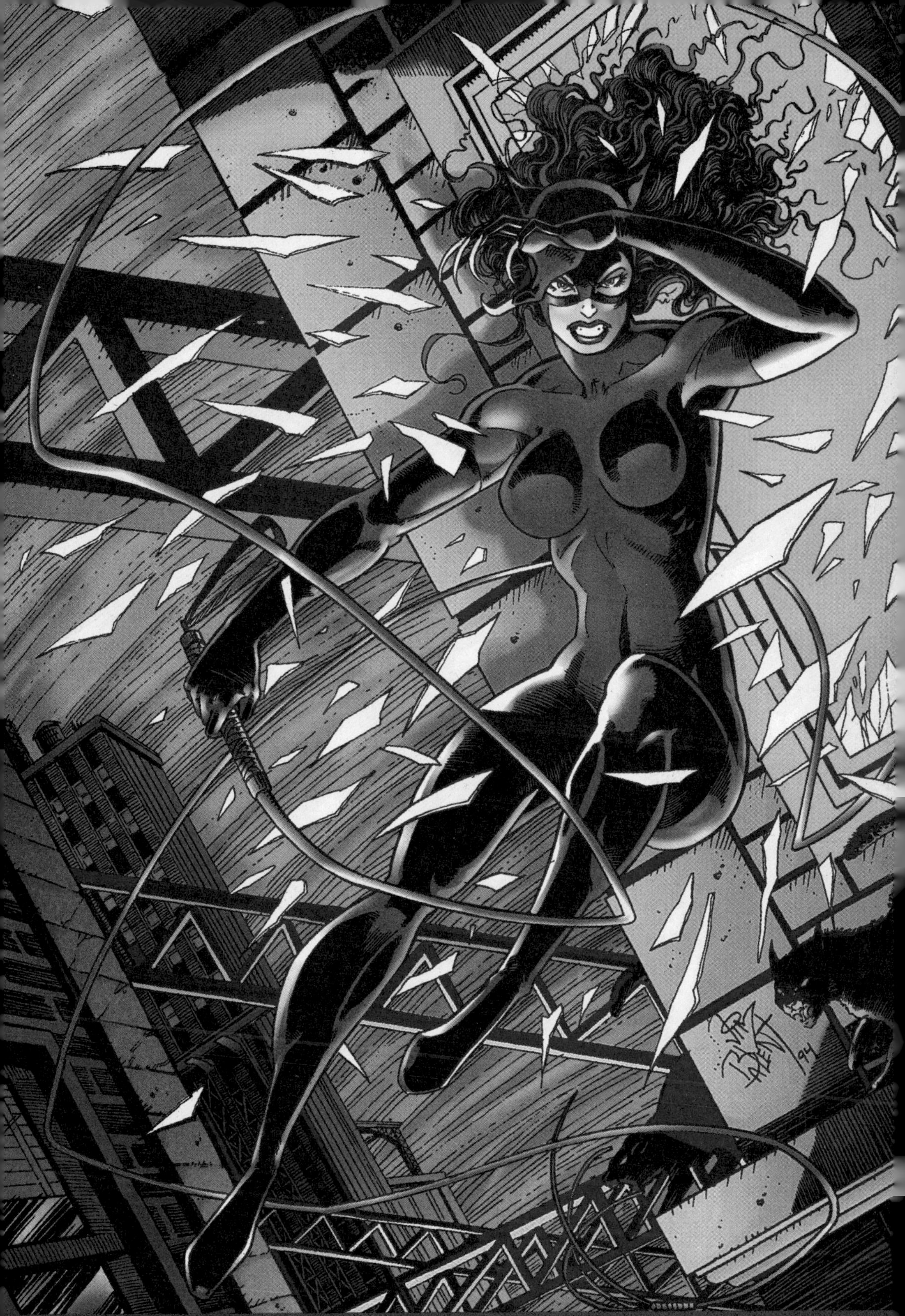

## Cat Shadows

**Doug Moench** Writer **Jim Balent** Penciller **Bob Smith** Inker
**Buzz Setzer** Colorist **Bob Pinaha** Letterer **Jim Balent** Cover Artist

Before Patience Philips was transformed into Catwoman, there was another who bore the Catwoman name. This is the origin of Selina Kyle.

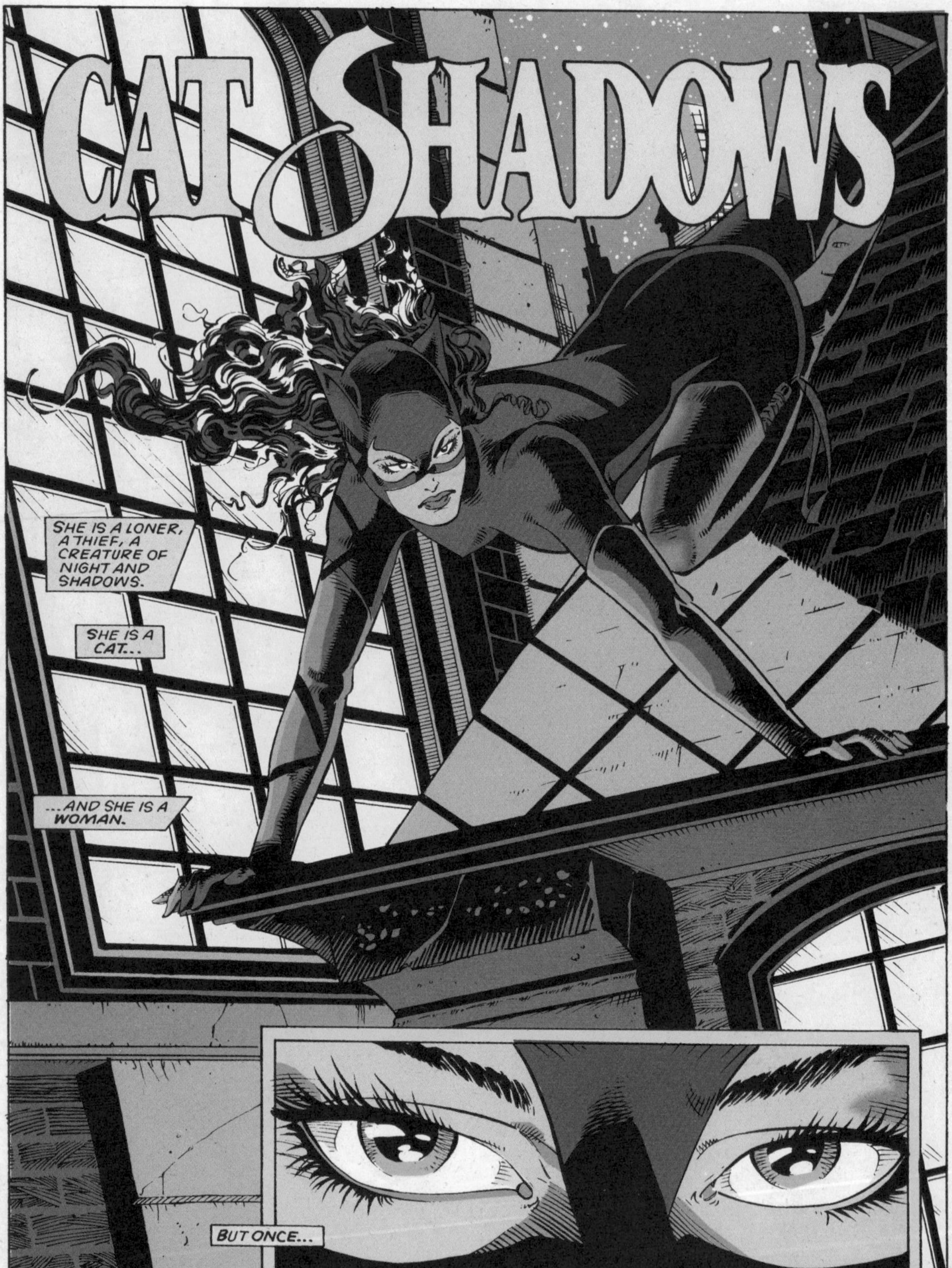
CAT SHADOWS
SHE IS A LONER, A THIEF, A CREATURE OF NIGHT AND SHADOWS.
SHE IS A CAT...
...AND SHE IS A WOMAN.
BUT ONCE...

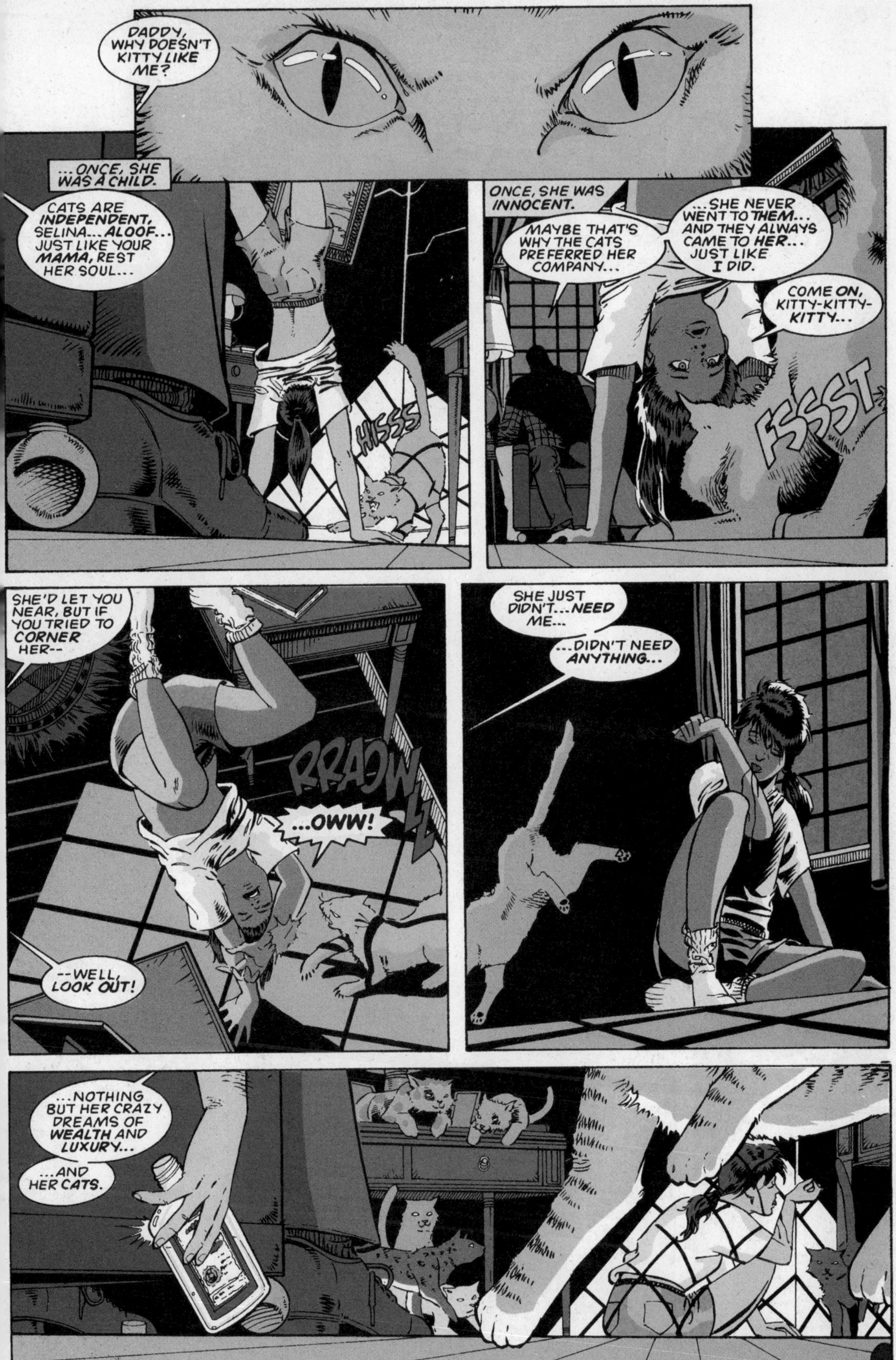
DADDY, WHY DOESN'T KITTY LIKE ME?
...ONCE, SHE WAS A CHILD.
CATS ARE INDEPENDENT, SELINA... ALOOF... JUST LIKE YOUR MAMA, REST HER SOUL...
HISSS
ONCE, SHE WAS INNOCENT.
MAYBE THAT'S WHY THE CATS PREFERRED HER COMPANY...
...SHE NEVER WENT TO THEM... AND THEY ALWAYS CAME TO HER... JUST LIKE I DID.
COME ON, KITTY-KITTY-KITTY...
FSSST
SHE'D LET YOU NEAR, BUT IF YOU TRIED TO CORNER HER--
RRAOWLL
...OWW!
--WELL, LOOK OUT!
SHE JUST DIDN'T... NEED ME...
...DIDN'T NEED ANYTHING...
...NOTHING BUT HER CRAZY DREAMS OF WEALTH AND LUXURY...
...AND HER CATS.

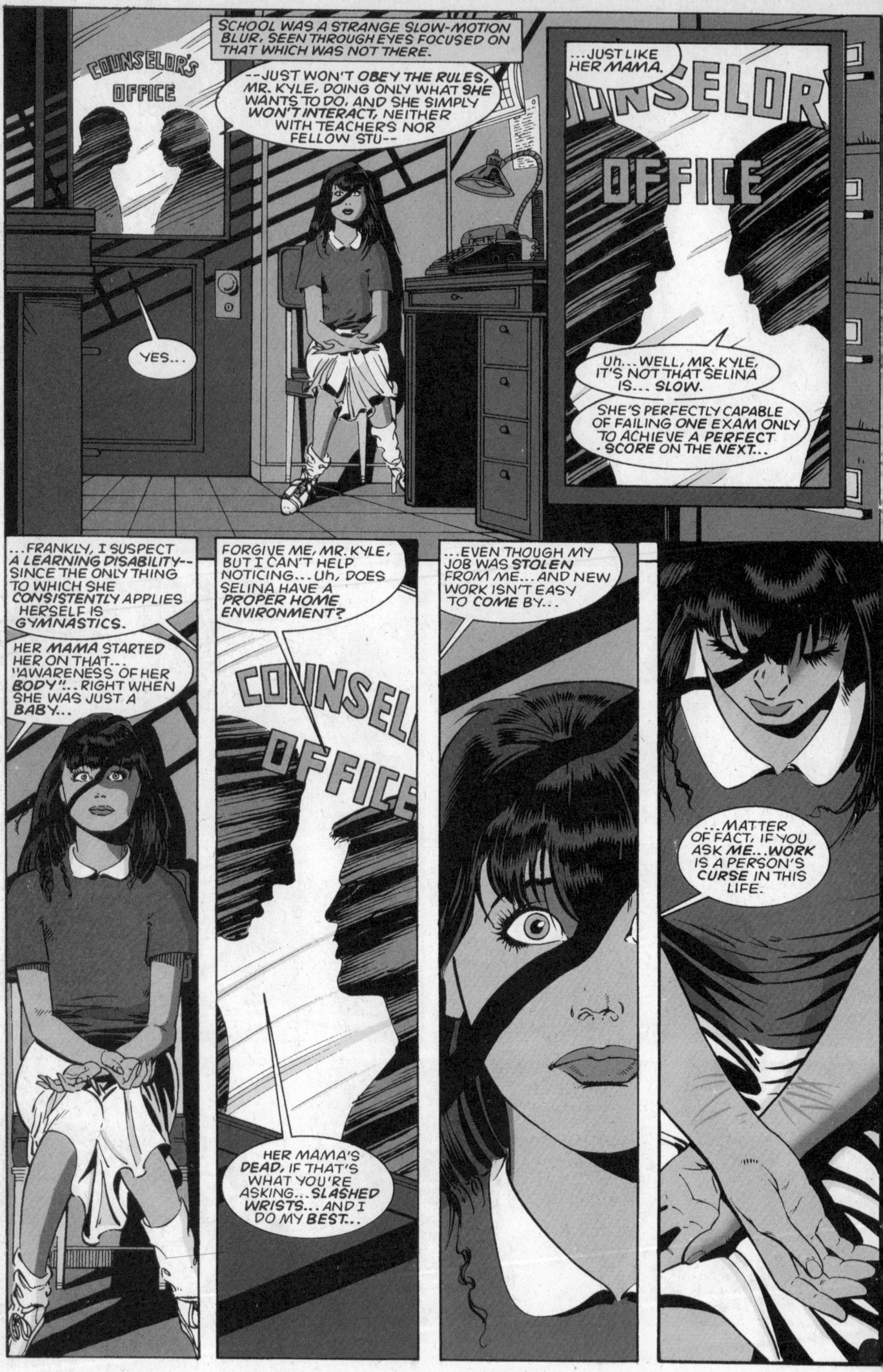
SCHOOL WAS A STRANGE SLOW-MOTION BLUR, SEEN THROUGH EYES FOCUSED ON THAT WHICH WAS NOT THERE.
COUNSELOR'S OFFICE
--JUST WON'T OBEY THE RULES, MR. KYLE, DOING ONLY WHAT SHE WANTS TO DO, AND SHE SIMPLY WON'T INTERACT, NEITHER WITH TEACHERS NOR FELLOW STU--
YES...
...JUST LIKE HER MAMA.
Uh... WELL, MR. KYLE, IT'S NOT THAT SELINA IS... SLOW.
SHE'S PERFECTLY CAPABLE OF FAILING ONE EXAM ONLY TO ACHIEVE A PERFECT SCORE ON THE NEXT...
...FRANKLY, I SUSPECT A LEARNING DISABILITY-- SINCE THE ONLY THING TO WHICH SHE CONSISTENTLY APPLIES HERSELF IS GYMNASTICS.
HER MAMA STARTED HER ON THAT... "AWARENESS OF HER BODY"... RIGHT WHEN SHE WAS JUST A BABY...
FORGIVE ME, MR. KYLE, BUT I CAN'T HELP NOTICING... Uh, DOES SELINA HAVE A PROPER HOME ENVIRONMENT?
HER MAMA'S DEAD, IF THAT'S WHAT YOU'RE ASKING... SLASHED WRISTS... AND I DO MY BEST...
...EVEN THOUGH MY JOB WAS STOLEN FROM ME... AND NEW WORK ISN'T EASY TO COME BY...
...MATTER OF FACT, IF YOU ASK ME... WORK IS A PERSON'S CURSE IN THIS LIFE.

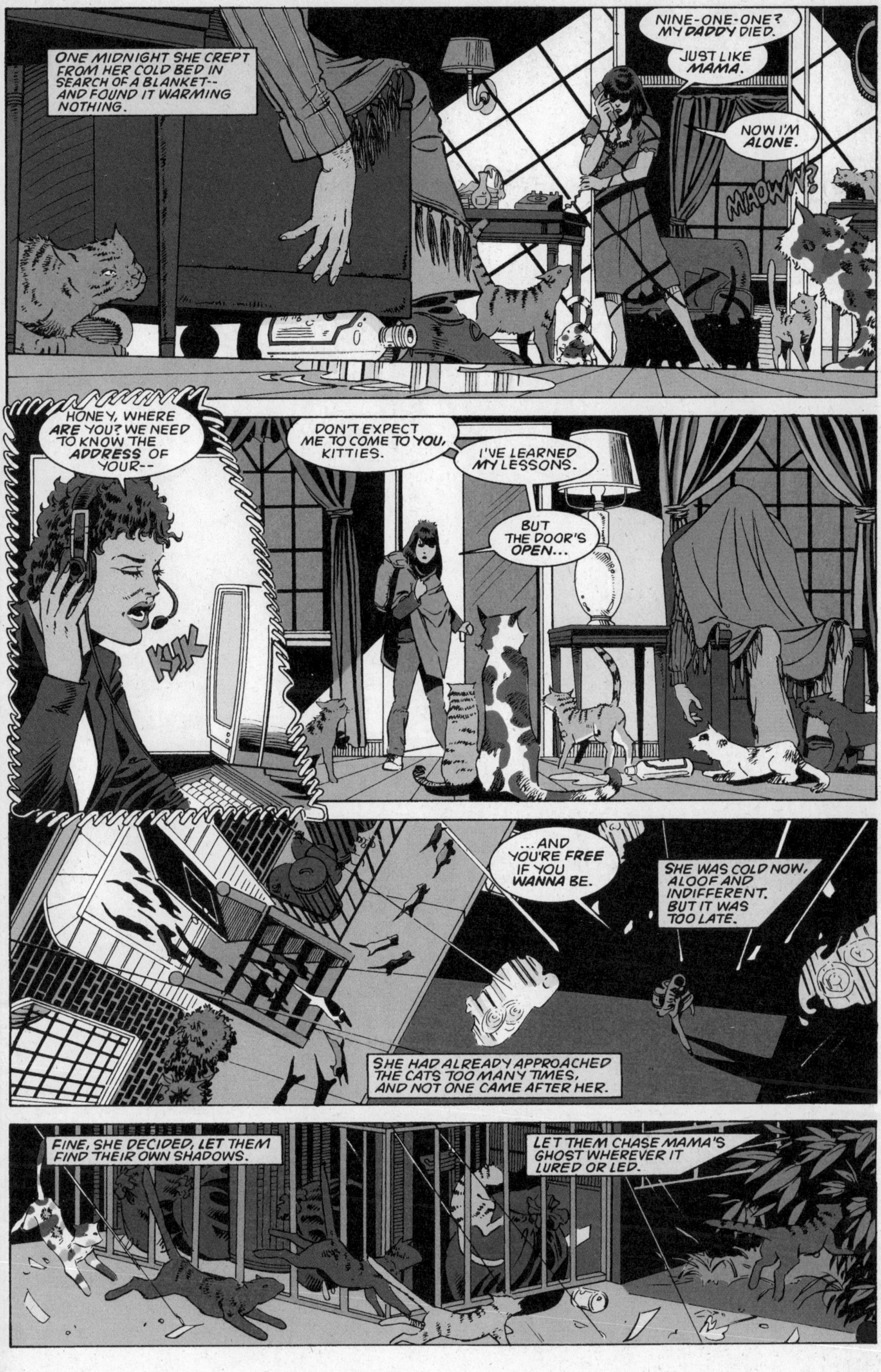
ONE MIDNIGHT SHE CREPT FROM HER COLD BED IN SEARCH OF A BLANKET-- AND FOUND IT WARMING NOTHING.
NINE-ONE-ONE? MY DADDY DIED.
JUST LIKE MAMA.
NOW I'M ALONE.
MAOWW?
HONEY, WHERE ARE YOU? WE NEED TO KNOW THE ADDRESS OF YOUR--
KLIK
DON'T EXPECT ME TO COME TO YOU, KITTIES.
I'VE LEARNED MY LESSONS.
BUT THE DOOR'S OPEN...
...AND YOU'RE FREE IF YOU WANNA BE.
SHE WAS COLD NOW, ALOOF AND INDIFFERENT. BUT IT WAS TOO LATE.
SHE HAD ALREADY APPROACHED THE CATS TOO MANY TIMES, AND NOT ONE CAME AFTER HER.
FINE, SHE DECIDED, LET THEM FIND THEIR OWN SHADOWS.
LET THEM CHASE MAMA'S GHOST WHEREVER IT LURED OR LED.

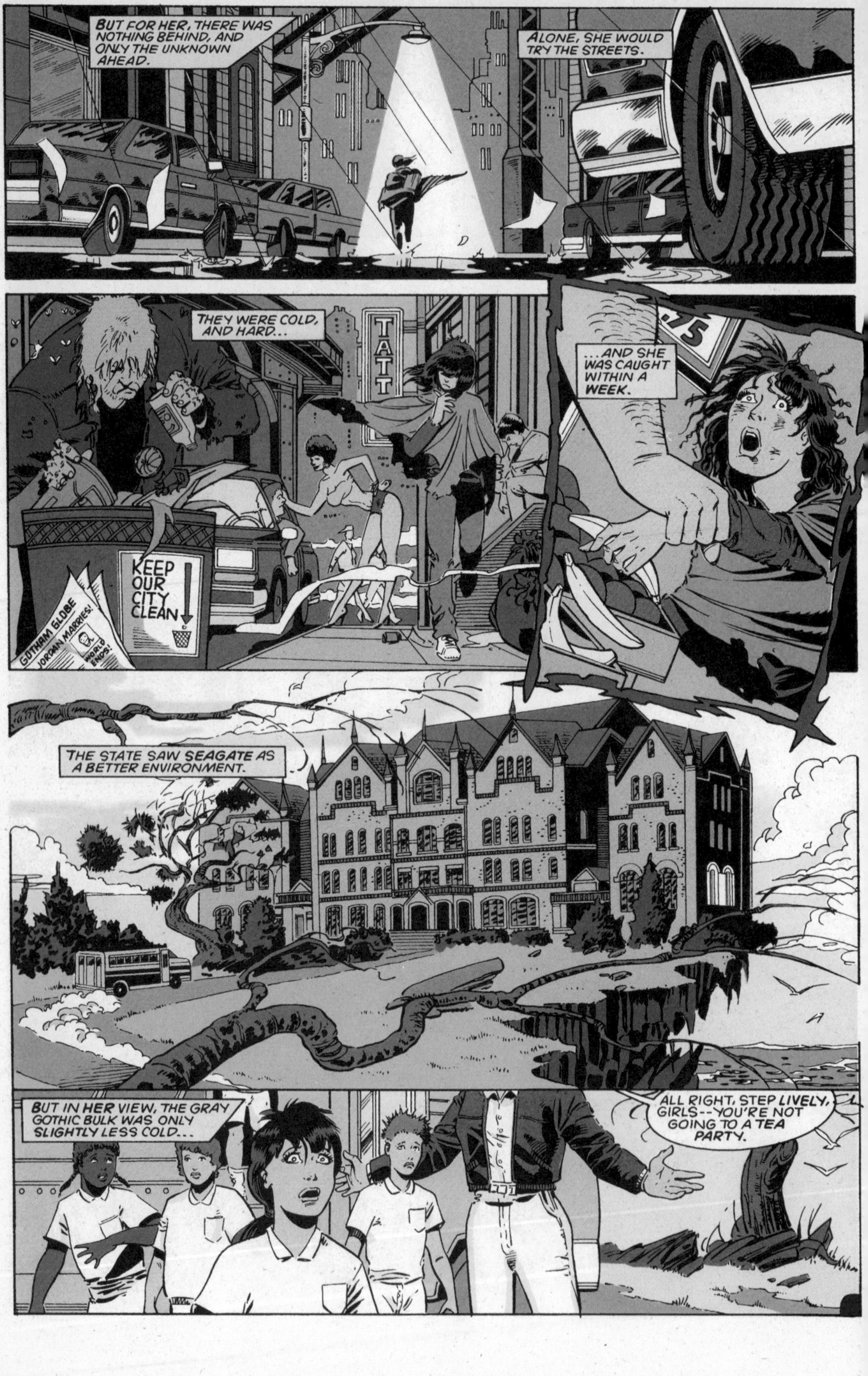
BUT FOR HER, THERE WAS NOTHING BEHIND, AND ONLY THE UNKNOWN AHEAD.
ALONE, SHE WOULD TRY THE STREETS.
THEY WERE COLD, AND HARD...
TATT
KEEP OUR CITY CLEAN
GOTHAM GLOBE
JORDAN MARRIES!
WORLD ENDS!
...AND SHE WAS CAUGHT WITHIN A WEEK.
THE STATE SAW SEAGATE AS A BETTER ENVIRONMENT.
BUT IN HER VIEW, THE GRAY GOTHIC BULK WAS ONLY SLIGHTLY LESS COLD...
ALL RIGHT, STEP LIVELY, GIRLS--YOU'RE NOT GOING TO A TEA PARTY.

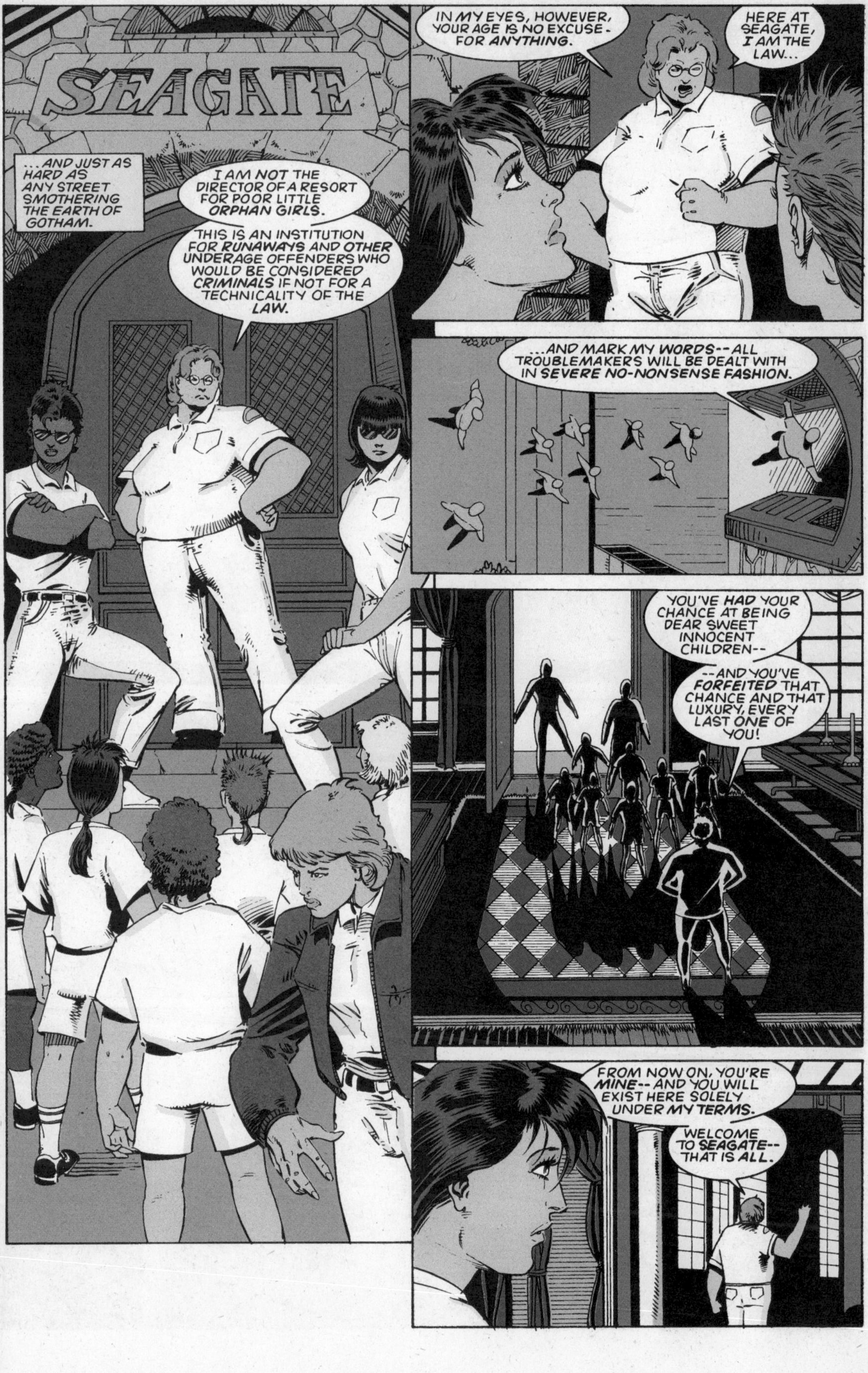
SEAGATE
...AND JUST AS HARD AS ANY STREET SMOTHERING THE EARTH OF GOTHAM.
I AM NOT THE DIRECTOR OF A RESORT FOR POOR LITTLE ORPHAN GIRLS.
THIS IS AN INSTITUTION FOR RUNAWAYS AND OTHER UNDERAGE OFFENDERS WHO WOULD BE CONSIDERED CRIMINALS IF NOT FOR A TECHNICALITY OF THE LAW.
IN MY EYES, HOWEVER, YOUR AGE IS NO EXCUSE-FOR ANYTHING.
HERE AT SEAGATE, I AM THE LAW...
...AND MARK MY WORDS--ALL TROUBLEMAKERS WILL BE DEALT WITH IN SEVERE NO-NONSENSE FASHION.
YOU'VE HAD YOUR CHANCE AT BEING DEAR SWEET INNOCENT CHILDREN--
--AND YOU'VE FORFEITED THAT CHANCE AND THAT LUXURY, EVERY LAST ONE OF YOU!
FROM NOW ON, YOU'RE MINE--AND YOU WILL EXIST HERE SOLELY UNDER MY TERMS.
WELCOME TO SEAGATE--THAT IS ALL.

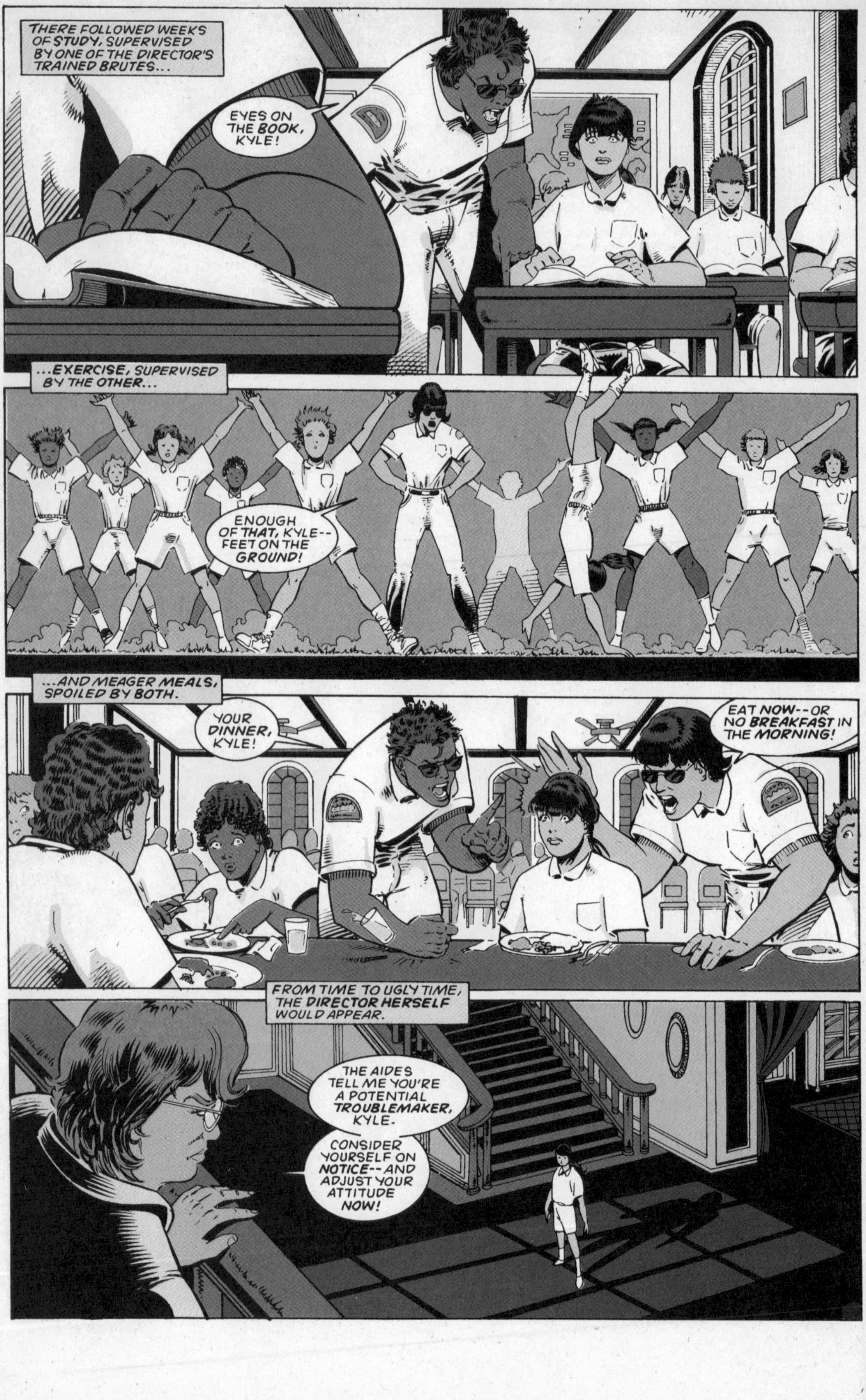

THERE FOLLOWED WEEKS OF STUDY, SUPERVISED BY ONE OF THE DIRECTOR'S TRAINED BRUTES...
EYES ON THE BOOK, KYLE!
...EXERCISE, SUPERVISED BY THE OTHER...
ENOUGH OF THAT, KYLE-- FEET ON THE GROUND!
...AND MEAGER MEALS, SPOILED BY BOTH.
YOUR DINNER, KYLE!
EAT NOW--OR NO BREAKFAST IN THE MORNING!
FROM TIME TO UGLY TIME, THE DIRECTOR HERSELF WOULD APPEAR.
THE AIDES TELL ME YOU'RE A POTENTIAL TROUBLEMAKER, KYLE.
CONSIDER YOURSELF ON NOTICE--AND ADJUST YOUR ATTITUDE NOW!

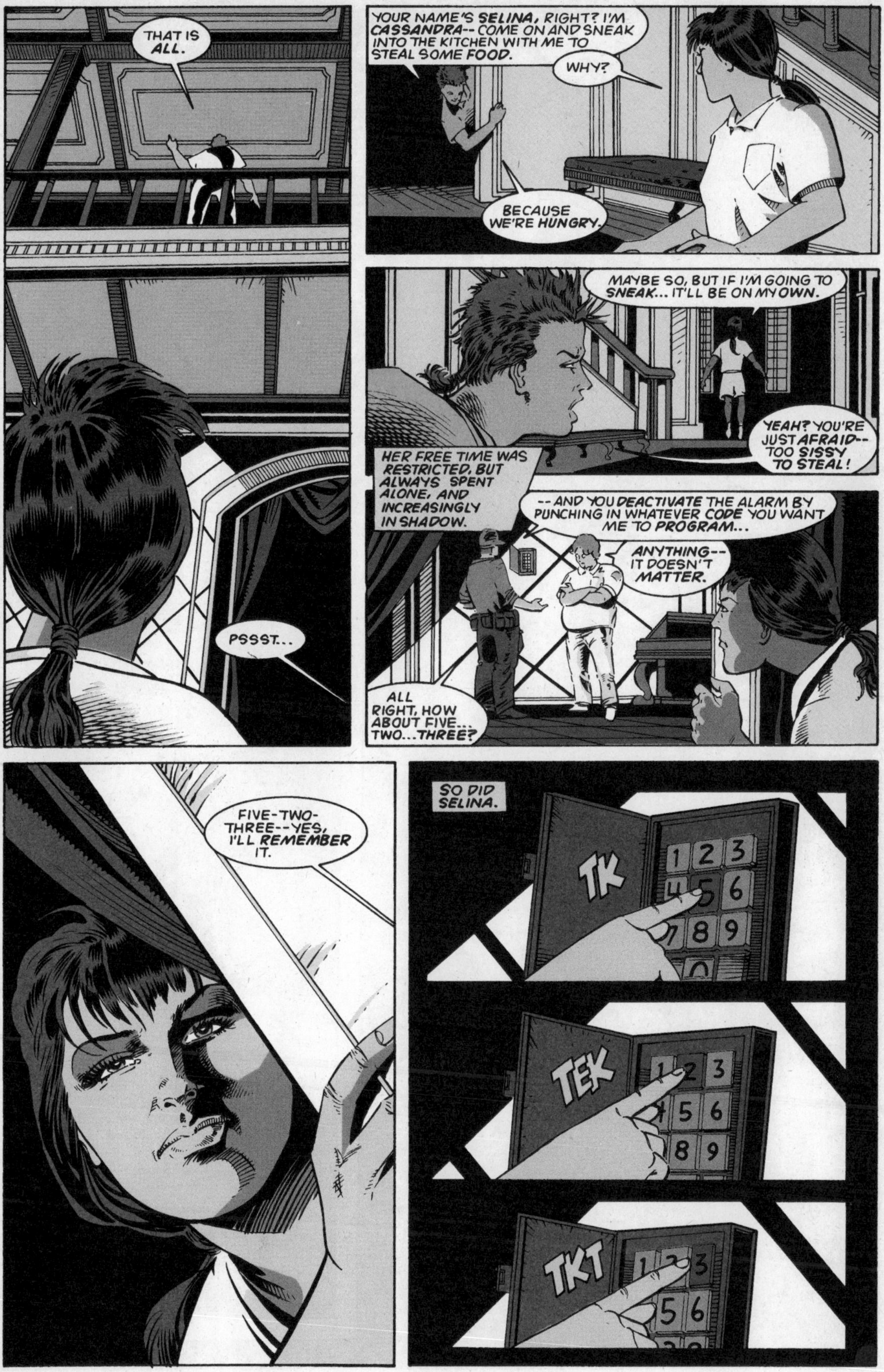
THAT IS ALL.
YOUR NAME'S SELINA, RIGHT? I'M CASSANDRA-- COME ON AND SNEAK INTO THE KITCHEN WITH ME TO STEAL SOME FOOD.
WHY?
BECAUSE WE'RE HUNGRY.
PSSST...
MAYBE SO, BUT IF I'M GOING TO SNEAK... IT'LL BE ON MY OWN.
YEAH? YOU'RE JUST AFRAID-- TOO SISSY TO STEAL!
HER FREE TIME WAS RESTRICTED, BUT ALWAYS SPENT ALONE, AND INCREASINGLY IN SHADOW.
--AND YOU DEACTIVATE THE ALARM BY PUNCHING IN WHATEVER CODE YOU WANT ME TO PROGRAM...
ANYTHING-- IT DOESN'T MATTER.
ALL RIGHT, HOW ABOUT FIVE... TWO... THREE?
FIVE-TWO-THREE--YES, I'LL REMEMBER IT.
SO DID SELINA.
TK
TEK
TKT

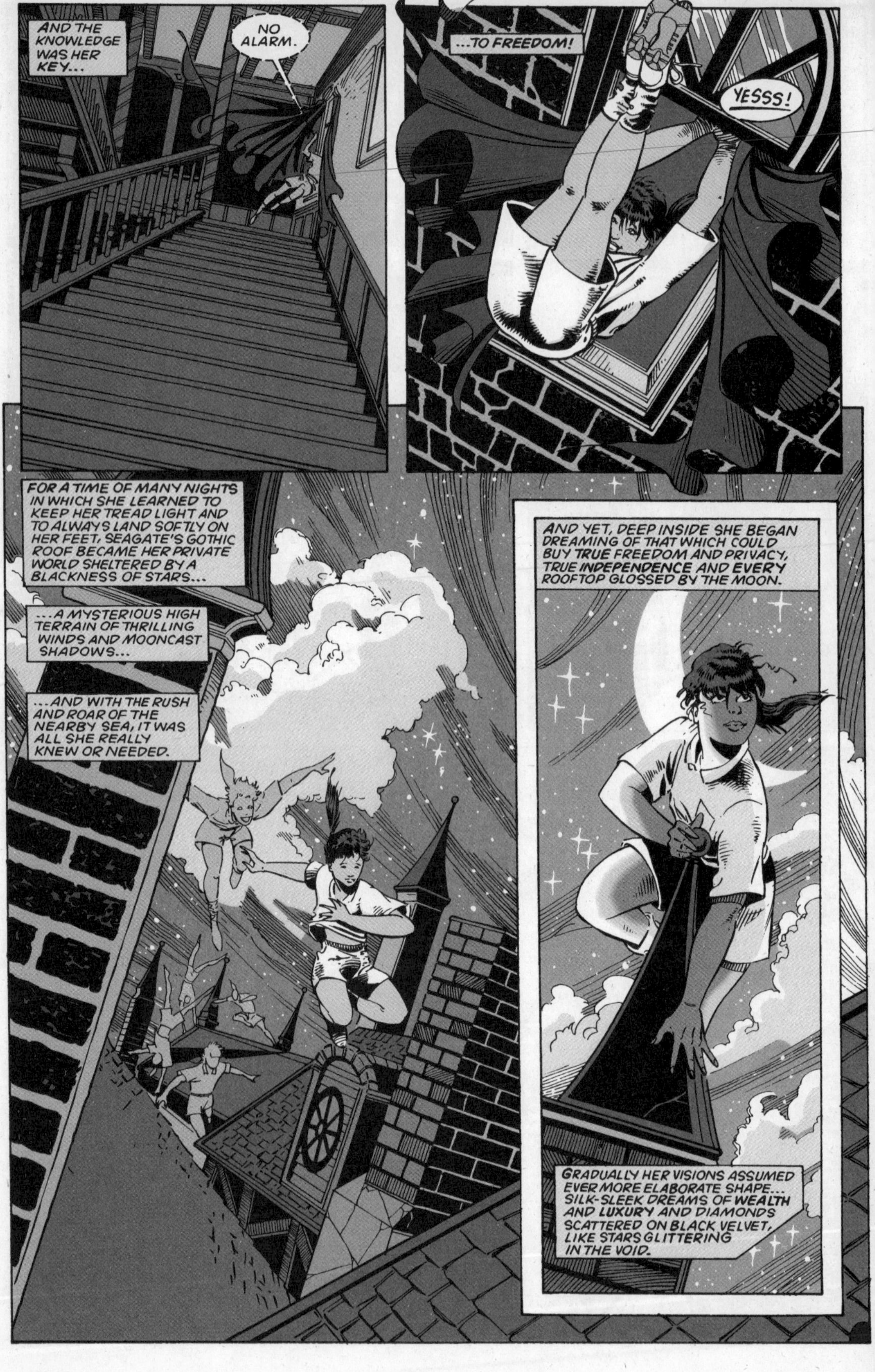
AND THE KNOWLEDGE WAS HER KEY...
NO ALARM.
...TO FREEDOM!
YESSS!
FOR A TIME OF MANY NIGHTS IN WHICH SHE LEARNED TO KEEP HER TREAD LIGHT AND TO ALWAYS LAND SOFTLY ON HER FEET, SEAGATE'S GOTHIC ROOF BECAME HER PRIVATE WORLD SHELTERED BY A BLACKNESS OF STARS...
...A MYSTERIOUS HIGH TERRAIN OF THRILLING WINDS AND MOONCAST SHADOWS...
...AND WITH THE RUSH AND ROAR OF THE NEARBY SEA, IT WAS ALL SHE REALLY KNEW OR NEEDED.
AND YET, DEEP INSIDE SHE BEGAN DREAMING OF THAT WHICH COULD BUY TRUE FREEDOM AND PRIVACY, TRUE INDEPENDENCE AND EVERY ROOFTOP GLOSSED BY THE MOON.
GRADUALLY HER VISIONS ASSUMED EVER MORE ELABORATE SHAPE... SILK-SLEEK DREAMS OF WEALTH AND LUXURY AND DIAMONDS SCATTERED ON BLACK VELVET, LIKE STARS GLITTERING IN THE VOID.

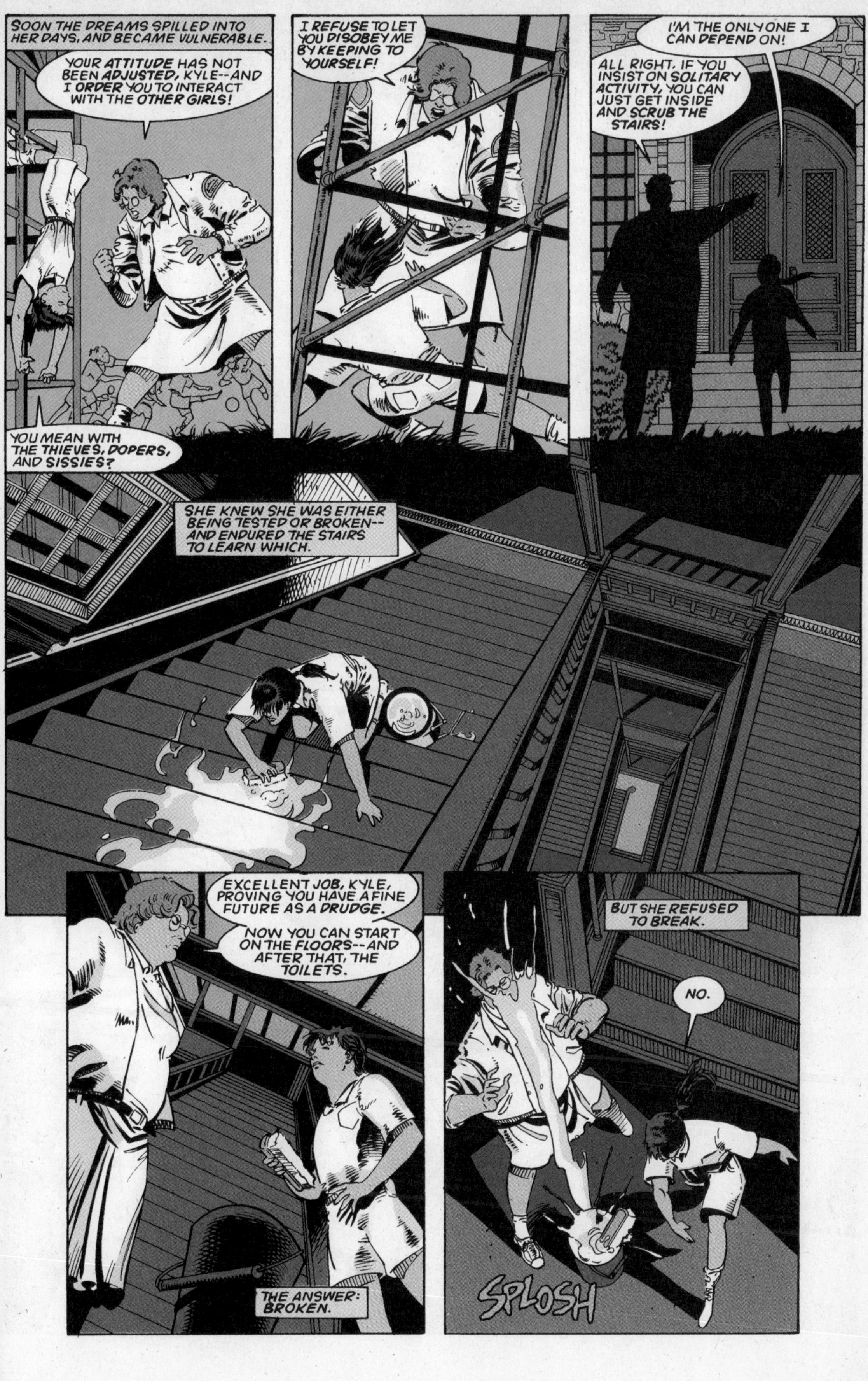
SOON THE DREAMS SPILLED INTO HER DAYS, AND BECAME VULNERABLE.
YOUR ATTITUDE HAS NOT BEEN ADJUSTED, KYLE--AND I ORDER YOU TO INTERACT WITH THE OTHER GIRLS!
YOU MEAN WITH THE THIEVES, DOPERS, AND SISSIES?
I REFUSE TO LET YOU DISOBEY ME BY KEEPING TO YOURSELF!
I'M THE ONLY ONE I CAN DEPEND ON!
ALL RIGHT. IF YOU INSIST ON SOLITARY ACTIVITY, YOU CAN JUST GET INSIDE AND SCRUB THE STAIRS!
SHE KNEW SHE WAS EITHER BEING TESTED OR BROKEN--AND ENDURED THE STAIRS TO LEARN WHICH.
EXCELLENT JOB, KYLE, PROVING YOU HAVE A FINE FUTURE AS A DRUDGE.
NOW YOU CAN START ON THE FLOORS--AND AFTER THAT, THE TOILETS.
THE ANSWER: BROKEN.
BUT SHE REFUSED TO BREAK.
NO.
SPLOSH

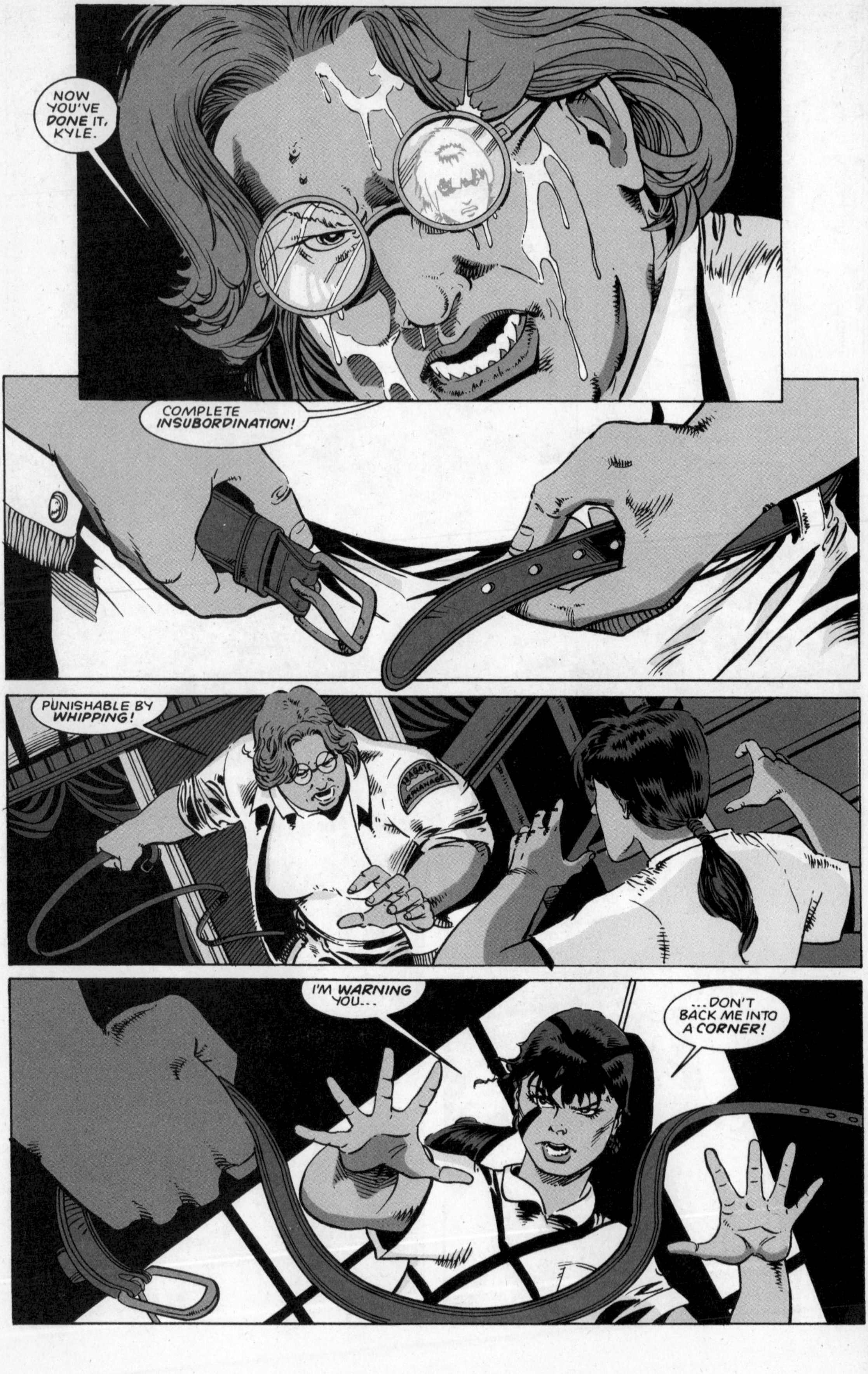
NOW YOU'VE DONE IT, KYLE.
COMPLETE INSUBORDINATION!
PUNISHABLE BY WHIPPING!
I'M WARNING YOU...
...DON'T BACK ME INTO A CORNER!

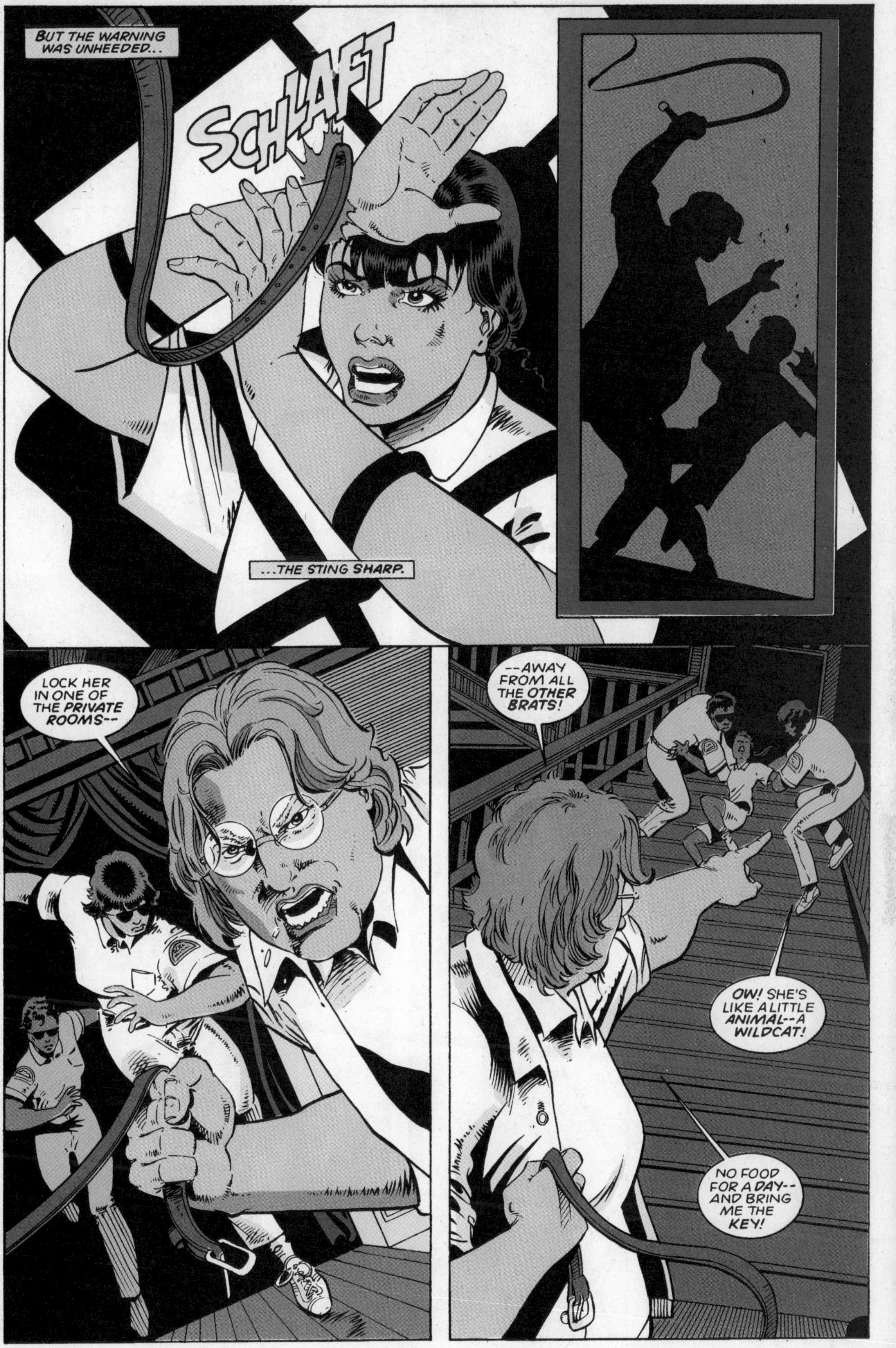

BUT THE WARNING WAS UNHEEDED...
SCHLAFT
...THE STING SHARP.
LOCK HER IN ONE OF THE PRIVATE ROOMS--
--AWAY FROM ALL THE OTHER BRATS!
OW! SHE'S LIKE A LITTLE ANIMAL--A WILDCAT!
NO FOOD FOR A DAY--AND BRING ME THE KEY!

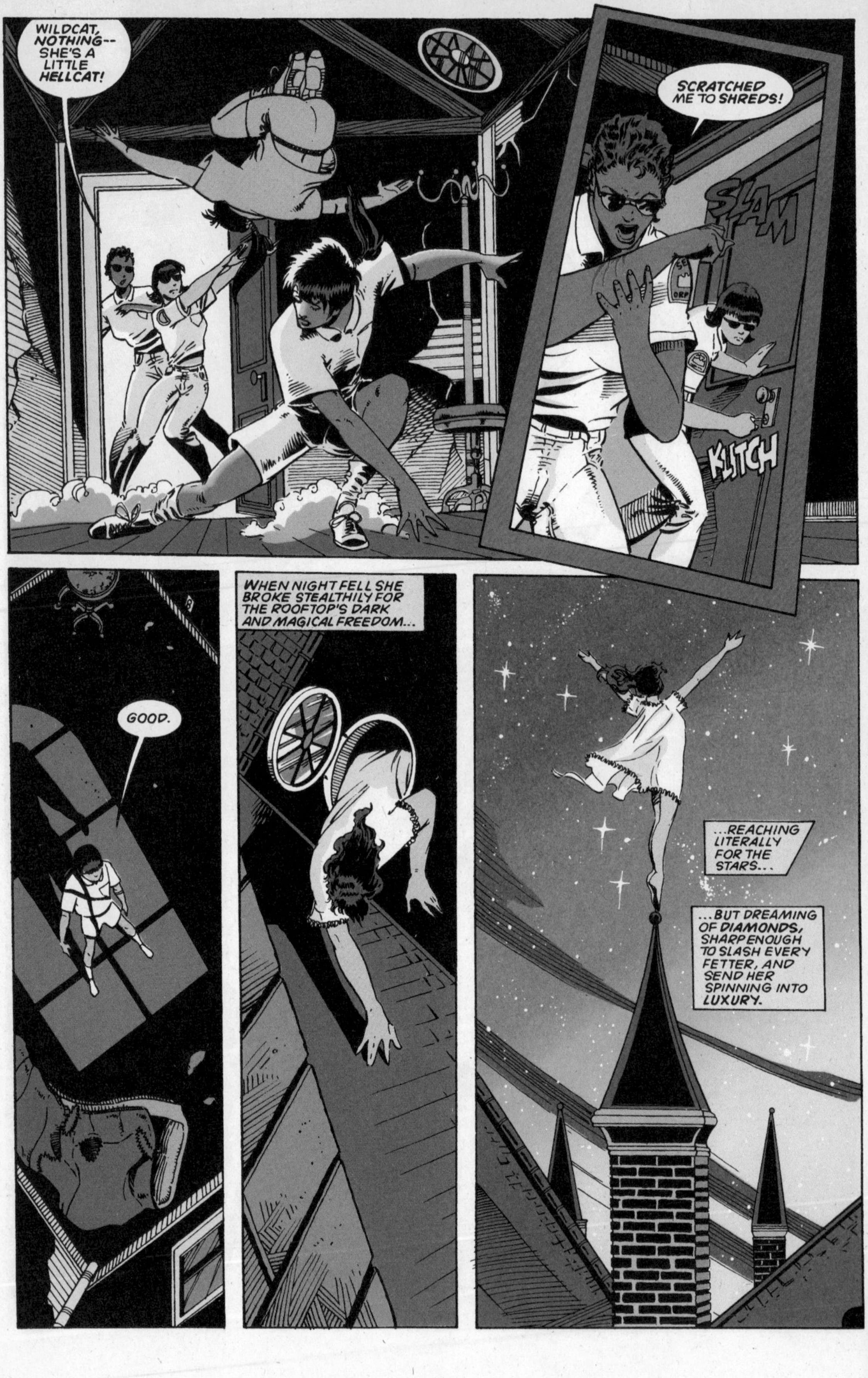
WILDCAT, NOTHING-- SHE'S A LITTLE HELLCAT!
SCRATCHED ME TO SHREDS!
SLAM
KLITCH
GOOD.
WHEN NIGHT FELL SHE BROKE STEALTHILY FOR THE ROOFTOP'S DARK AND MAGICAL FREEDOM...
...REACHING LITERALLY FOR THE STARS...
...BUT DREAMING OF DIAMONDS, SHARP ENOUGH TO SLASH EVERY FETTER, AND SEND HER SPINNING INTO LUXURY.

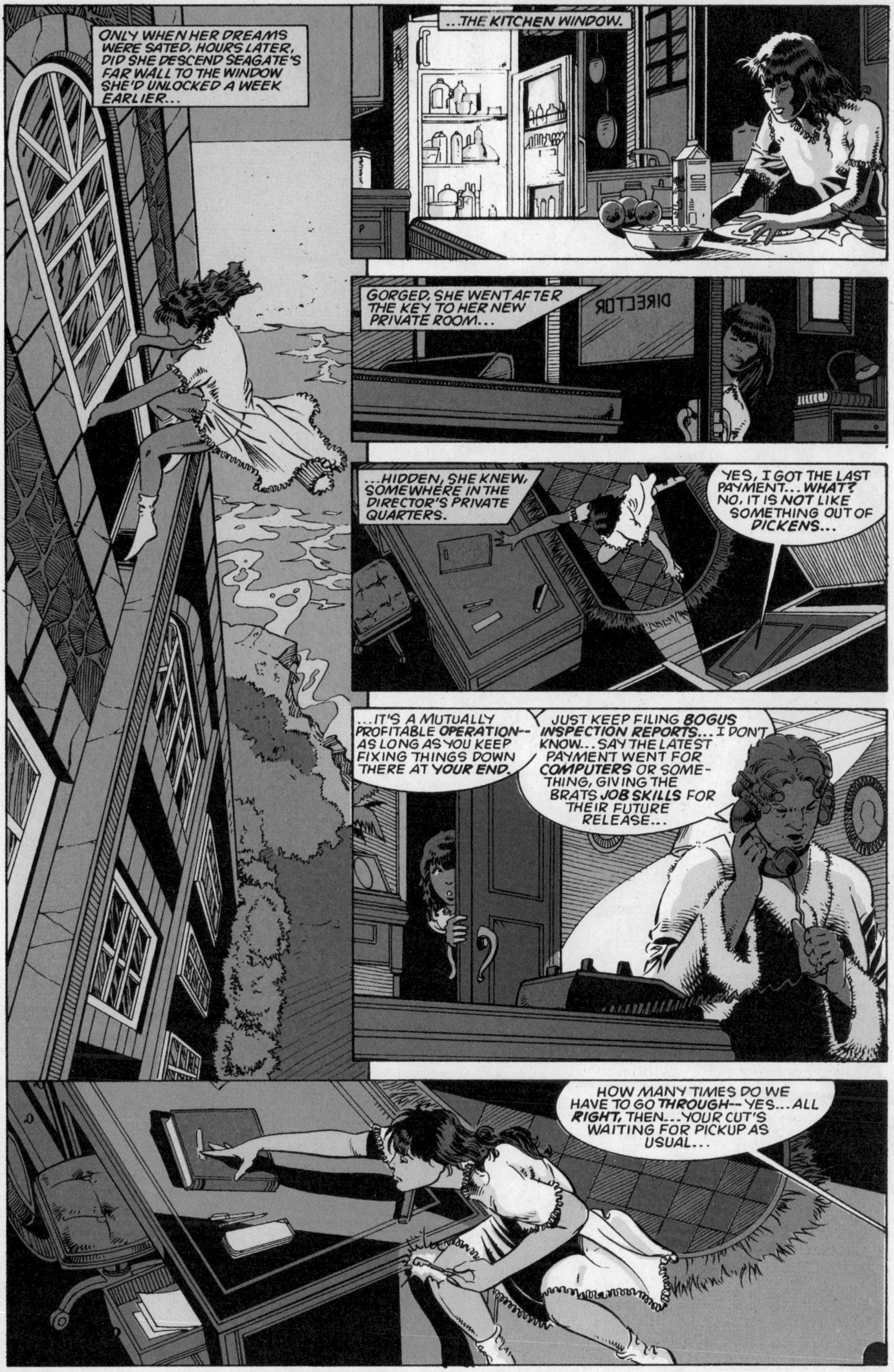
ONLY WHEN HER DREAMS WERE SATED, HOURS LATER, DID SHE DESCEND SEAGATE'S FAR WALL TO THE WINDOW SHE'D UNLOCKED A WEEK EARLIER...
...THE KITCHEN WINDOW.
GORGED, SHE WENT AFTER THE KEY TO HER NEW PRIVATE ROOM...
DIRECTOR
...HIDDEN, SHE KNEW, SOMEWHERE IN THE DIRECTOR'S PRIVATE QUARTERS.
YES, I GOT THE LAST PAYMENT... WHAT? NO, IT IS NOT LIKE SOMETHING OUT OF DICKENS...
...IT'S A MUTUALLY PROFITABLE OPERATION-- AS LONG AS YOU KEEP FIXING THINGS DOWN THERE AT YOUR END.
JUST KEEP FILING BOGUS INSPECTION REPORTS... I DON'T KNOW... SAY THE LATEST PAYMENT WENT FOR COMPUTERS OR SOMETHING, GIVING THE BRATS JOB SKILLS FOR THEIR FUTURE RELEASE...
HOW MANY TIMES DO WE HAVE TO GO THROUGH-- YES... ALL RIGHT, THEN... YOUR CUT'S WAITING FOR PICKUP AS USUAL...

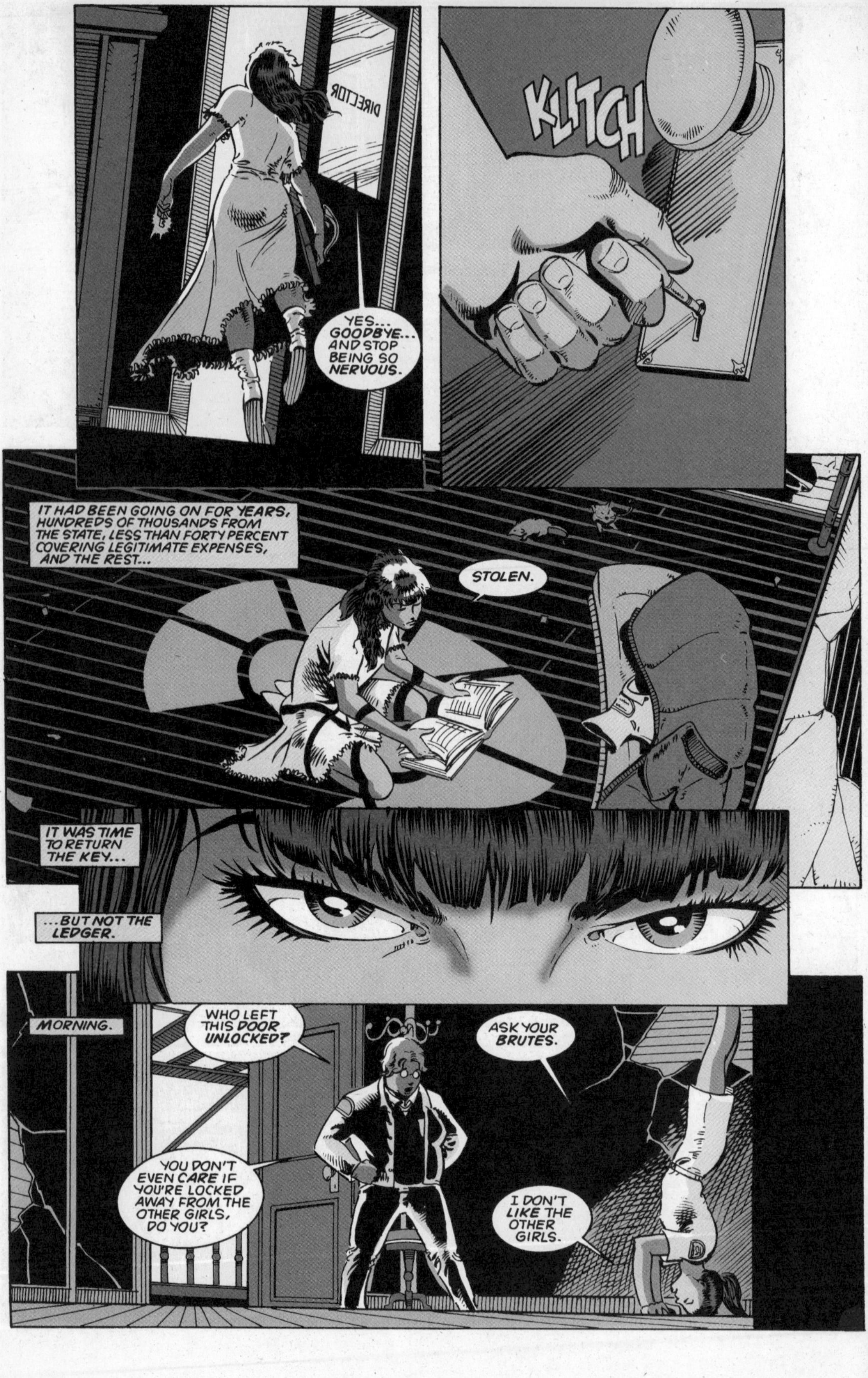
DIRECTOR
YES... GOODBYE... AND STOP BEING SO NERVOUS.
KLITCH
IT HAD BEEN GOING ON FOR YEARS, HUNDREDS OF THOUSANDS FROM THE STATE, LESS THAN FORTY PERCENT COVERING LEGITIMATE EXPENSES, AND THE REST...
STOLEN.
IT WAS TIME TO RETURN THE KEY...
...BUT NOT THE LEDGER.
MORNING.
WHO LEFT THIS DOOR UNLOCKED?
ASK YOUR BRUTES.
YOU DON'T EVEN CARE IF YOU'RE LOCKED AWAY FROM THE OTHER GIRLS, DO YOU?
I DON'T LIKE THE OTHER GIRLS.

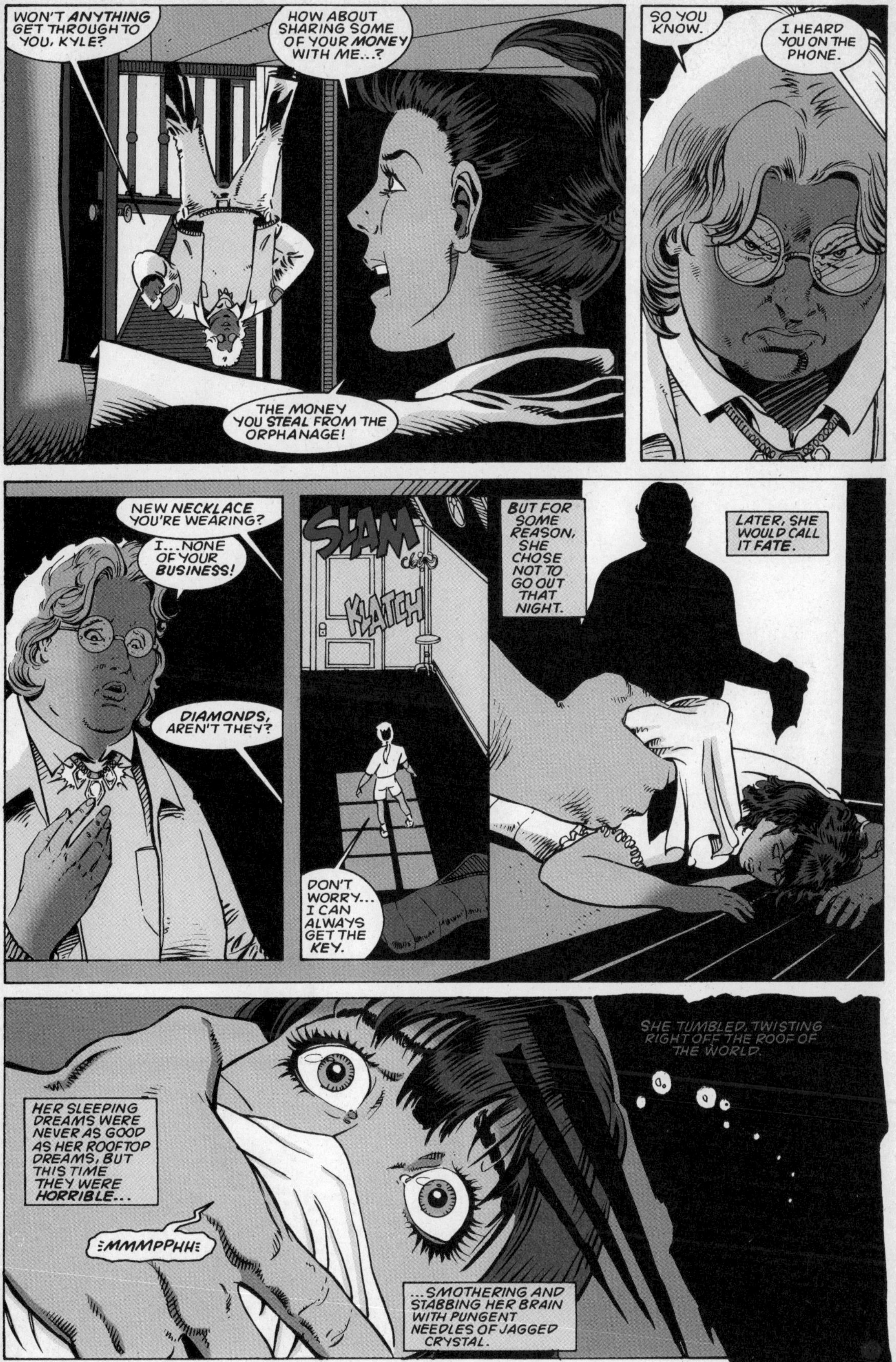
WON'T ANYTHING GET THROUGH TO YOU, KYLE?
HOW ABOUT SHARING SOME OF YOUR MONEY WITH ME...?
THE MONEY YOU STEAL FROM THE ORPHANAGE!
SO YOU KNOW.
I HEARD YOU ON THE PHONE.
NEW NECKLACE YOU'RE WEARING?
I...NONE OF YOUR BUSINESS!
DIAMONDS, AREN'T THEY?
SLAM
KLATCH
DON'T WORRY... I CAN ALWAYS GET THE KEY.
BUT FOR SOME REASON, SHE CHOSE NOT TO GO OUT THAT NIGHT.
LATER, SHE WOULD CALL IT FATE.
HER SLEEPING DREAMS WERE NEVER AS GOOD AS HER ROOFTOP DREAMS, BUT THIS TIME THEY WERE HORRIBLE...
MMMPPHH
...SMOTHERING AND STABBING HER BRAIN WITH PUNGENT NEEDLES OF JAGGED CRYSTAL.
SHE TUMBLED, TWISTING RIGHT OFF THE ROOF OF THE WORLD.

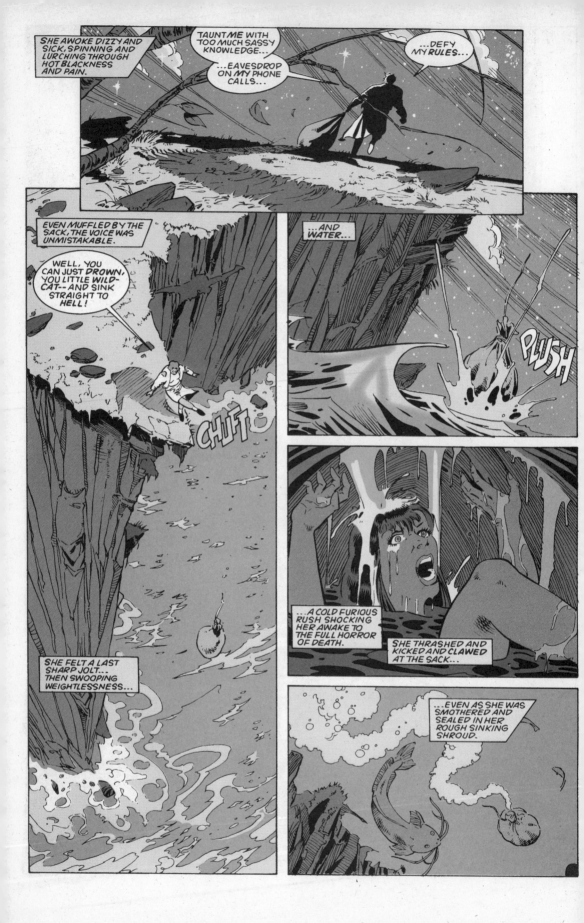

SHE AWOKE DIZZY AND SICK, SPINNING AND LURCHING THROUGH HOT BLACKNESS AND PAIN.

TAUNT ME WITH TOO MUCH SASSY KNOWLEDGE...

...EAVESDROP ON MY PHONE CALLS...

...DEFY MY RULES...

EVEN MUFFLED BY THE SACK, THE VOICE WAS UNMISTAKABLE.

WELL, YOU CAN JUST DROWN, YOU LITTLE WILD-CAT-- AND SINK STRAIGHT TO HELL!

CHUF!

...AND WATER...

PLUSH

SHE FELT A LAST SHARP JOLT... THEN SWOOPING WEIGHTLESSNESS...

...A COLD FURIOUS RUSH SHOCKING HER AWAKE TO THE FULL HORROR OF DEATH.

SHE THRASHED AND KICKED AND CLAWED AT THE SACK...

...EVEN AS SHE WAS SMOTHERED AND SEALED IN HER ROUGH SINKING SHROUD.

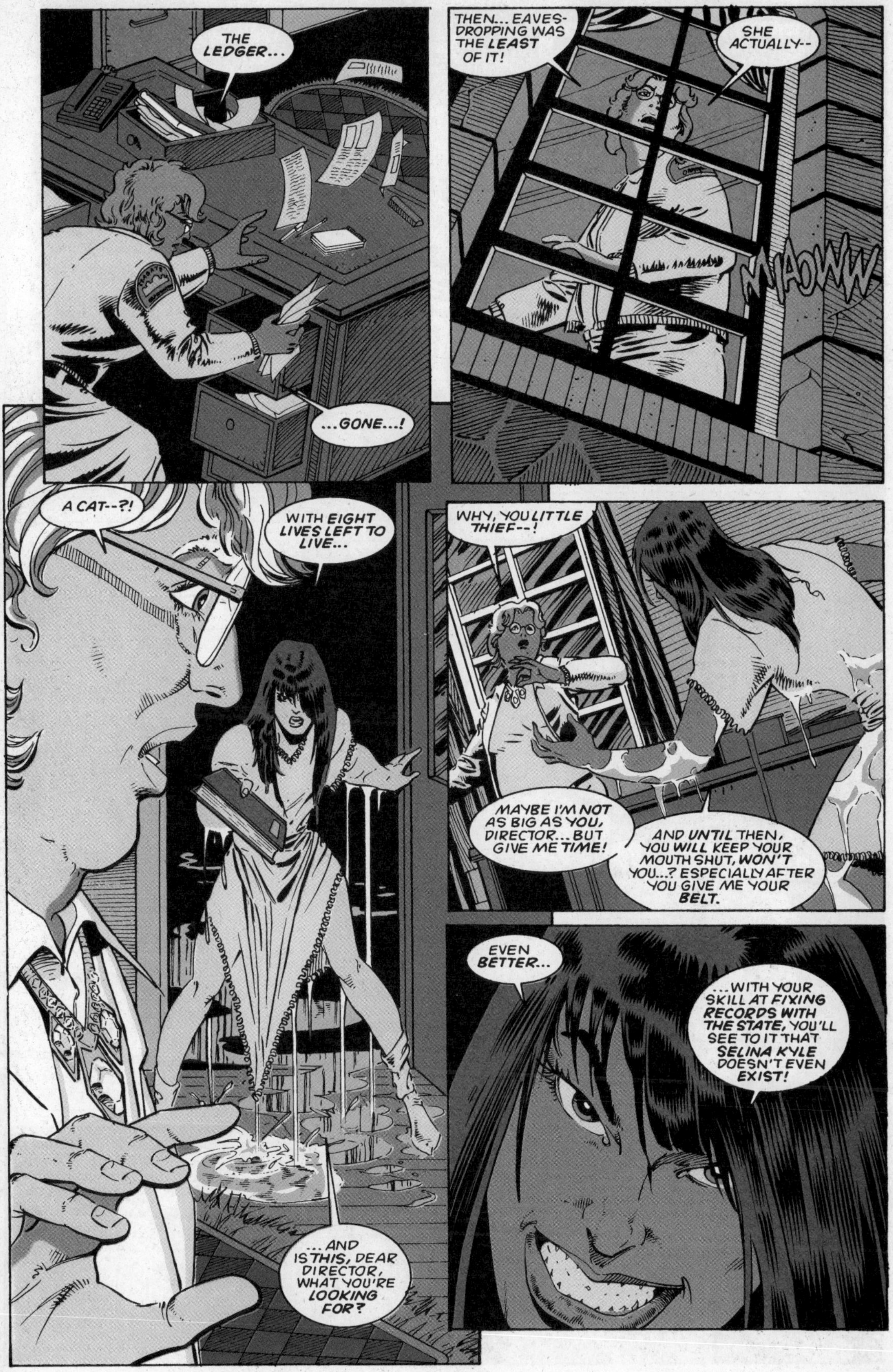
THE LEDGER...
...GONE...!
THEN... EAVES-DROPPING WAS THE LEAST OF IT!
SHE ACTUALLY--
MAOWW
A CAT--?!
WITH EIGHT LIVES LEFT TO LIVE...
...AND IS THIS, DEAR DIRECTOR, WHAT YOU'RE LOOKING FOR?
WHY, YOU LITTLE THIEF--!
MAYBE I'M NOT AS BIG AS YOU, DIRECTOR... BUT GIVE ME TIME!
AND UNTIL THEN, YOU WILL KEEP YOUR MOUTH SHUT, WON'T YOU...? ESPECIALLY AFTER YOU GIVE ME YOUR BELT.
EVEN BETTER...
...WITH YOUR SKILL AT FIXING RECORDS WITH THE STATE, YOU'LL SEE TO IT THAT SELINA KYLE DOESN'T EVEN EXIST!

WHEN SHE WAS DONE WITH THE DIRECTOR, SHE DRIED, DRESSED AND DEACTIVATED THE ALARM.

THE DOOR IS OPEN... THE JAILERS ARE SLEEPING...

TK
TK
TEK

"...AND THE WARDEN IS ALL TIED UP..."

≡MNNMPHHH≡

...SO YOU'RE FREE, KIDDIES, IF YOU WANNA BE.

HEY, SELINA-- WAIT UP, WILLYA?

WHAT'S WITH THE BOOK?

INFORMATION-- A VALUABLE COMMODITY.

SO WHAT'S IT WORTH?

NOT ONE DIME, BUT EVERY- THING IN THE WORLD-- FREEDOM.

YEAH? WELL, IF YOU'RE HEADED FOR GOTHAM, IT CAN BE TOUGH...

SO CAN I.

...WE'LL HAVE TO STEAL, YOU KNOW.

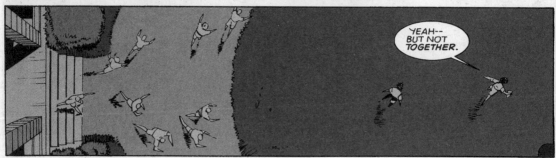

YEAH-- BUT NOT TOGETHER.

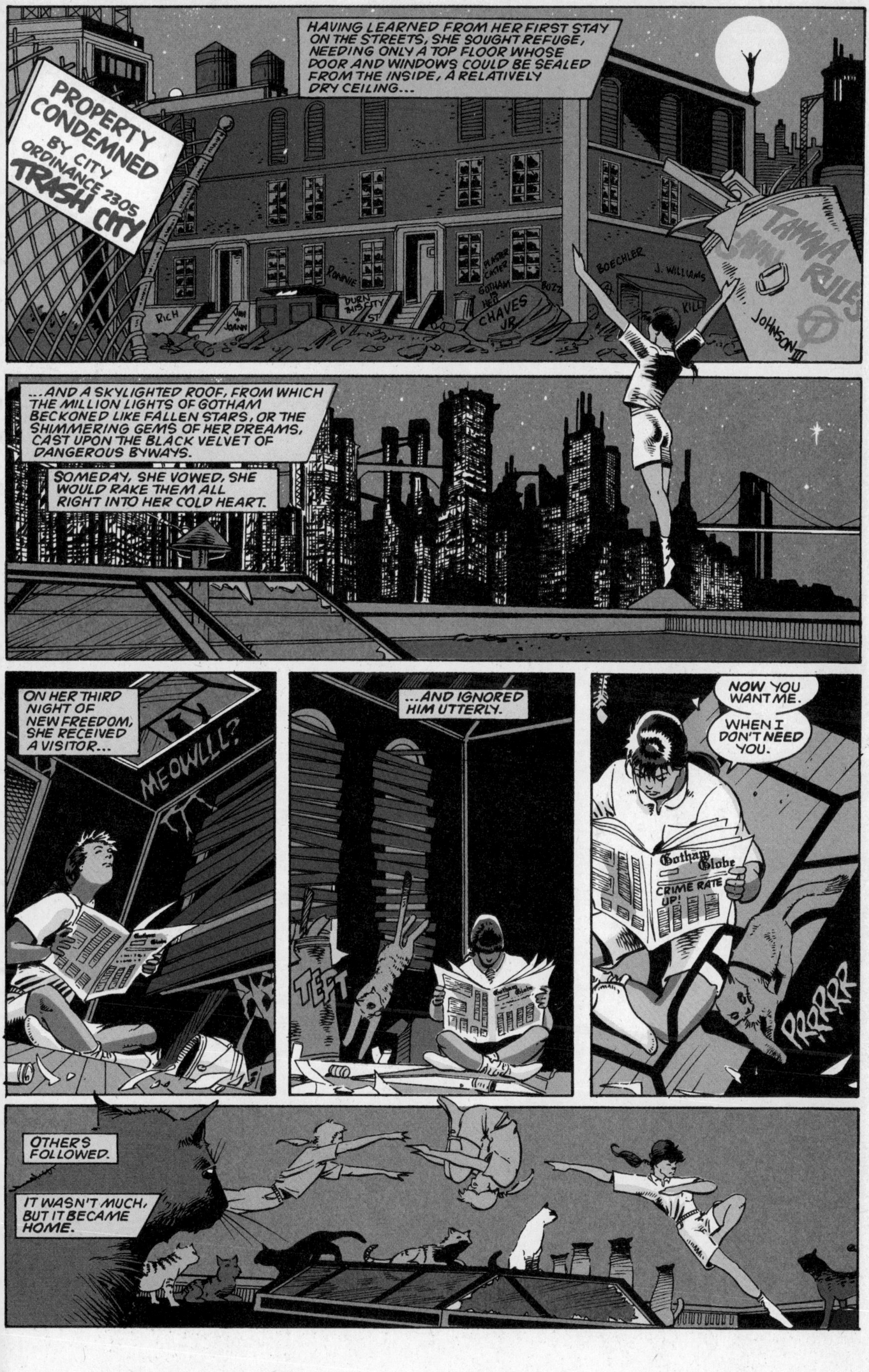
HAVING LEARNED FROM HER FIRST STAY ON THE STREETS, SHE SOUGHT REFUGE, NEEDING ONLY A TOP FLOOR WHOSE DOOR AND WINDOWS COULD BE SEALED FROM THE INSIDE, A RELATIVELY DRY CEILING...
PROPERTY CONDEMNED BY CITY ORDINANCE 2305
TRASH CITY
CHAVES JR
BOECHLER
J. WILLIAMS
JOHNSON III
...AND A SKYLIGHTED ROOF, FROM WHICH THE MILLION LIGHTS OF GOTHAM BECKONED LIKE FALLEN STARS, OR THE SHIMMERING GEMS OF HER DREAMS, CAST UPON THE BLACK VELVET OF DANGEROUS BYWAYS.
SOMEDAY, SHE VOWED, SHE WOULD RAKE THEM ALL RIGHT INTO HER COLD HEART.
ON HER THIRD NIGHT OF NEW FREEDOM, SHE RECEIVED A VISITOR...
MEOWLLL?
...AND IGNORED HIM UTTERLY.
TEFT
NOW YOU WANT ME.
WHEN I DON'T NEED YOU.
Gotham Globe
CRIME RATE UP!
PRRRRR
OTHERS FOLLOWED.
IT WASN'T MUCH, BUT IT BECAME HOME.

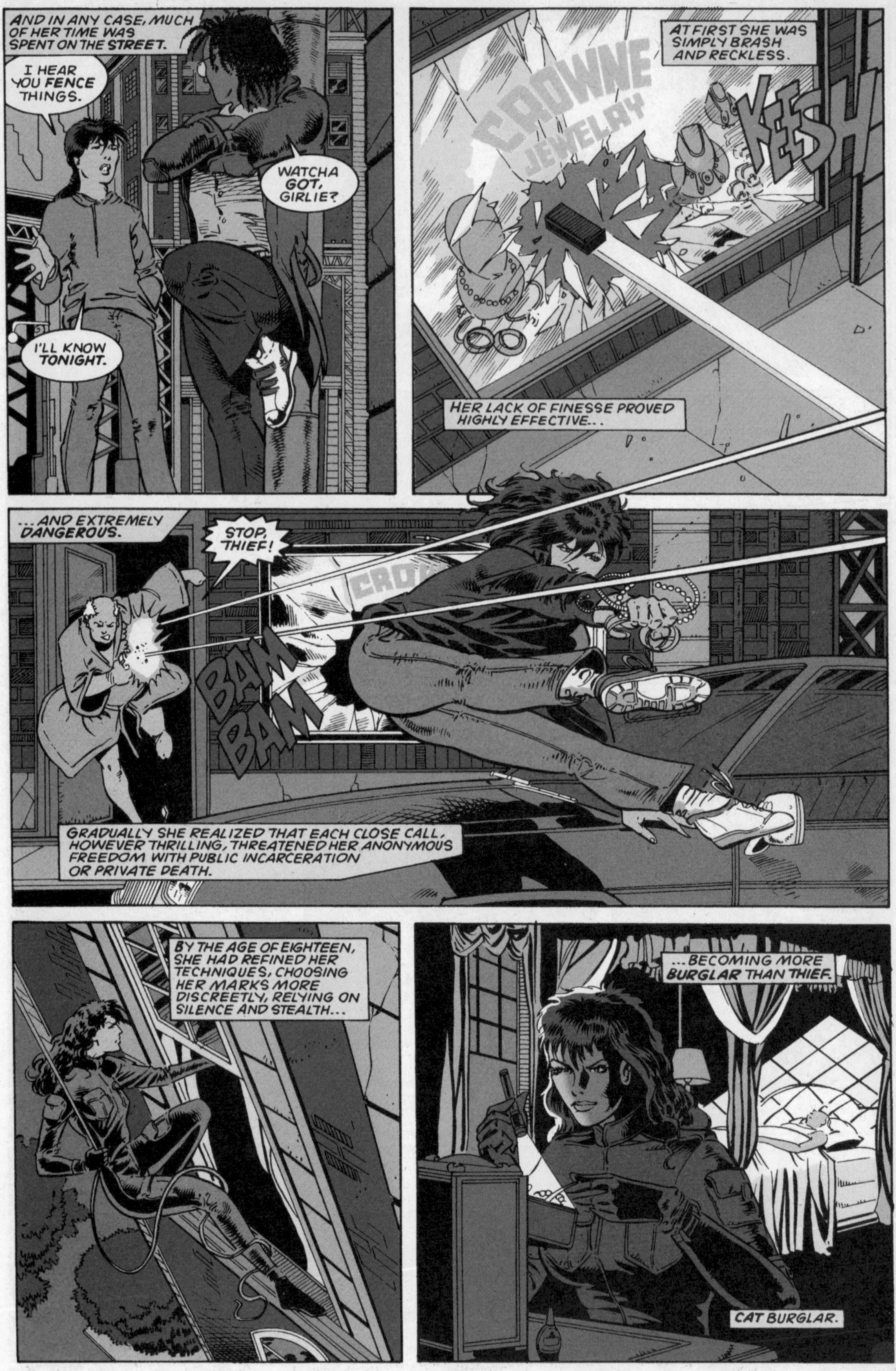
AND IN ANY CASE, MUCH OF HER TIME WAS SPENT ON THE STREET.
I HEAR YOU FENCE THINGS.
WATCHA GOT, GIRLIE?
I'LL KNOW TONIGHT.
AT FIRST SHE WAS SIMPLY BRASH AND RECKLESS.
CROWNE JEWELRY
KEESH
HER LACK OF FINESSE PROVED HIGHLY EFFECTIVE...
...AND EXTREMELY DANGEROUS.
STOP, THIEF!
BAM BAM
GRADUALLY SHE REALIZED THAT EACH CLOSE CALL, HOWEVER THRILLING, THREATENED HER ANONYMOUS FREEDOM WITH PUBLIC INCARCERATION OR PRIVATE DEATH.
BY THE AGE OF EIGHTEEN, SHE HAD REFINED HER TECHNIQUES, CHOOSING HER MARKS MORE DISCREETLY, RELYING ON SILENCE AND STEALTH...
...BECOMING MORE BURGLAR THAN THIEF.
CAT BURGLAR.

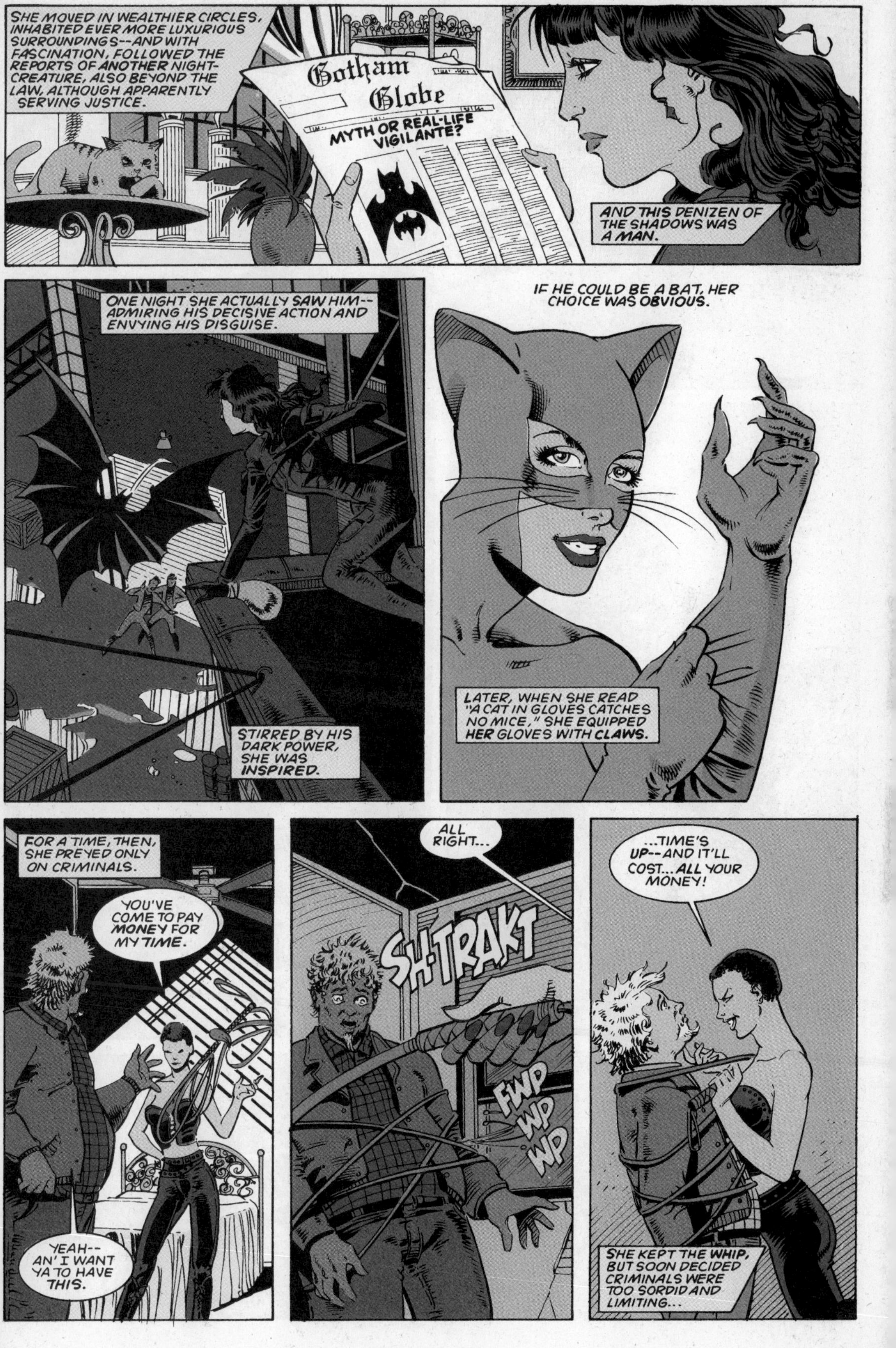

SHE MOVED IN WEALTHIER CIRCLES, INHABITED EVER MORE LUXURIOUS SURROUNDINGS--AND WITH FASCINATION, FOLLOWED THE REPORTS OF ANOTHER NIGHT-CREATURE, ALSO BEYOND THE LAW, ALTHOUGH APPARENTLY SERVING JUSTICE.
Gotham Globe
MYTH OR REAL-LIFE VIGILANTE?
AND THIS DENIZEN OF THE SHADOWS WAS A MAN.
ONE NIGHT SHE ACTUALLY SAW HIM--ADMIRING HIS DECISIVE ACTION AND ENVYING HIS DISGUISE.
STIRRED BY HIS DARK POWER, SHE WAS INSPIRED.
IF HE COULD BE A BAT, HER CHOICE WAS OBVIOUS.
LATER, WHEN SHE READ "A CAT IN GLOVES CATCHES NO MICE," SHE EQUIPPED HER GLOVES WITH CLAWS.
FOR A TIME, THEN, SHE PREYED ONLY ON CRIMINALS.
YOU'VE COME TO PAY MONEY FOR MY TIME.
YEAH-- AN' I WANT YA TO HAVE THIS.
ALL RIGHT...
SH-TRAKT
FWP WP WP
...TIME'S UP--AND IT'LL COST... ALL YOUR MONEY!
SHE KEPT THE WHIP, BUT SOON DECIDED CRIMINALS WERE TOO SORDID AND LIMITING...

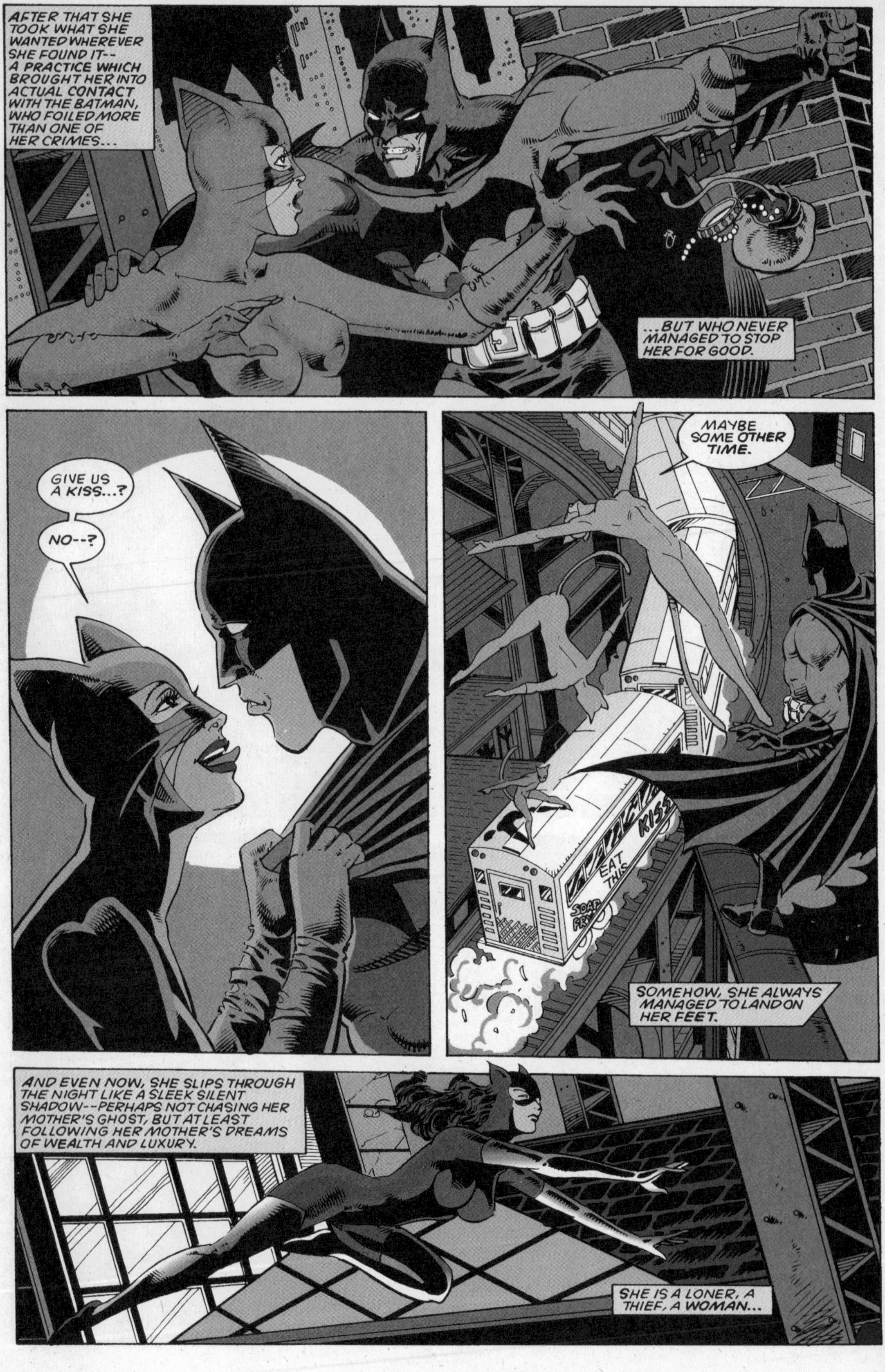
AFTER THAT SHE TOOK WHAT SHE WANTED WHEREVER SHE FOUND IT-- A PRACTICE WHICH BROUGHT HER INTO ACTUAL CONTACT WITH THE BATMAN, WHO FOILED MORE THAN ONE OF HER CRIMES...
SWIT
...BUT WHO NEVER MANAGED TO STOP HER FOR GOOD.
GIVE US A KISS...?
NO--?
MAYBE SOME OTHER TIME.
KISS
EAT THIS
SOMEHOW, SHE ALWAYS MANAGED TO LAND ON HER FEET.
AND EVEN NOW, SHE SLIPS THROUGH THE NIGHT LIKE A SLEEK SILENT SHADOW--PERHAPS NOT CHASING HER MOTHER'S GHOST, BUT AT LEAST FOLLOWING HER MOTHER'S DREAMS OF WEALTH AND LUXURY.
SHE IS A LONER, A THIEF, A WOMAN...

...AND A CAT.

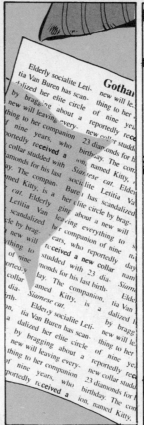

Gotha...

Elderly socialite Letitia Van Buren has scandalized her elite circle by bragging about a new will leaving everything to her companion of nine years, who reportedly received a collar studded with 23 diamonds for his last birthday. The companion, named Kitty, is a Siamese cat.

COME ON, KITTY-KITTY-KITTY...

PRRRRRR

...KITTY, YOU COULD STAND TO LOSE SOME WEIGHT...

...AND THIS'LL DO...FOR STARTERS.

NOW MAKE YOURSELF AT HOME...IN THE LAP OF LUXURY.

BUT WHATEVER YOU DO...DON'T DEPEND ON ME.

MIAOW?

THE END

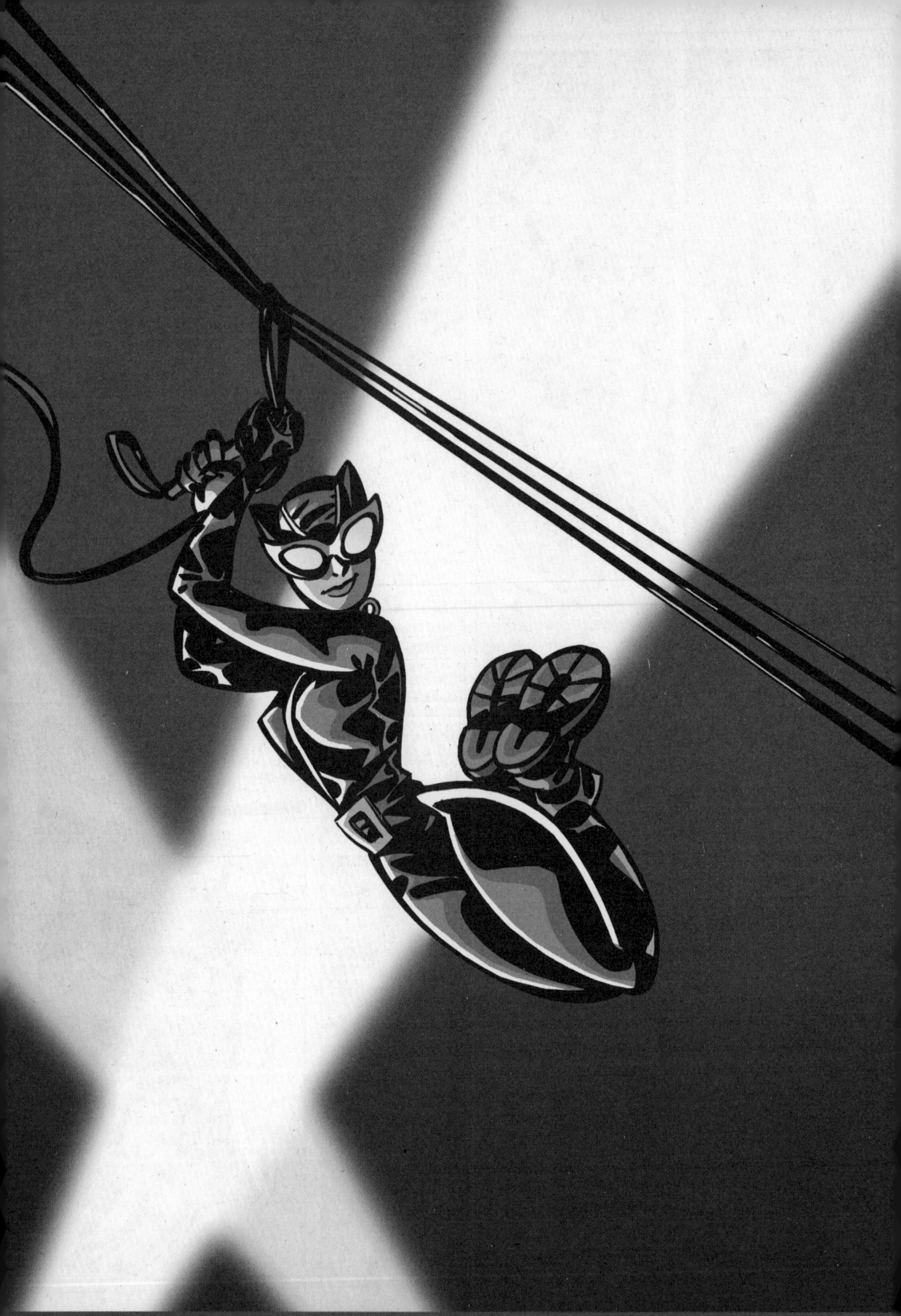

## Final Report

**Steven Grant** Writer **Brad Rader** Penciller **Mark Lipka** **Dan Davis** Inkers
**Lee Loughridge** Colorist **Sean Konot** Letterer **Jeff Parker** Cover Artist

A tale from the current CATWOMAN series,
this story shows Selina using her talents to the fullest!

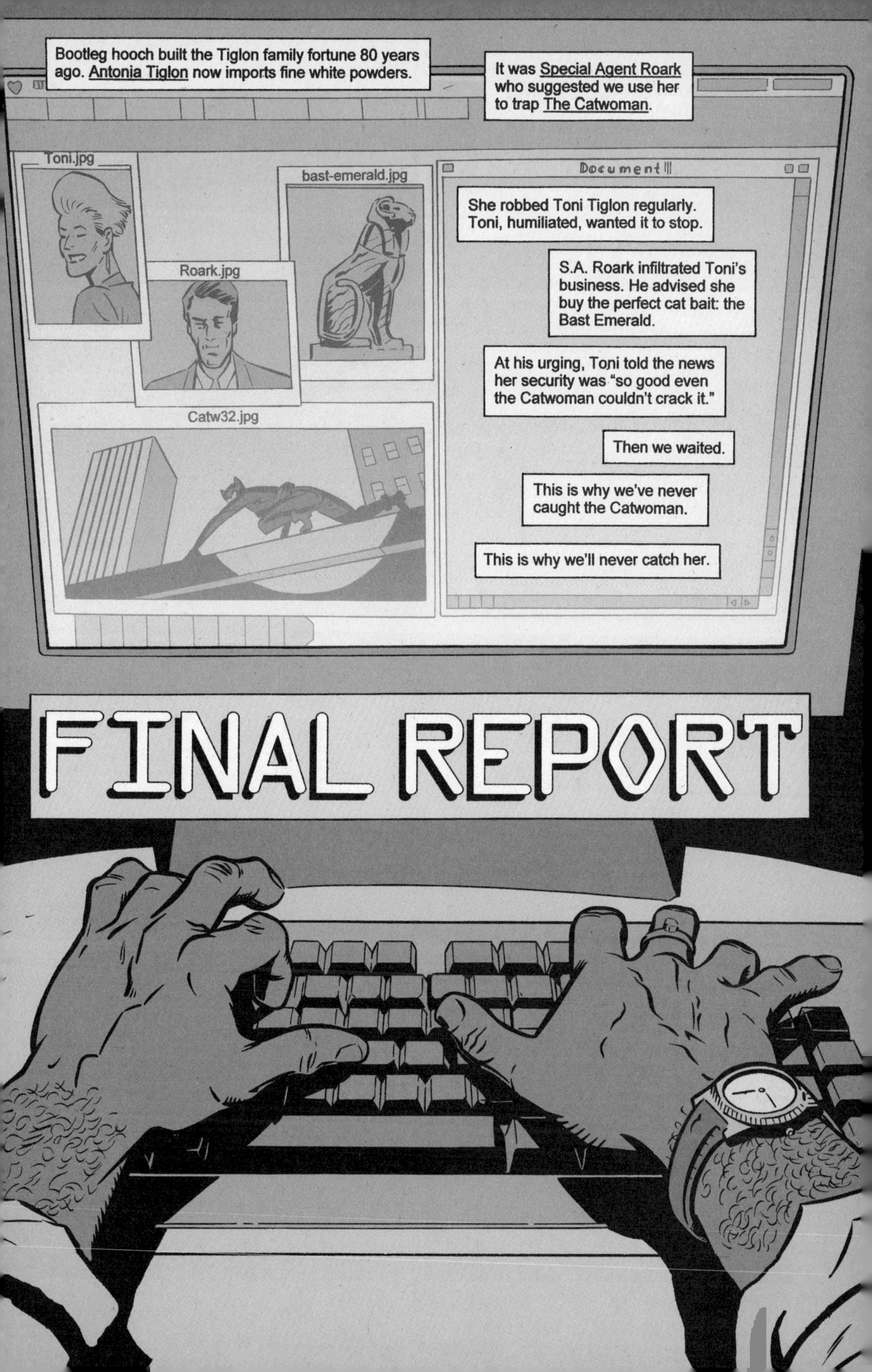
Bootleg hooch built the Tiglon family fortune 80 years ago. Antonia Tiglon now imports fine white powders.
It was Special Agent Roark who suggested we use her to trap The Catwoman.
Toni.jpg
Roark.jpg
bast-emerald.jpg
Catw32.jpg
Document
She robbed Toni Tiglon regularly. Toni, humiliated, wanted it to stop.
S.A. Roark infiltrated Toni's business. He advised she buy the perfect cat bait: the Bast Emerald.
At his urging, Toni told the news her security was "so good even the Catwoman couldn't crack it."
Then we waited.
This is why we've never caught the Catwoman.
This is why we'll never catch her.
FINAL REPORT

The Catwoman never showed.

Then we lost contact with Roark.

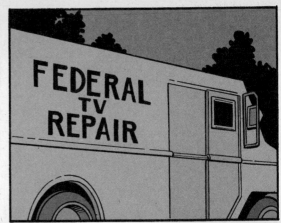

FEDERAL TV REPAIR

FEDERAL TV REPAIR

SEE, THE PROBLEM'S ALL THAT SECURITY WE GOT HER TO INSTALL IS BLOCKING US, TOO.

SO FOR ALL WE KNOW HE'S DEAD?

SATELLITE GIVES US FIVE HEAT READINGS. THAT ACCOUNTS FOR HIM, BUT WHICH IS HIM I COULDN'T SAY.

WHOOP! SIX READINGS!

INCOMING!

GOT HER.

ALL UNITS, FULL ALERT.

MAINTAIN YOUR POSITIONS. REPEAT: MAINTAIN POSITIONS...

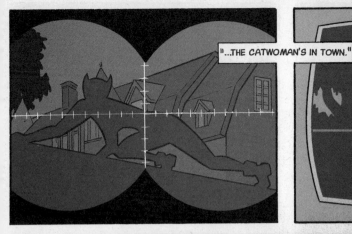

"...THE CATWOMAN'S IN TOWN."

SOMEONE'S ON THE WALL.

NOT "SOMEONE," ZURIN. HER.

HEAR THAT, ROARK? YOU'RE A SUCCESS. YOUR GIRL-FRIEND'S FINALLY ON HER WAY.

OF COURSE, WHEN SHE TOUCHED THE WALL, SHE ELECTRIFIED THE ENTIRE GROUNDS.

"UNLESS SHE CAN FLY, SHE'S FRIED."

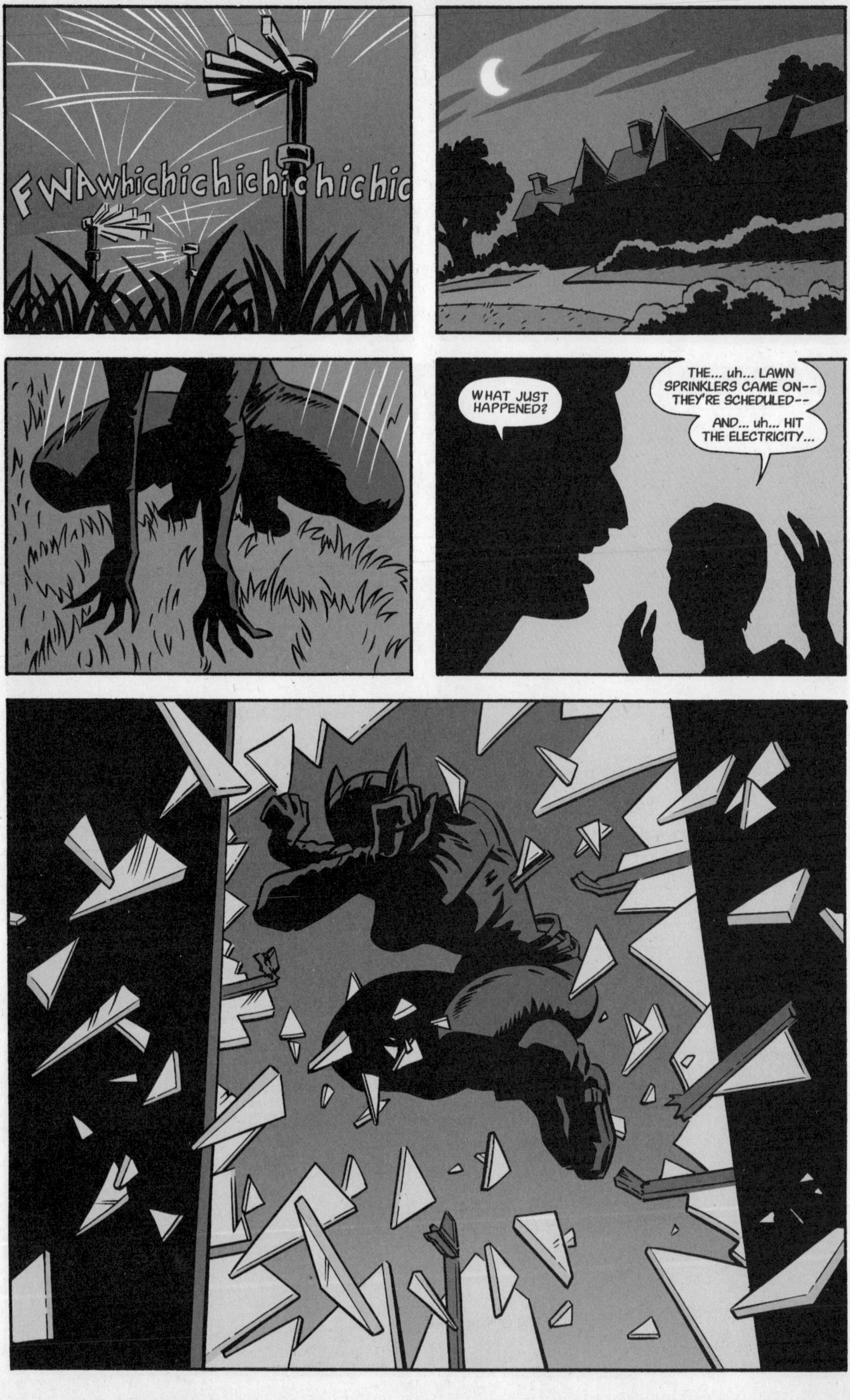
FWAwhichichichichichic
WHAT JUST HAPPENED?
THE... uh... LAWN SPRINKLERS CAME ON-- THEY'RE SCHEDULED--
AND... uh... HIT THE ELECTRICITY...

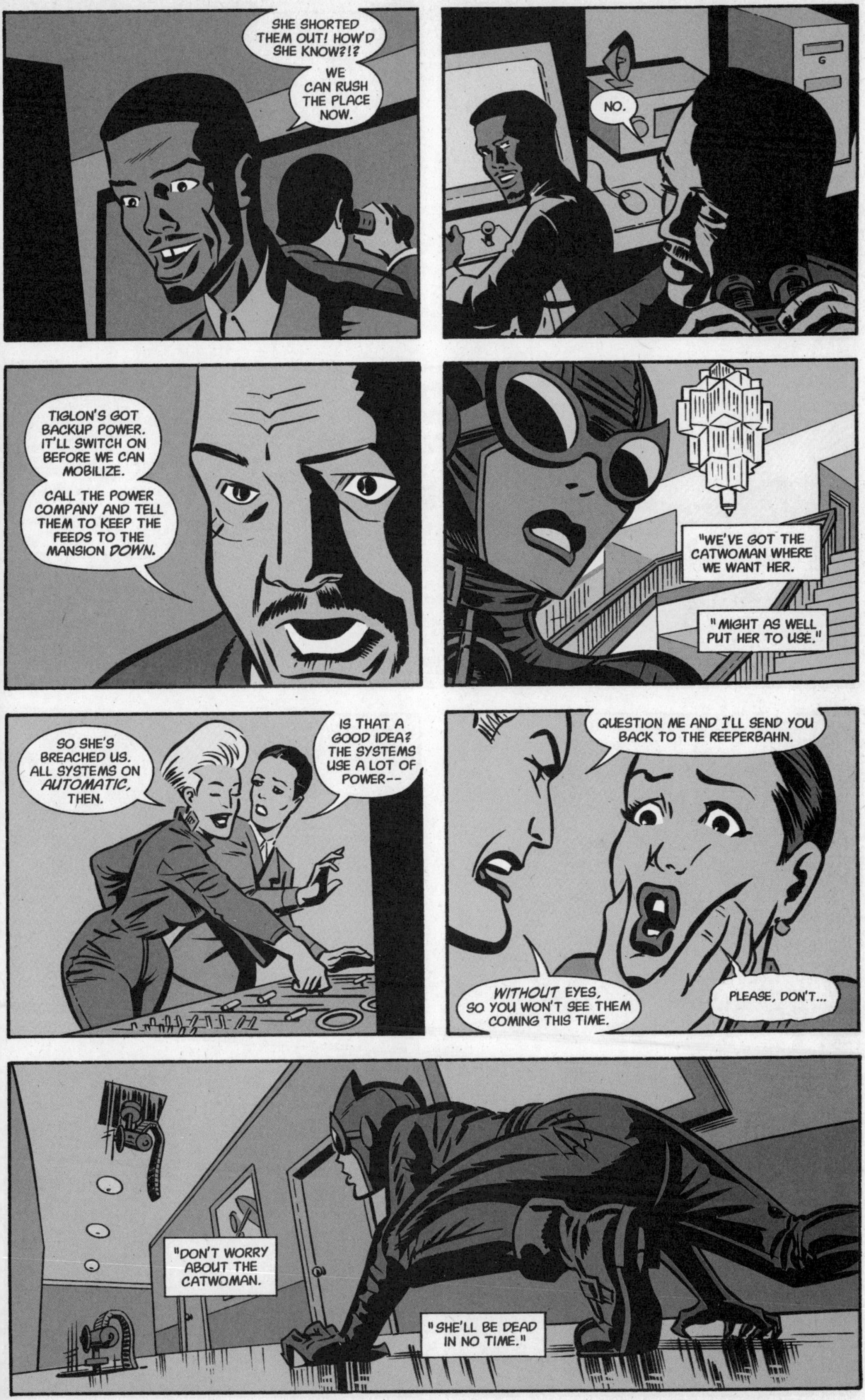

SHE SHORTED THEM OUT! HOW'D SHE KNOW?!?
WE CAN RUSH THE PLACE NOW.
NO.
TIGLON'S GOT BACKUP POWER. IT'LL SWITCH ON BEFORE WE CAN MOBILIZE.
CALL THE POWER COMPANY AND TELL THEM TO KEEP THE FEEDS TO THE MANSION *DOWN*.
"WE'VE GOT THE CATWOMAN WHERE WE WANT HER.
"MIGHT AS WELL PUT HER TO USE."
SO SHE'S BREACHED US. ALL SYSTEMS ON *AUTOMATIC*, THEN.
IS THAT A GOOD IDEA? THE SYSTEMS USE A LOT OF POWER--
QUESTION ME AND I'LL SEND YOU BACK TO THE REEPERBAHN.
*WITHOUT* EYES, SO YOU WON'T SEE THEM COMING THIS TIME.
PLEASE, DON'T...
"DON'T WORRY ABOUT THE CATWOMAN.
"SHE'LL BE DEAD IN NO TIME."

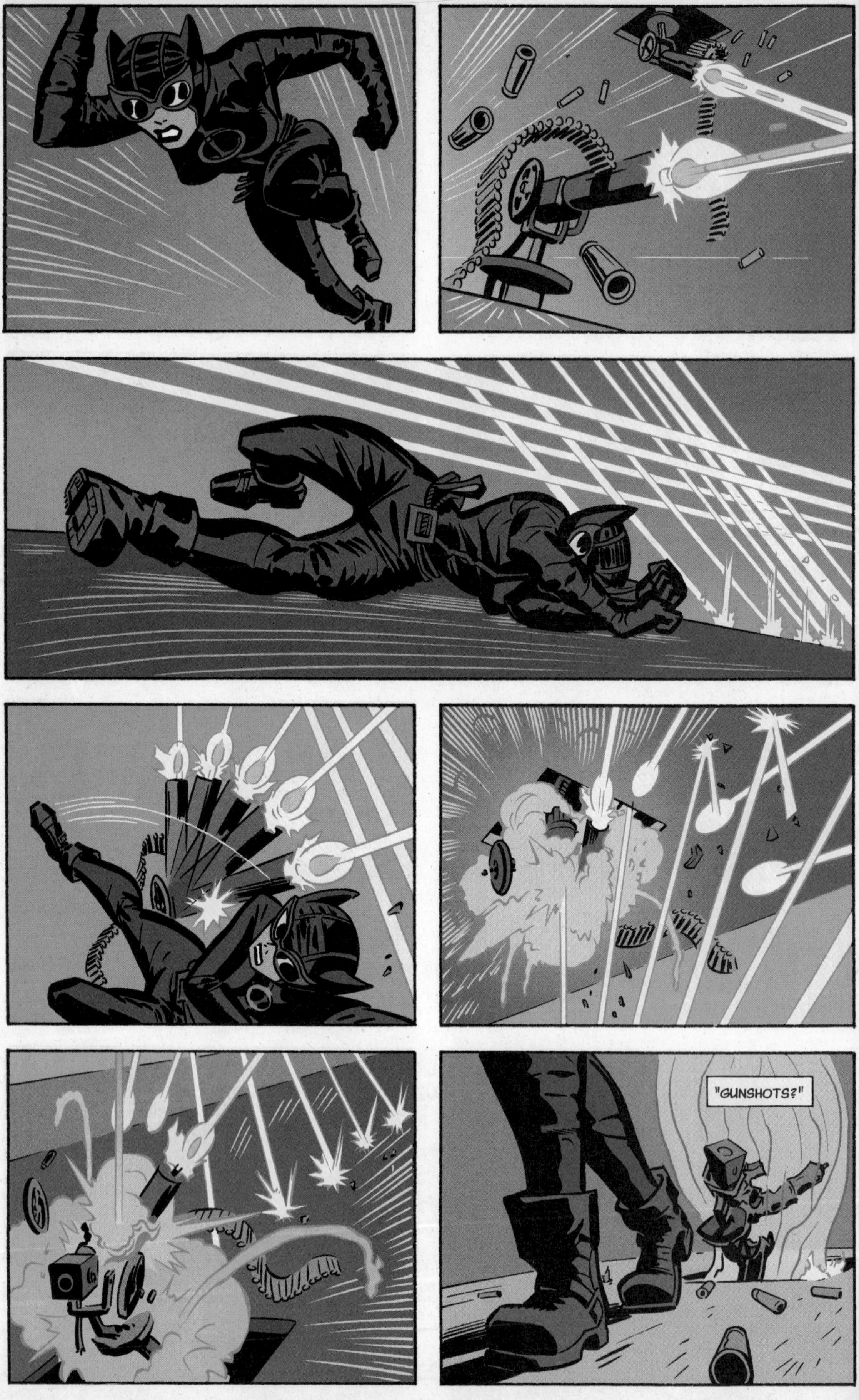
"GUNSHOTS?"

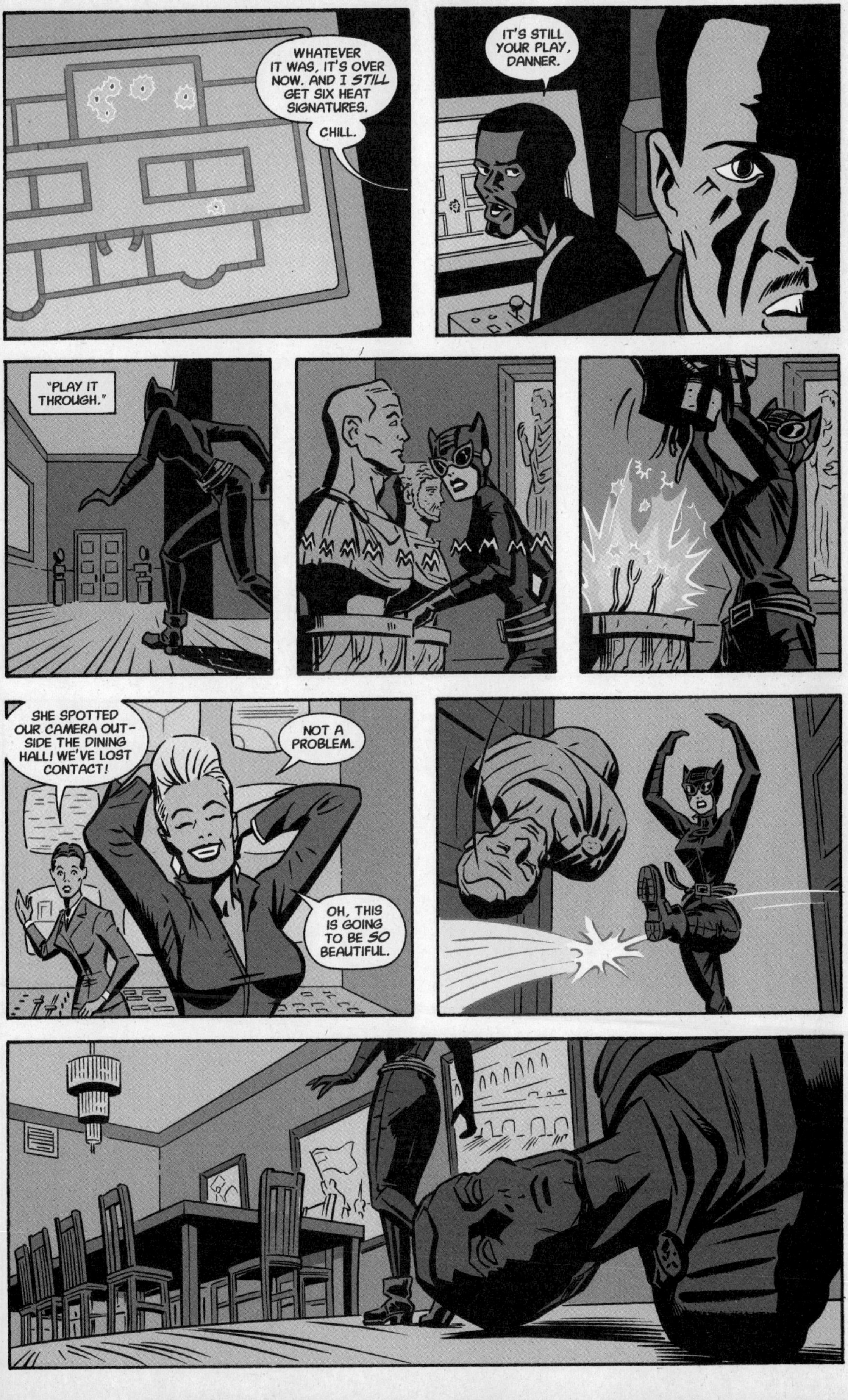

WHATEVER IT WAS, IT'S OVER NOW. AND I STILL GET SIX HEAT SIGNATURES.
CHILL.
IT'S STILL YOUR PLAY, DANNER.
"PLAY IT THROUGH."
SHE SPOTTED OUR CAMERA OUT-SIDE THE DINING HALL! WE'VE LOST CONTACT!
NOT A PROBLEM.
OH, THIS IS GOING TO BE SO BEAUTIFUL.

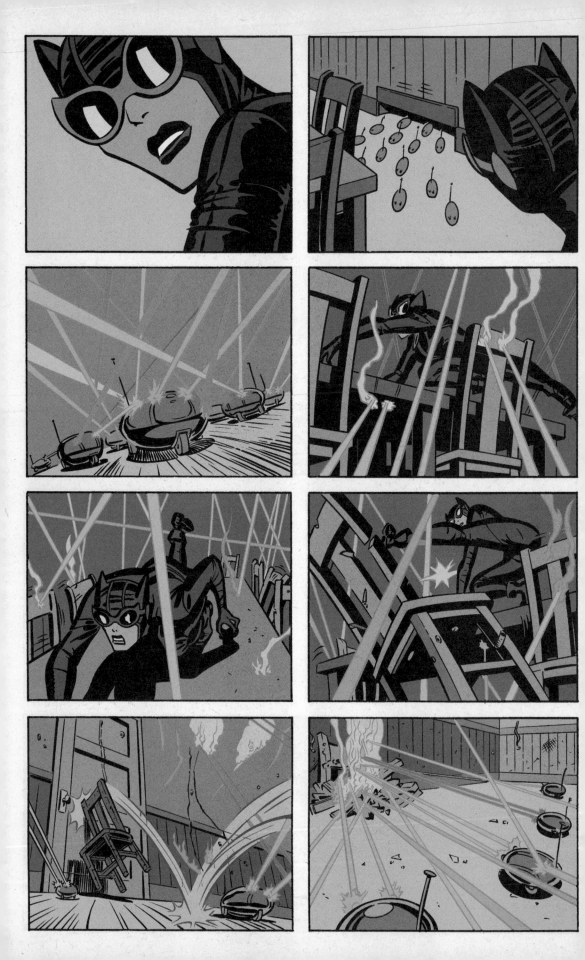

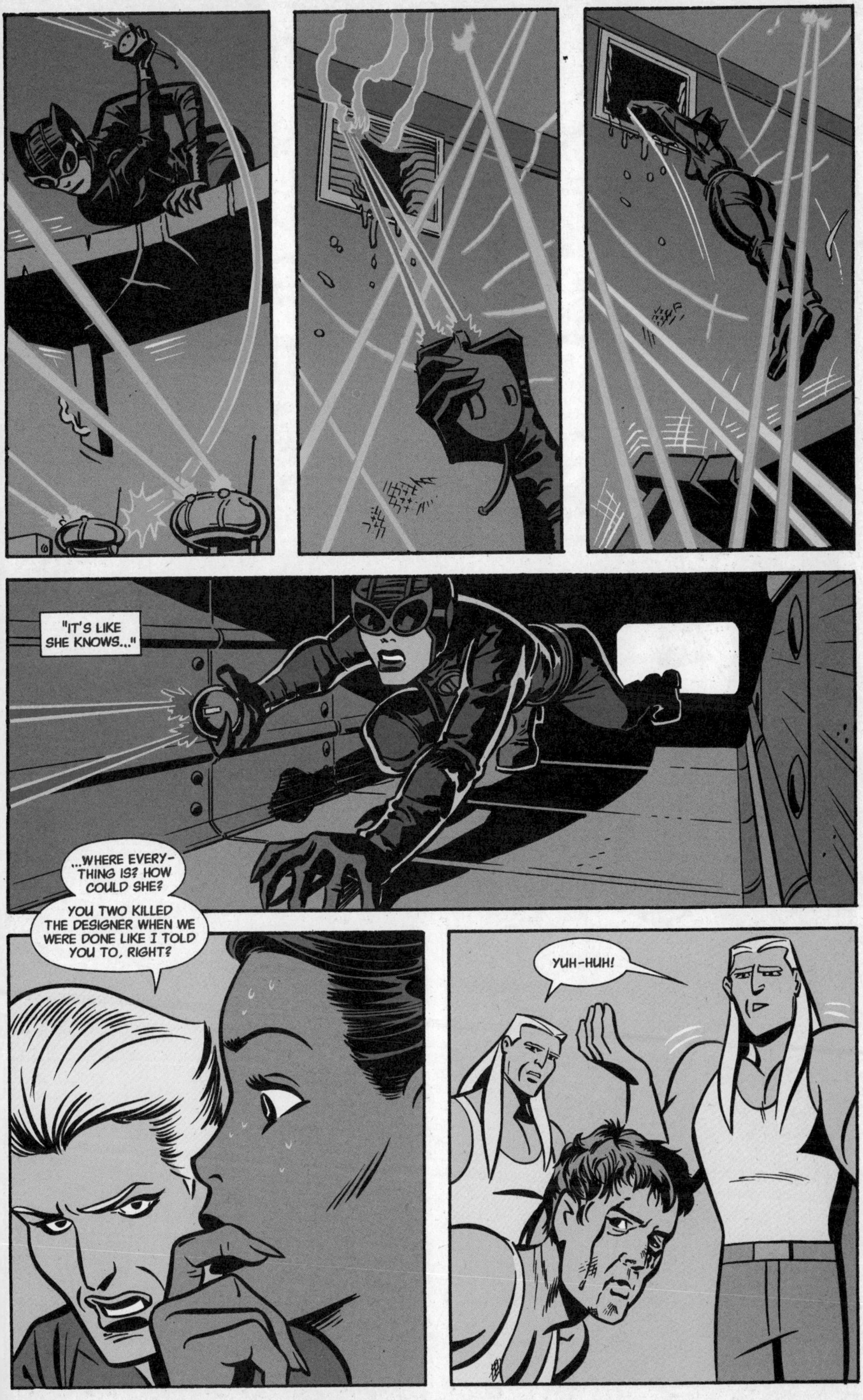
"IT'S LIKE SHE KNOWS..."
...WHERE EVERYTHING IS? HOW COULD SHE?
YOU TWO KILLED THE DESIGNER WHEN WE WERE DONE LIKE I TOLD YOU TO, RIGHT?
YUH-HUH!

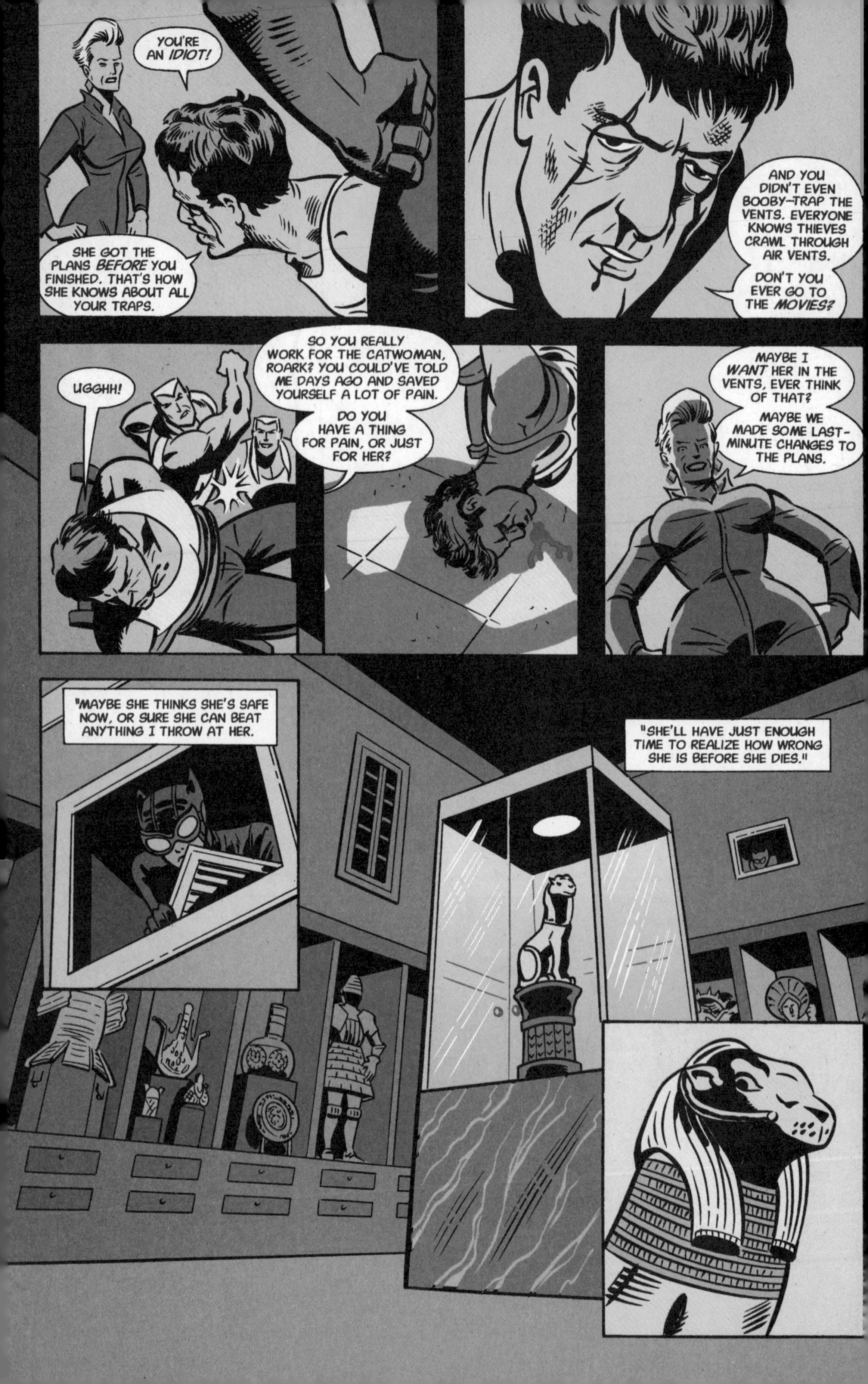

YOU'RE AN IDIOT!
SHE GOT THE PLANS BEFORE YOU FINISHED. THAT'S HOW SHE KNOWS ABOUT ALL YOUR TRAPS.
AND YOU DIDN'T EVEN BOOBY-TRAP THE VENTS. EVERYONE KNOWS THIEVES CRAWL THROUGH AIR VENTS.
DON'T YOU EVER GO TO THE MOVIES?
UGGHH!
SO YOU REALLY WORK FOR THE CATWOMAN, ROARK? YOU COULD'VE TOLD ME DAYS AGO AND SAVED YOURSELF A LOT OF PAIN.
DO YOU HAVE A THING FOR PAIN, OR JUST FOR HER?
MAYBE I WANT HER IN THE VENTS, EVER THINK OF THAT?
MAYBE WE MADE SOME LAST-MINUTE CHANGES TO THE PLANS.
"MAYBE SHE THINKS SHE'S SAFE NOW, OR SURE SHE CAN BEAT ANYTHING I THROW AT HER.
"SHE'LL HAVE JUST ENOUGH TIME TO REALIZE HOW WRONG SHE IS BEFORE SHE DIES."

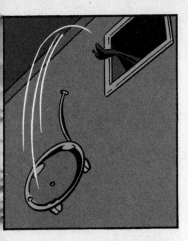

JUST REGISTERED A MAJOR POWER SURGE IN TIGLON'S DISPLAY ROOM.

CATWOMAN?

DUNNO, FRIED OUT THE HEATSCAN. IT'LL TAKE ANOTHER COUPLE SECONDS TO RECALIBRATE.

TO BE HONEST, I'D'VE BEEN A BIT LET DOWN IF THE OTHER TRAPS HAD GOTTEN HER.

I WANTED HER. OVERCONFIDENT, SECURE SHE COULD HANDLE ANYTHING I THREW AT HER.

THEN RIGHT WHEN SHE WAS FLUSHED WITH TRIUMPH, *BOOM!* A TRAP THAT'D TRIGGER ONLY AFTER SHE WAS TOO FAR IN TO GET OUT.

WHAT'S BEST IS IT'LL TAKE HER HOURS TO DIE, IF SHE WASN'T DUMB ENOUGH TO GET HIT IN THE HEAD OR HEART.

SO I GET TO RUB IN WHO FINALLY KILLED--

SHE'S NOT HERE!

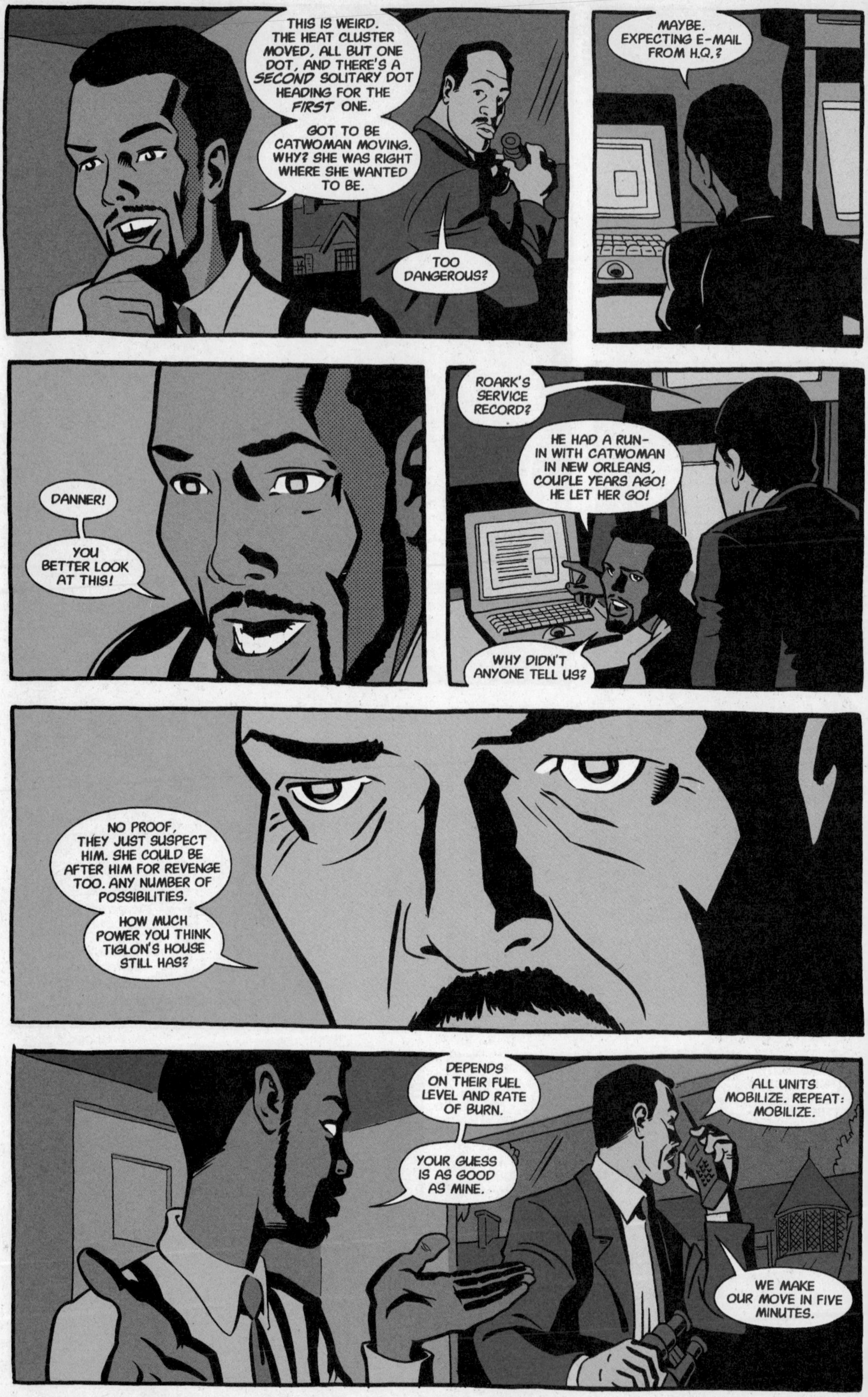
THIS IS WEIRD. THE HEAT CLUSTER MOVED, ALL BUT ONE DOT, AND THERE'S A SECOND SOLITARY DOT HEADING FOR THE FIRST ONE.
GOT TO BE CATWOMAN MOVING. WHY? SHE WAS RIGHT WHERE SHE WANTED TO BE.
TOO DANGEROUS?
MAYBE. EXPECTING E-MAIL FROM H.Q.?
DANNER!
YOU BETTER LOOK AT THIS!
ROARK'S SERVICE RECORD?
HE HAD A RUN-IN WITH CATWOMAN IN NEW ORLEANS, COUPLE YEARS AGO! HE LET HER GO!
WHY DIDN'T ANYONE TELL US?
NO PROOF, THEY JUST SUSPECT HIM. SHE COULD BE AFTER HIM FOR REVENGE TOO. ANY NUMBER OF POSSIBILITIES.
HOW MUCH POWER YOU THINK TIGLON'S HOUSE STILL HAS?
DEPENDS ON THEIR FUEL LEVEL AND RATE OF BURN.
YOUR GUESS IS AS GOOD AS MINE.
ALL UNITS MOBILIZE. REPEAT: MOBILIZE.
WE MAKE OUR MOVE IN FIVE MINUTES.

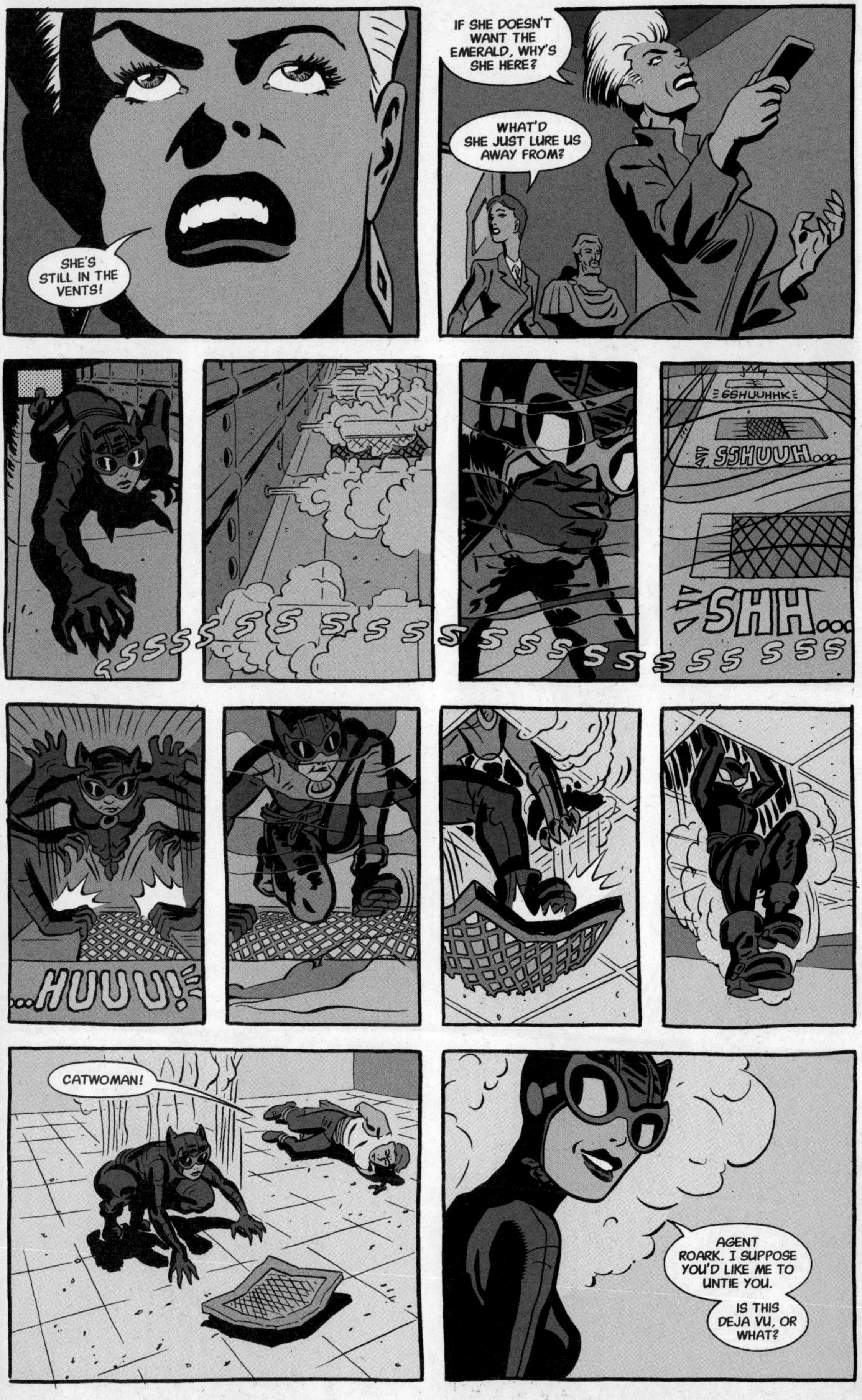
SHE'S STILL IN THE VENTS!
IF SHE DOESN'T WANT THE EMERALD, WHY'S SHE HERE?
WHAT'D SHE JUST LURE US AWAY FROM?
SSSSSSSSSSSSSSSSSSSSS
SSHUUHHK
SSHUUH...
SHH...
...HUUU!
CATWOMAN!
AGENT ROARK. I SUPPOSE YOU'D LIKE ME TO UNTIE YOU.
IS THIS DEJA VU, OR WHAT?

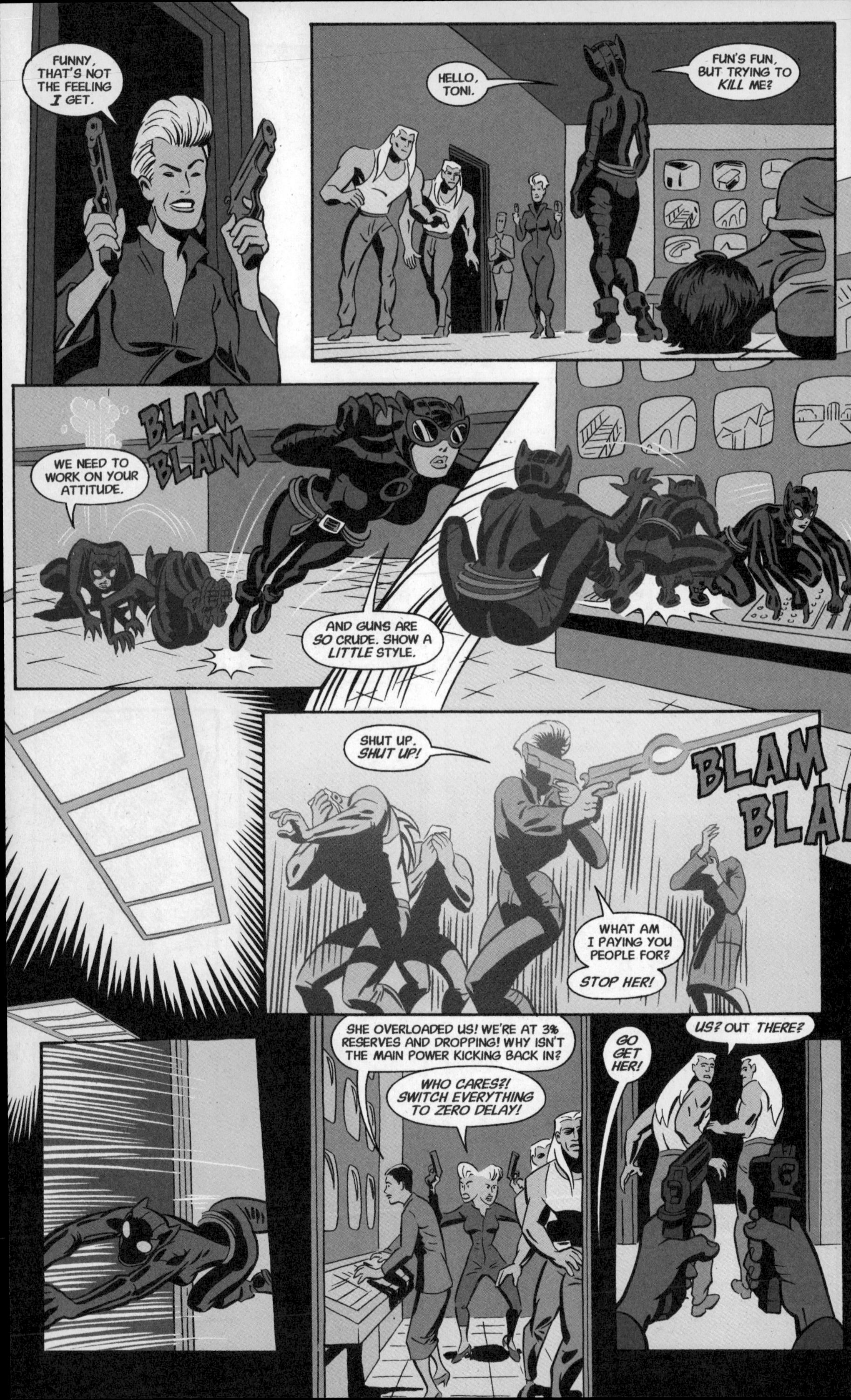
FUNNY, THAT'S NOT THE FEELING *I* GET.
HELLO, TONI.
FUN'S FUN, BUT TRYING TO *KILL ME?*
BLAM BLAM
WE NEED TO WORK ON YOUR ATTITUDE.
AND GUNS ARE *SO* CRUDE. SHOW A *LITTLE* STYLE.
SHUT UP. *SHUT UP!*
BLAM BLA
WHAT AM I PAYING YOU PEOPLE FOR?
*STOP HER!*
SHE OVERLOADED US! WE'RE AT 3% RESERVES AND DROPPING! WHY ISN'T THE MAIN POWER KICKING BACK IN?
*WHO CARES?! SWITCH EVERYTHING TO ZERO DELAY!*
*GO GET HER!*
*US? OUT THERE?*

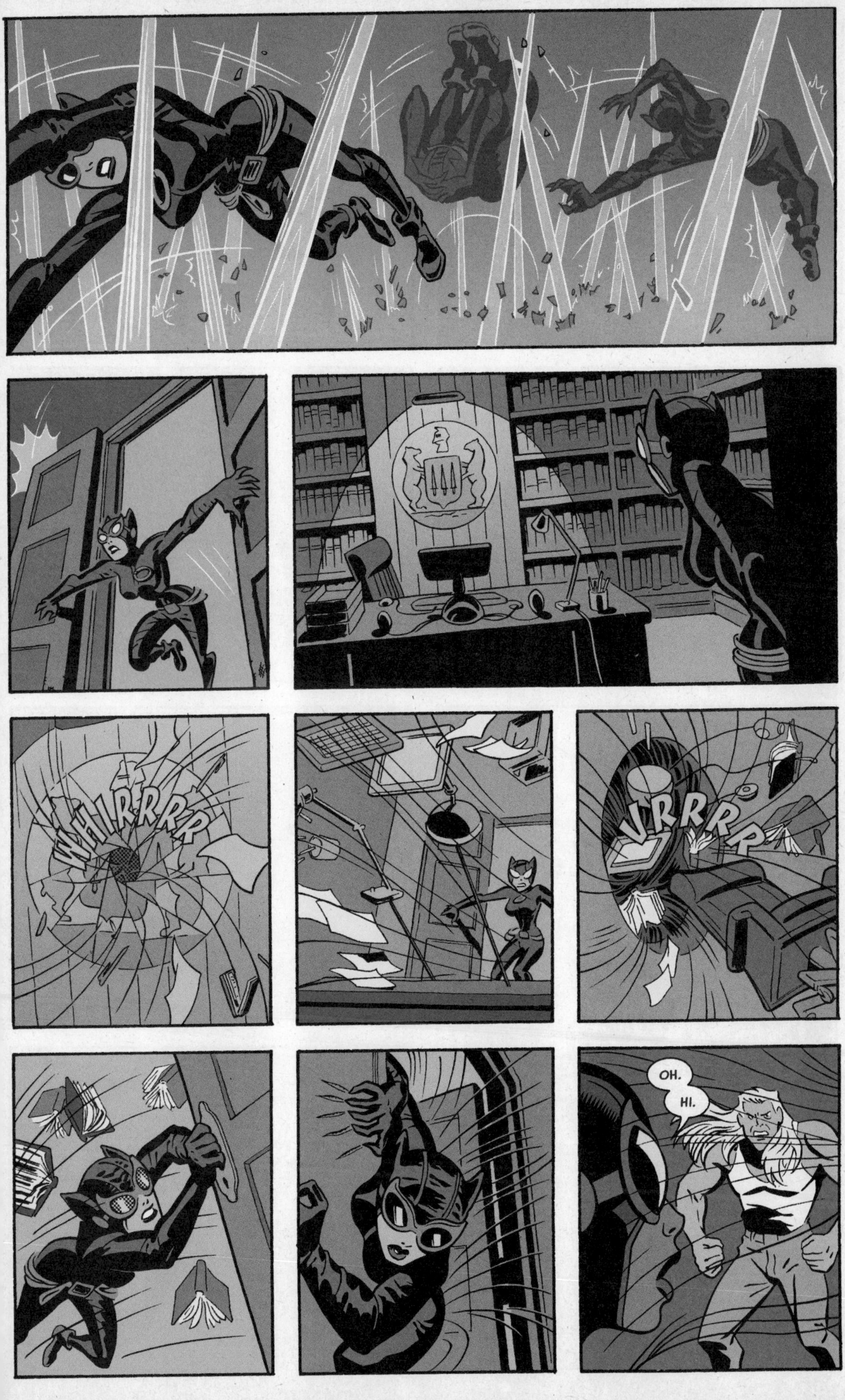
WHIRRRRR
VRRRRR
OH.
HI.

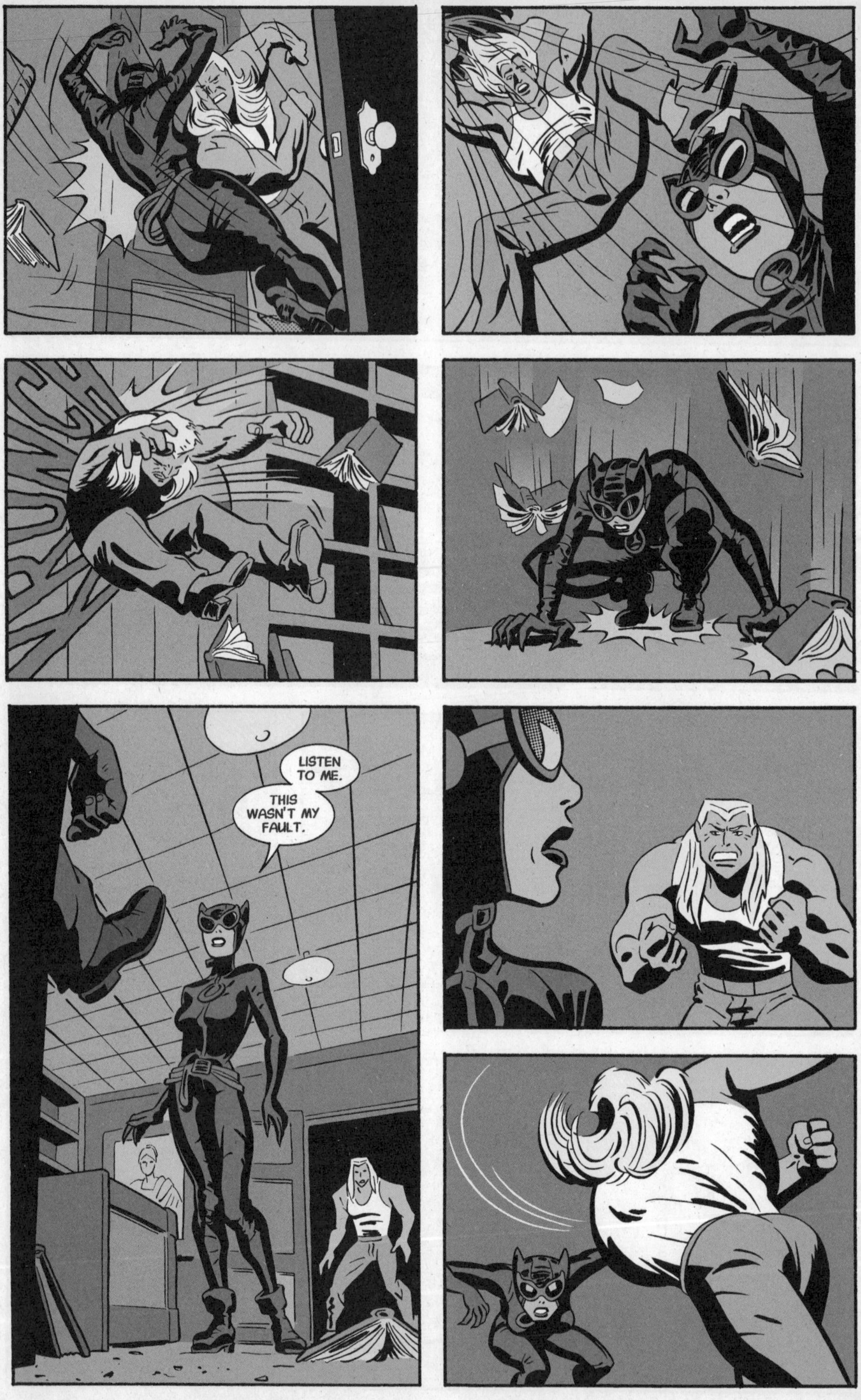
LISTEN TO ME.
THIS WASN'T MY FAULT.

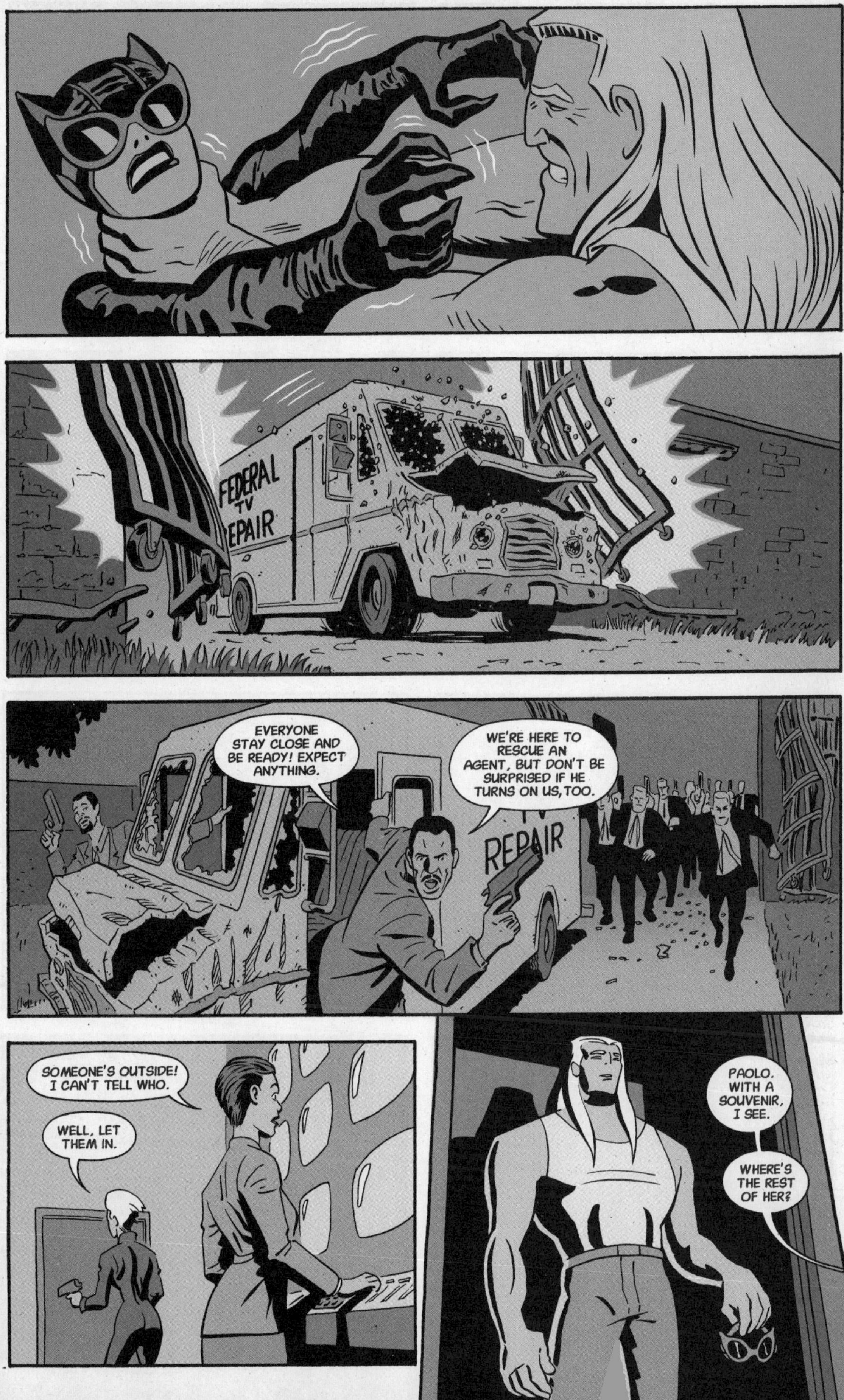
FEDERAL TV REPAIR
EVERYONE STAY CLOSE AND BE READY! EXPECT ANYTHING.
WE'RE HERE TO RESCUE AN AGENT, BUT DON'T BE SURPRISED IF HE TURNS ON US, TOO.
TV REPAIR
SOMEONE'S OUTSIDE! I CAN'T TELL WHO.
WELL, LET THEM IN.
PAOLO. WITH A SOUVENIR, I SEE.
WHERE'S THE REST OF HER?

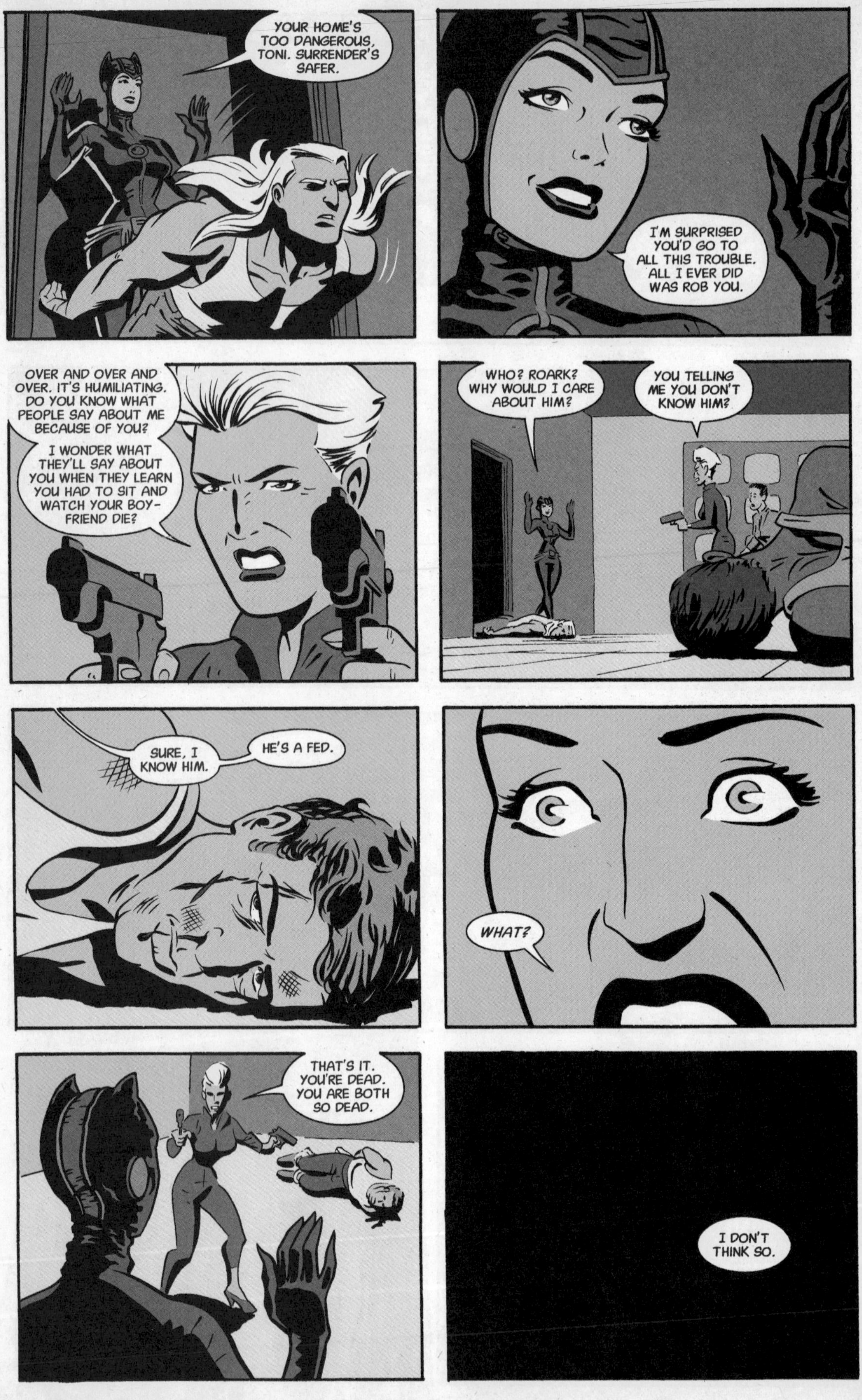
YOUR HOME'S TOO DANGEROUS, TONI. SURRENDER'S SAFER.
I'M SURPRISED YOU'D GO TO ALL THIS TROUBLE. ALL I EVER DID WAS ROB YOU.
OVER AND OVER. IT'S HUMILIATING. DO YOU KNOW WHAT PEOPLE SAY ABOUT ME BECAUSE OF YOU?
I WONDER WHAT THEY'LL SAY ABOUT YOU WHEN THEY LEARN YOU HAD TO SIT AND WATCH YOUR BOY-FRIEND DIE?
WHO? ROARK? WHY WOULD I CARE ABOUT HIM?
YOU TELLING ME YOU DON'T KNOW HIM?
SURE, I KNOW HIM.
HE'S A FED.
WHAT?
THAT'S IT. YOU'RE DEAD. YOU ARE BOTH SO DEAD.
I DON'T THINK SO.

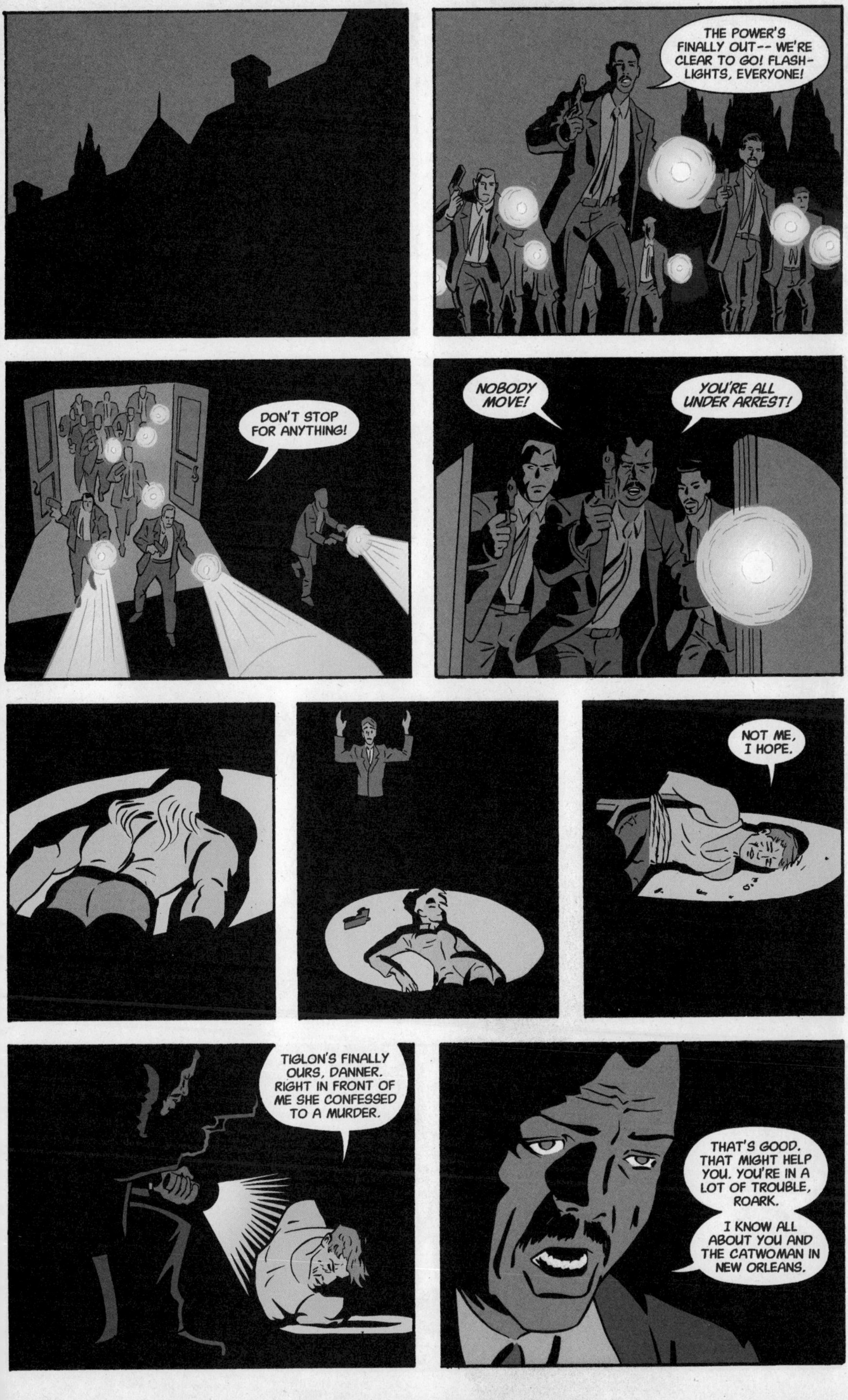
THE POWER'S FINALLY OUT-- WE'RE CLEAR TO GO! FLASH-LIGHTS, EVERYONE!
DON'T STOP FOR ANYTHING!
NOBODY MOVE!
YOU'RE ALL UNDER ARREST!
NOT ME, I HOPE.
TIGLON'S FINALLY OURS, DANNER. RIGHT IN FRONT OF ME SHE CONFESSED TO A MURDER.
THAT'S GOOD. THAT MIGHT HELP YOU. YOU'RE IN A LOT OF TROUBLE, ROARK.
I KNOW ALL ABOUT YOU AND THE CATWOMAN IN NEW ORLEANS.

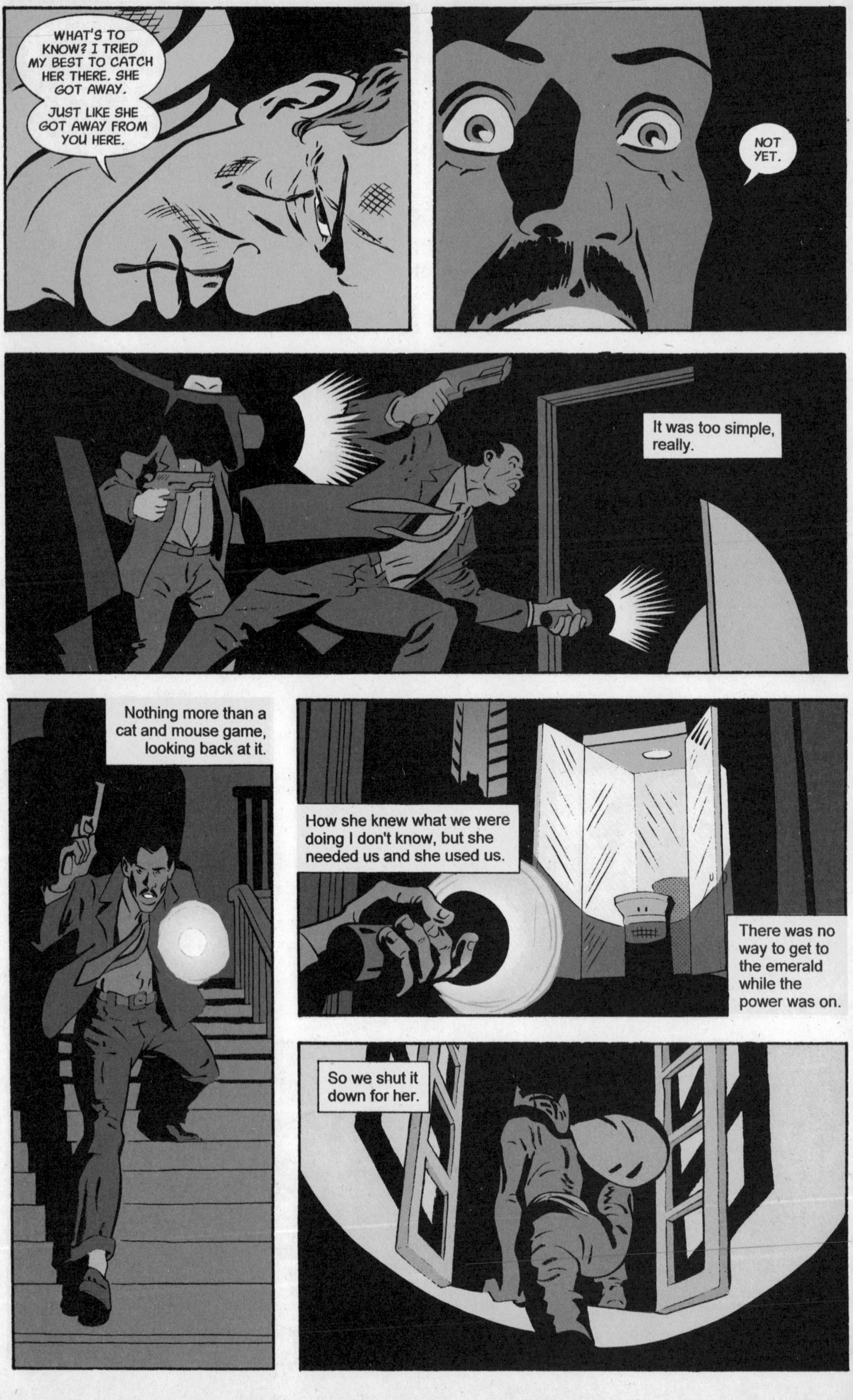
WHAT'S TO KNOW? I TRIED MY BEST TO CATCH HER THERE. SHE GOT AWAY.
JUST LIKE SHE GOT AWAY FROM YOU HERE.
NOT YET.
It was too simple, really.
Nothing more than a cat and mouse game, looking back at it.
How she knew what we were doing I don't know, but she needed us and she used us.
There was no way to get to the emerald while the power was on.
So we shut it down for her.

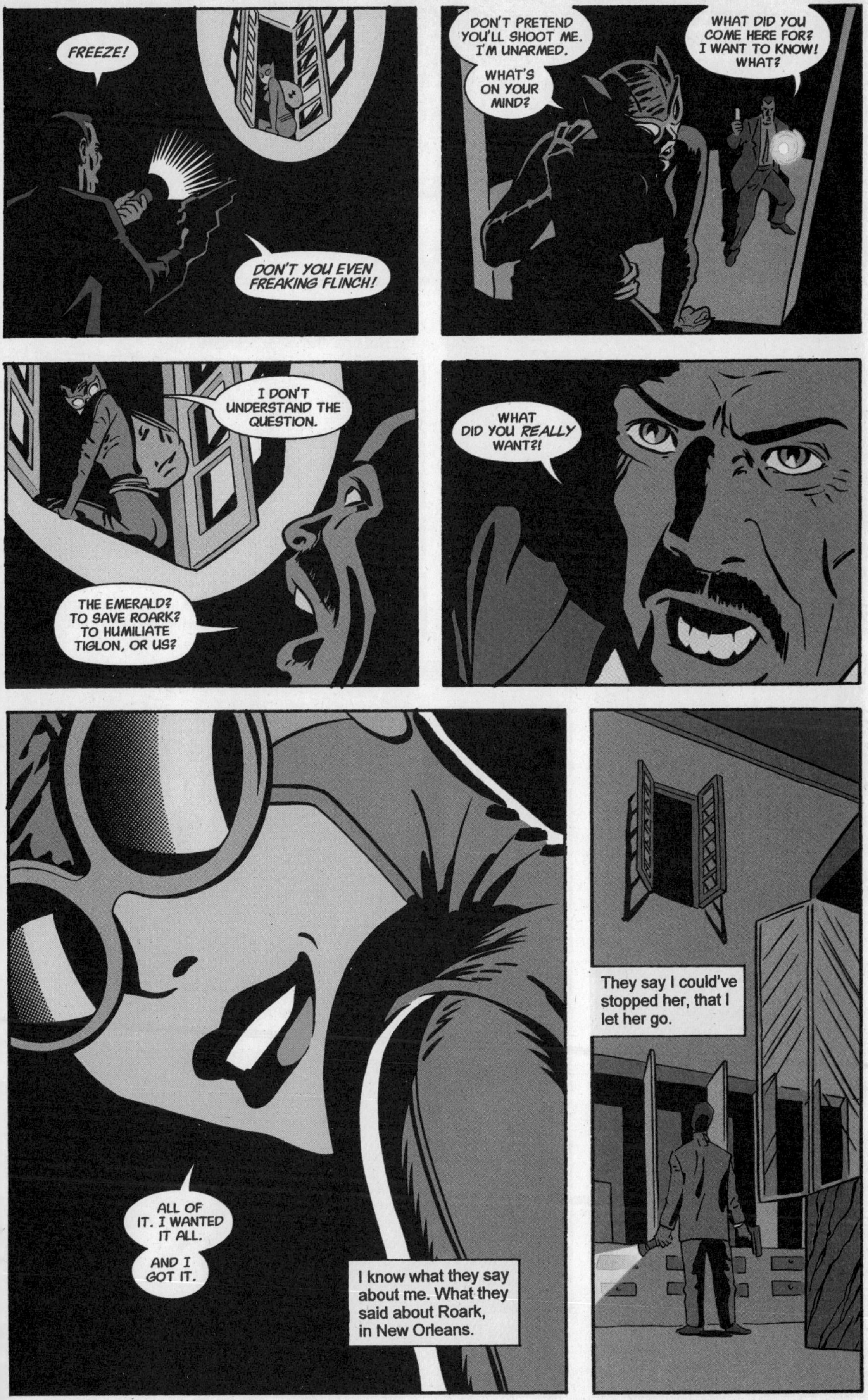
FREEZE!
DON'T YOU EVEN FREAKING FLINCH!
DON'T PRETEND YOU'LL SHOOT ME. I'M UNARMED.
WHAT'S ON YOUR MIND?
WHAT DID YOU COME HERE FOR? I WANT TO KNOW! WHAT?
I DON'T UNDERSTAND THE QUESTION.
THE EMERALD? TO SAVE ROARK? TO HUMILIATE TIGLON, OR US?
WHAT DID YOU REALLY WANT?!
ALL OF IT. I WANTED IT ALL.
AND I GOT IT.
I know what they say about me. What they said about Roark, in New Orleans.
They say I could've stopped her, that I let her go.

They're wrong.

They think she thinks like us.

They're wrong.

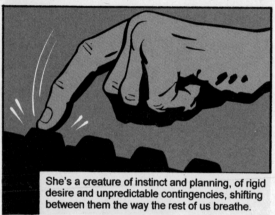

She's a creature of instinct and planning, of rigid desire and unpredictable contingencies, shifting between them the way the rest of us breathe.

There's not one rule of ours she plays by. Not one she even acknowledges.

She lives in the eternal now. And no one else is in there with her.

Except prey. What she can toy with.

She's a cat.

She's nothing we'll ever truly understand. That's why you'll never catch her.

No one ever will.

RESIGNATION

**THE END**

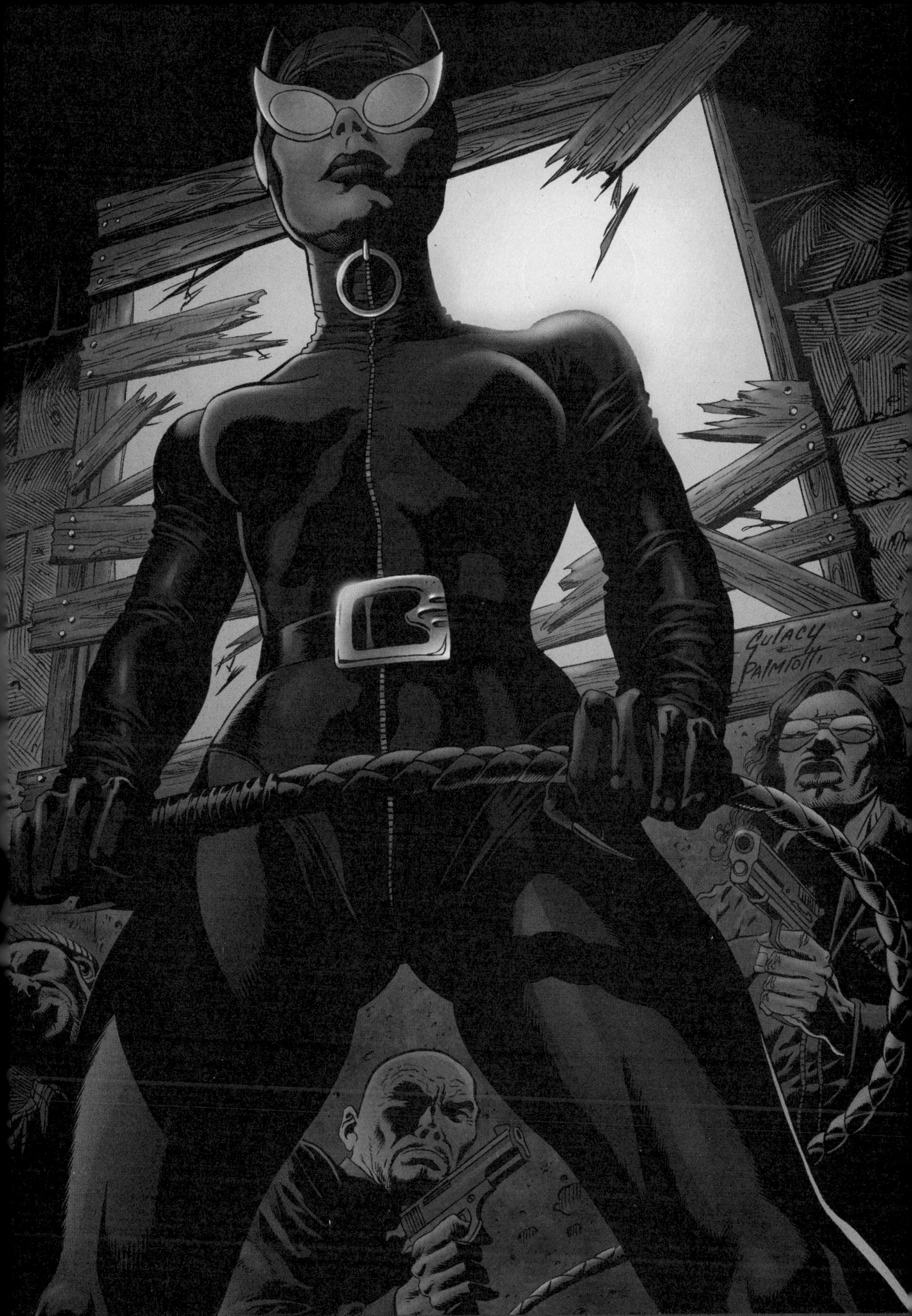
GULACY
PALMIOTTI

## Fire with Fire

**Ed Brubaker** Writer **Paul Gulacy** Penciller **Jimmy Palmiotti** Inker

**Laurie Kronenberg** Colorist **Clem Robins** Letterer **Paul Gulacy & Jimmy Palmiotti** Cover Artists

The current creative team on CATWOMAN tells a tale of Selina fighting "Fire with Fire," as the local gangs start exerting their control over Gotham City!

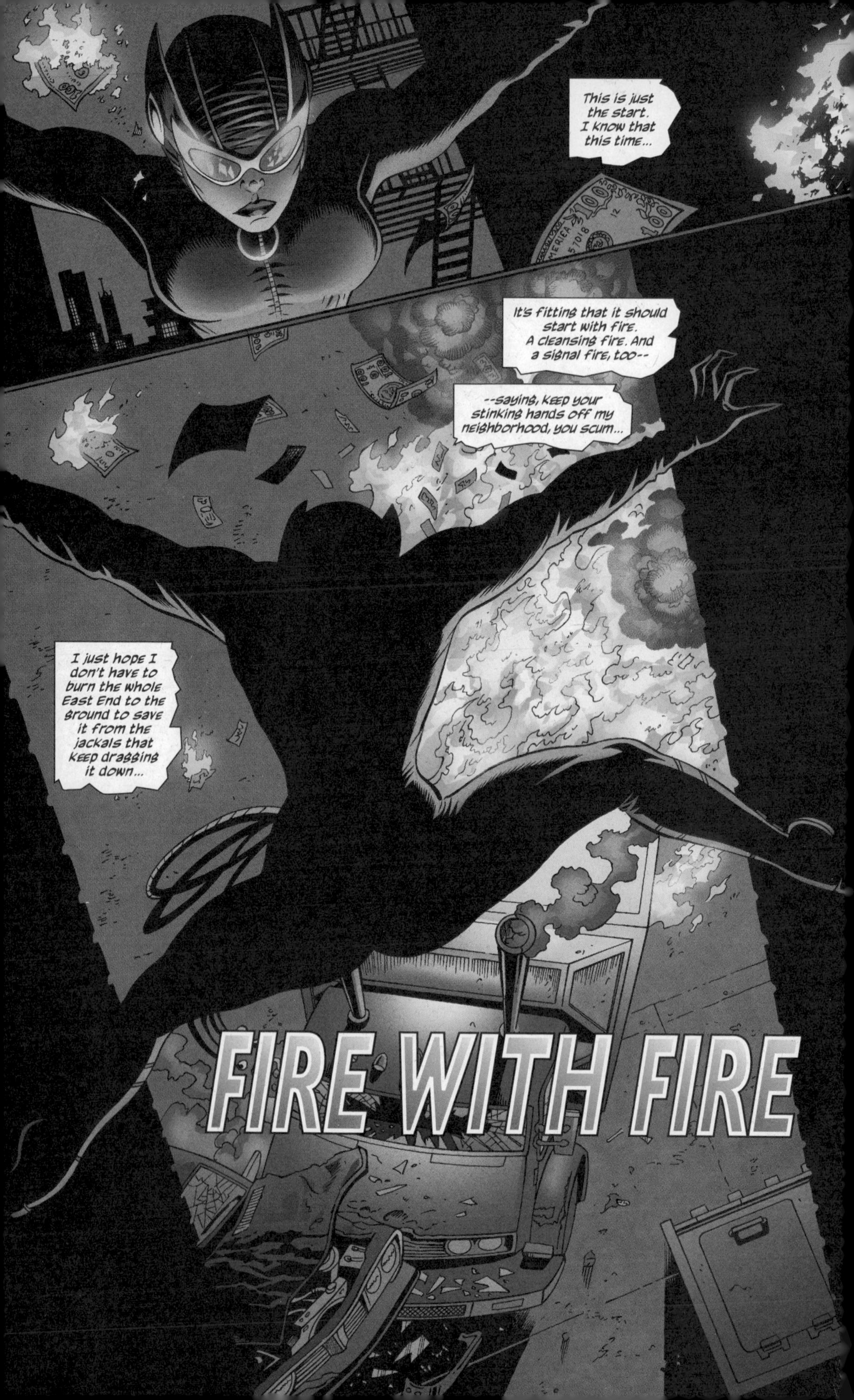
This is just the start. I know that this time...
It's fitting that it should start with fire. A cleansing fire. And a signal fire, too--
--saying, keep your stinking hands off my neighborhood, you scum...
I just hope I don't have to burn the whole East End to the ground to save it from the jackals that keep dragging it down...
FIRE WITH FIRE

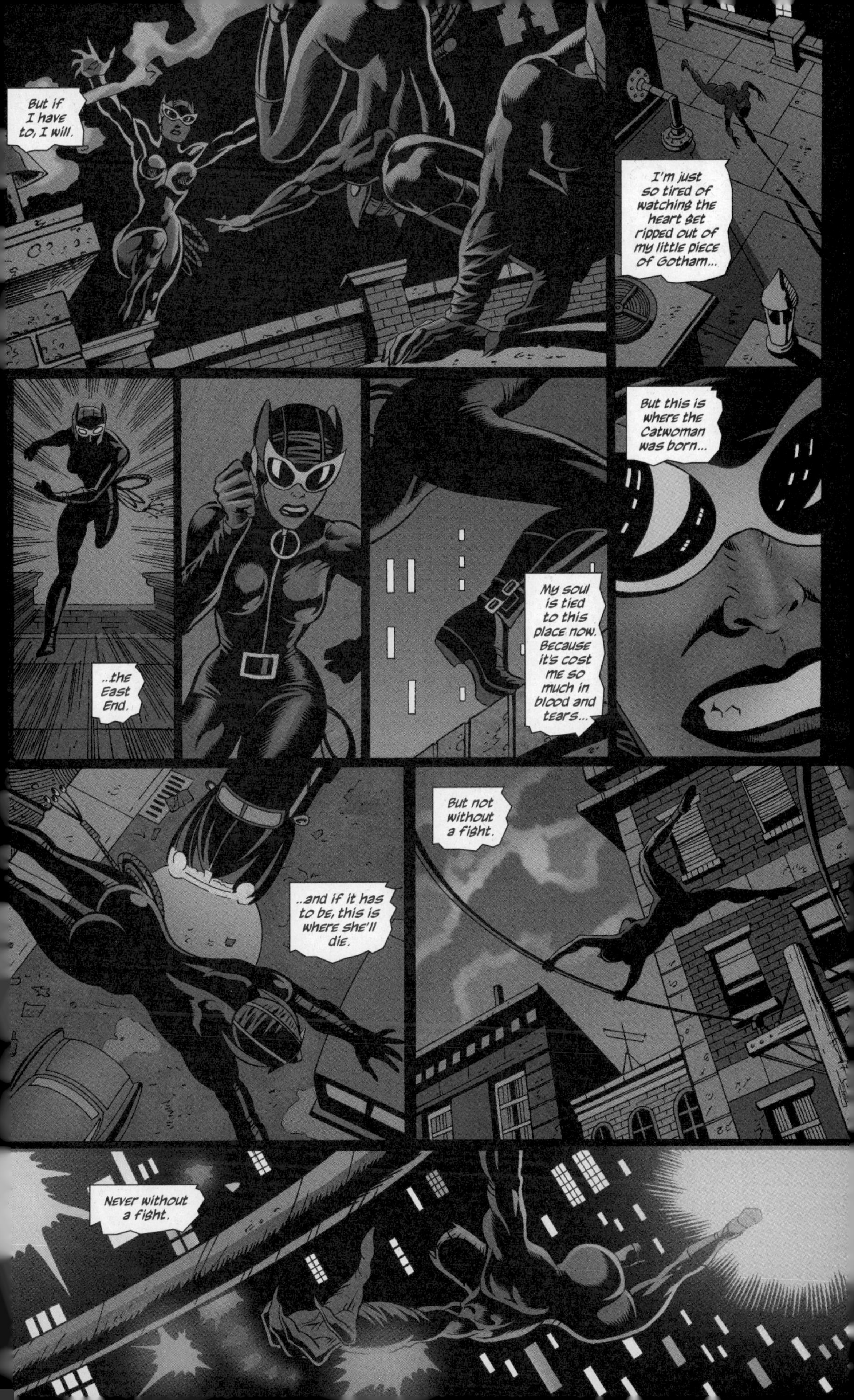
But if I have to, I will.
I'm just so tired of watching the heart get ripped out of my little piece of Gotham...
..the East End.
But this is where the Catwoman was born...
My soul is tied to this place now. Because it's cost me so much in blood and tears...
..and if it has to be, this is where she'll die.
But not without a fight.
Never without a fight.

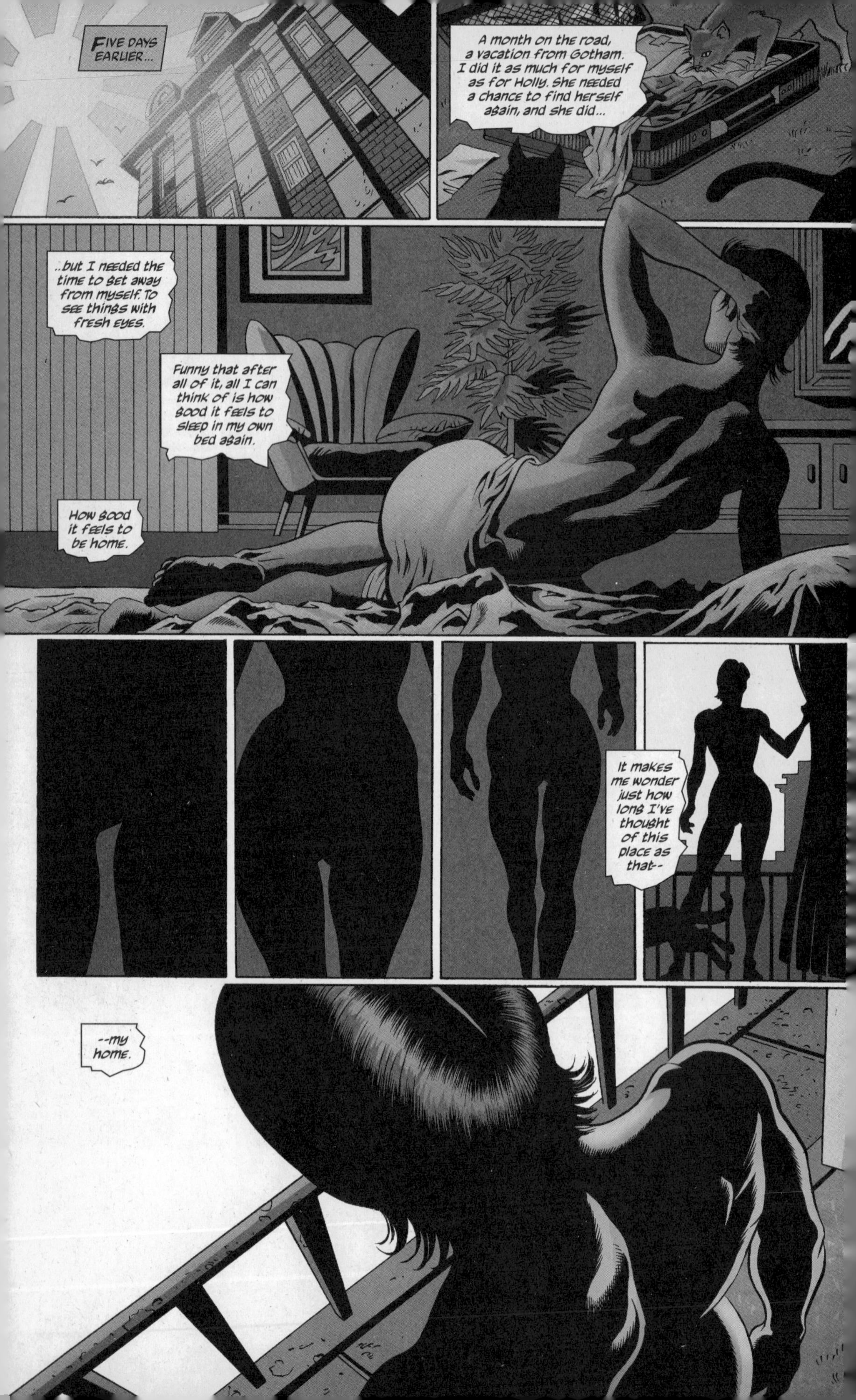
Five days earlier...
A month on the road, a vacation from Gotham. I did it as much for myself as for Holly. She needed a chance to find herself again, and she did...
..but I needed the time to get away from myself. To see things with fresh eyes.
Funny that after all of it, all I can think of is how good it feels to sleep in my own bed again.
How good it feels to be home.
It makes me wonder just how long I've thought of this place as that-
--my home.

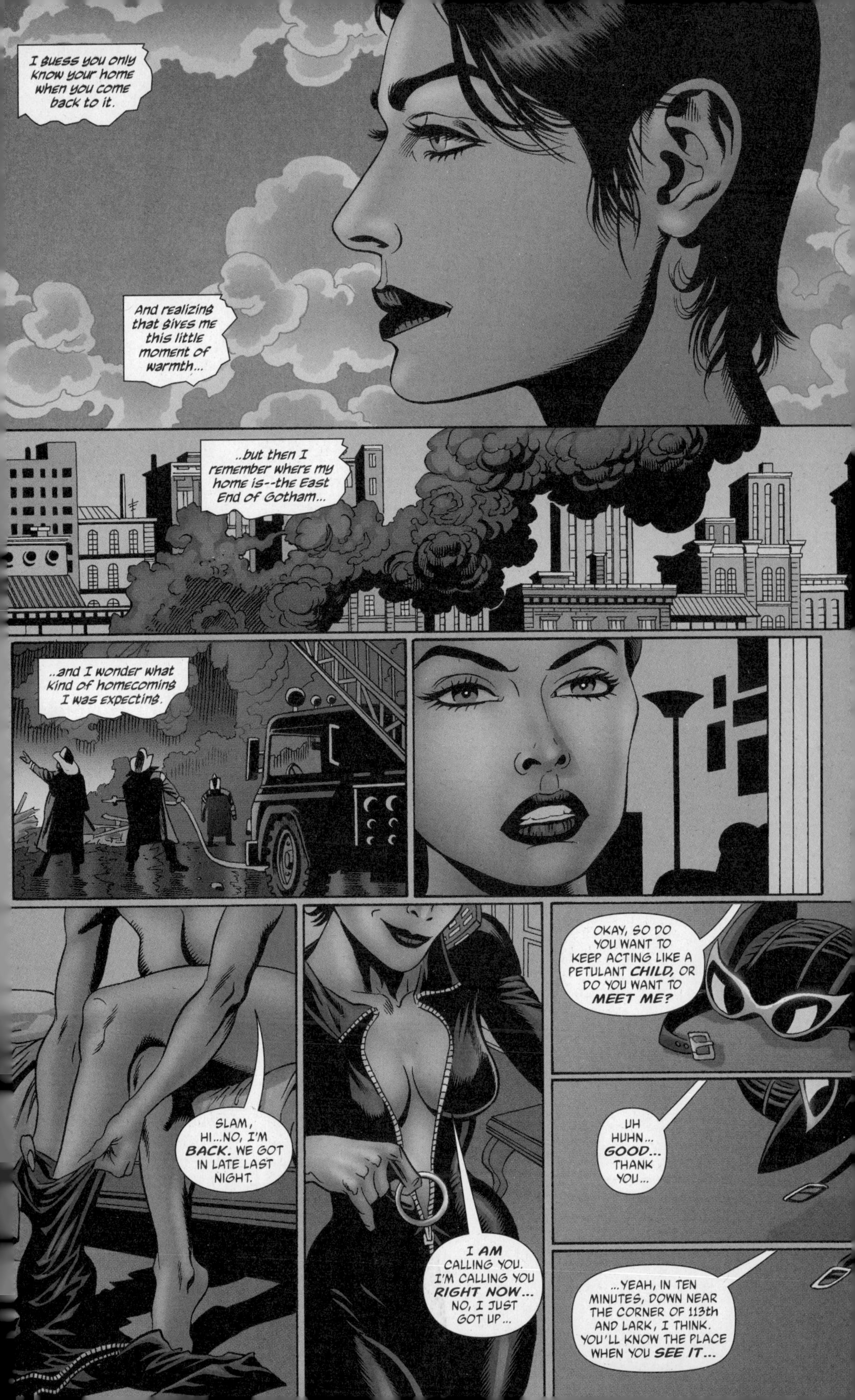

I guess you only know your home when you come back to it.
And realizing that gives me this little moment of warmth...
..but then I remember where my home is--the East End of Gotham...
..and I wonder what kind of homecoming I was expecting.
SLAM, HI...NO, I'M **BACK.** WE GOT IN LATE LAST NIGHT.
I **AM** CALLING YOU. I'M CALLING YOU **RIGHT NOW...** NO, I JUST GOT UP...
OKAY, SO DO YOU WANT TO KEEP ACTING LIKE A PETULANT **CHILD,** OR DO YOU WANT TO **MEET ME?**
UH HUHN... **GOOD...** THANK YOU...
...YEAH, IN TEN MINUTES, DOWN NEAR THE CORNER OF 113th AND LARK, I THINK. YOU'LL KNOW THE PLACE WHEN YOU **SEE IT...**

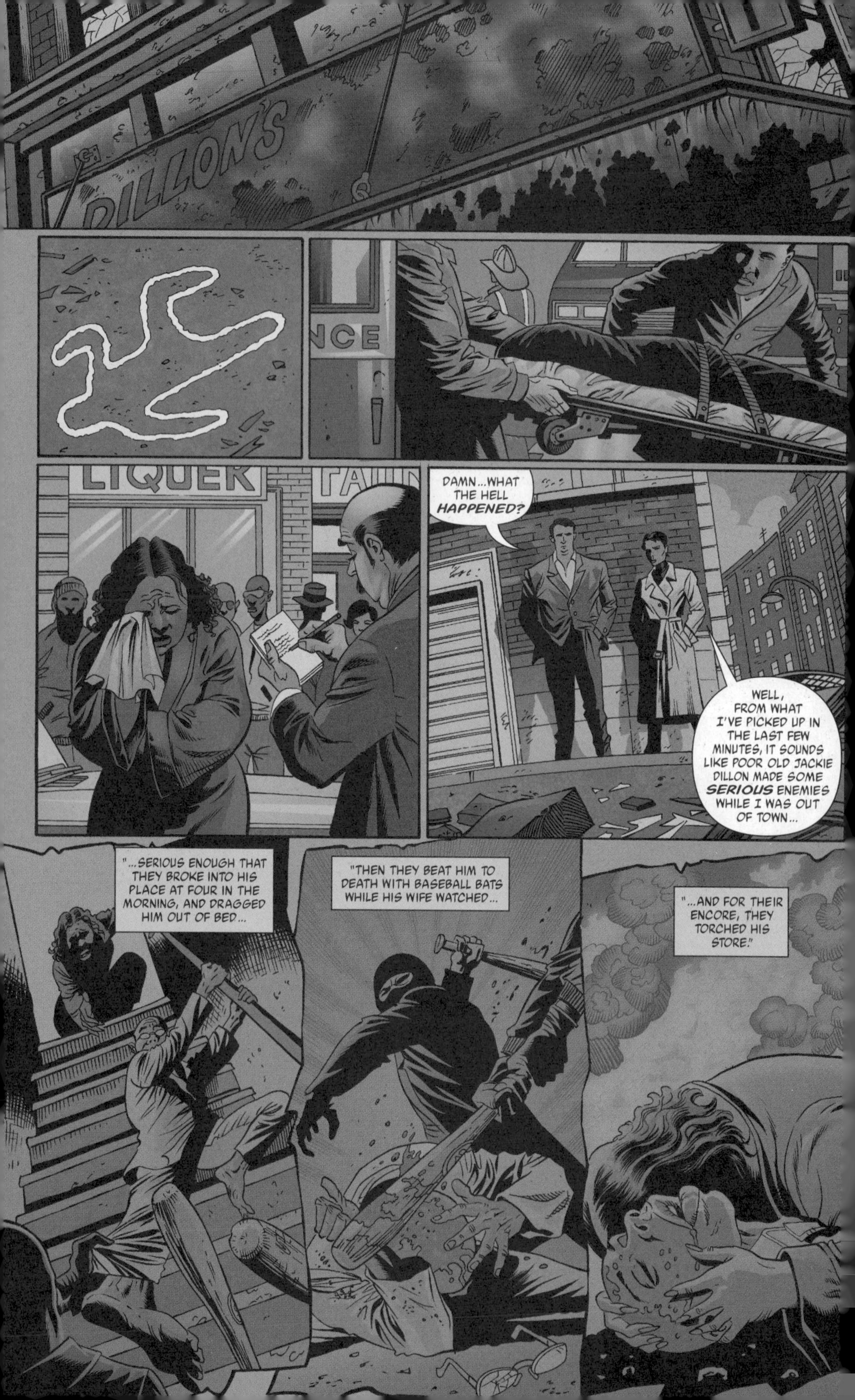
DILLON'S
NCE
LIQUER
DAMN...WHAT THE HELL HAPPENED?
WELL, FROM WHAT I'VE PICKED UP IN THE LAST FEW MINUTES, IT SOUNDS LIKE POOR OLD JACKIE DILLON MADE SOME SERIOUS ENEMIES WHILE I WAS OUT OF TOWN...
"...SERIOUS ENOUGH THAT THEY BROKE INTO HIS PLACE AT FOUR IN THE MORNING, AND DRAGGED HIM OUT OF BED...
"THEN THEY BEAT HIM TO DEATH WITH BASEBALL BATS WHILE HIS WIFE WATCHED...
"...AND FOR THEIR ENCORE, THEY TORCHED HIS STORE."

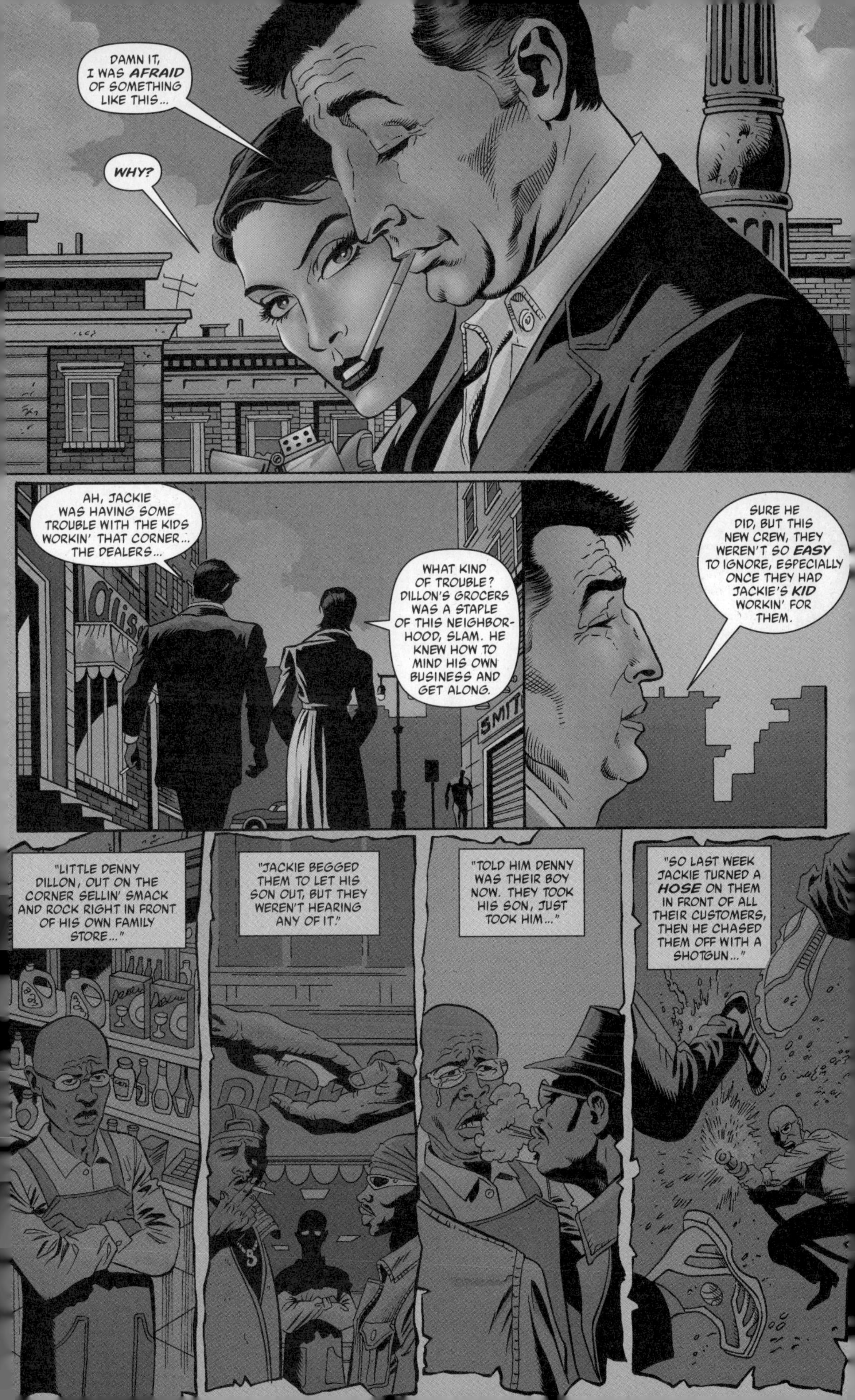

DAMN IT, I WAS AFRAID OF SOMETHING LIKE THIS...
WHY?
AH, JACKIE WAS HAVING SOME TROUBLE WITH THE KIDS WORKIN' THAT CORNER... THE DEALERS...
WHAT KIND OF TROUBLE? DILLON'S GROCERS WAS A STAPLE OF THIS NEIGHBORHOOD, SLAM. HE KNEW HOW TO MIND HIS OWN BUSINESS AND GET ALONG.
SURE HE DID, BUT THIS NEW CREW, THEY WEREN'T SO EASY TO IGNORE, ESPECIALLY ONCE THEY HAD JACKIE'S KID WORKIN' FOR THEM.
"LITTLE DENNY DILLON, OUT ON THE CORNER SELLIN' SMACK AND ROCK RIGHT IN FRONT OF HIS OWN FAMILY STORE..."
"JACKIE BEGGED THEM TO LET HIS SON OUT, BUT THEY WEREN'T HEARING ANY OF IT."
"TOLD HIM DENNY WAS THEIR BOY NOW. THEY TOOK HIS SON, JUST TOOK HIM..."
"SO LAST WEEK JACKIE TURNED A HOSE ON THEM IN FRONT OF ALL THEIR CUSTOMERS, THEN HE CHASED THEM OFF WITH A SHOTGUN..."

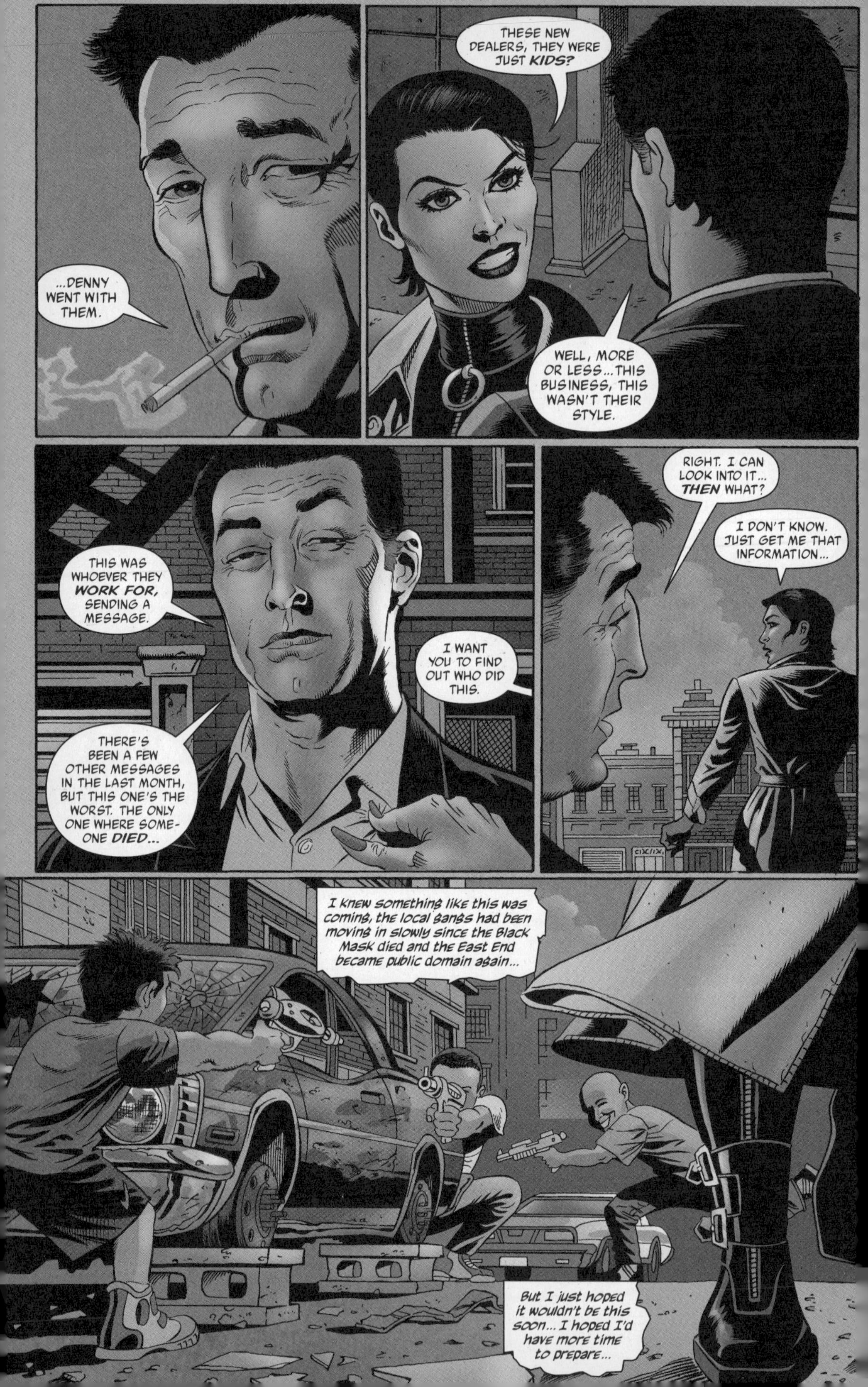
...DENNY WENT WITH THEM.
THESE NEW DEALERS, THEY WERE JUST KIDS?
WELL, MORE OR LESS... THIS BUSINESS, THIS WASN'T THEIR STYLE.
THIS WAS WHOEVER THEY WORK FOR, SENDING A MESSAGE.
THERE'S BEEN A FEW OTHER MESSAGES IN THE LAST MONTH, BUT THIS ONE'S THE WORST. THE ONLY ONE WHERE SOME-ONE DIED...
I WANT YOU TO FIND OUT WHO DID THIS.
RIGHT. I CAN LOOK INTO IT... THEN WHAT?
I DON'T KNOW. JUST GET ME THAT INFORMATION...
I knew something like this was coming, the local gangs had been moving in slowly since the Black Mask died and the East End became public domain again...
But I just hoped it wouldn't be this soon... I hoped I'd have more time to prepare...

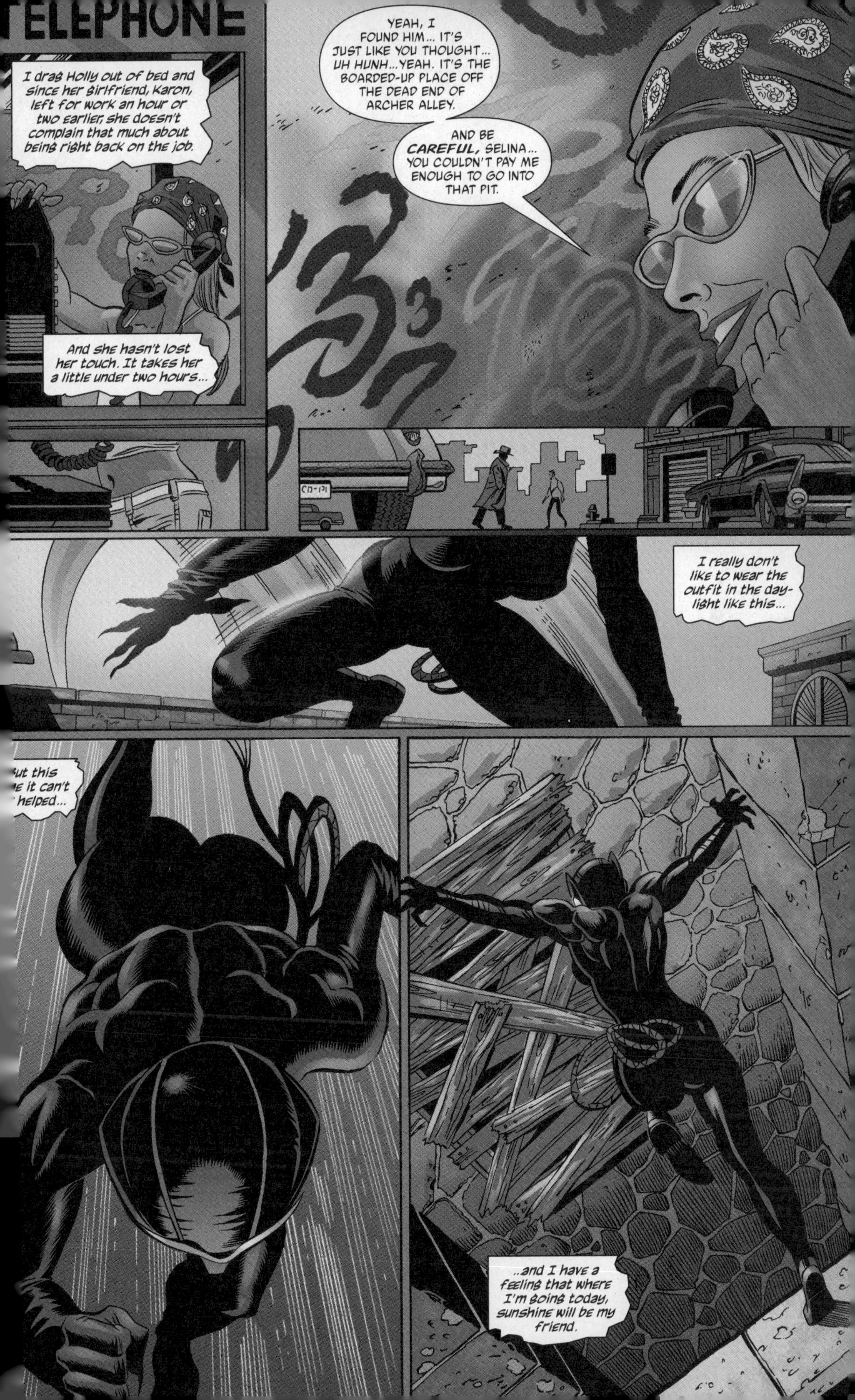
TELEPHONE
I drag Holly out of bed and since her girlfriend, Karon, left for work an hour or two earlier, she doesn't complain that much about being right back on the job.
And she hasn't lost her touch. It takes her a little under two hours...
YEAH, I FOUND HIM... IT'S JUST LIKE YOU THOUGHT... UH HUNH...YEAH. IT'S THE BOARDED-UP PLACE OFF THE DEAD END OF ARCHER ALLEY.
AND BE CAREFUL, SELINA... YOU COULDN'T PAY ME ENOUGH TO GO INTO THAT PIT.
I really don't like to wear the outfit in the day-light like this...
..and I have a feeling that where I'm going today, sunshine will be my friend.

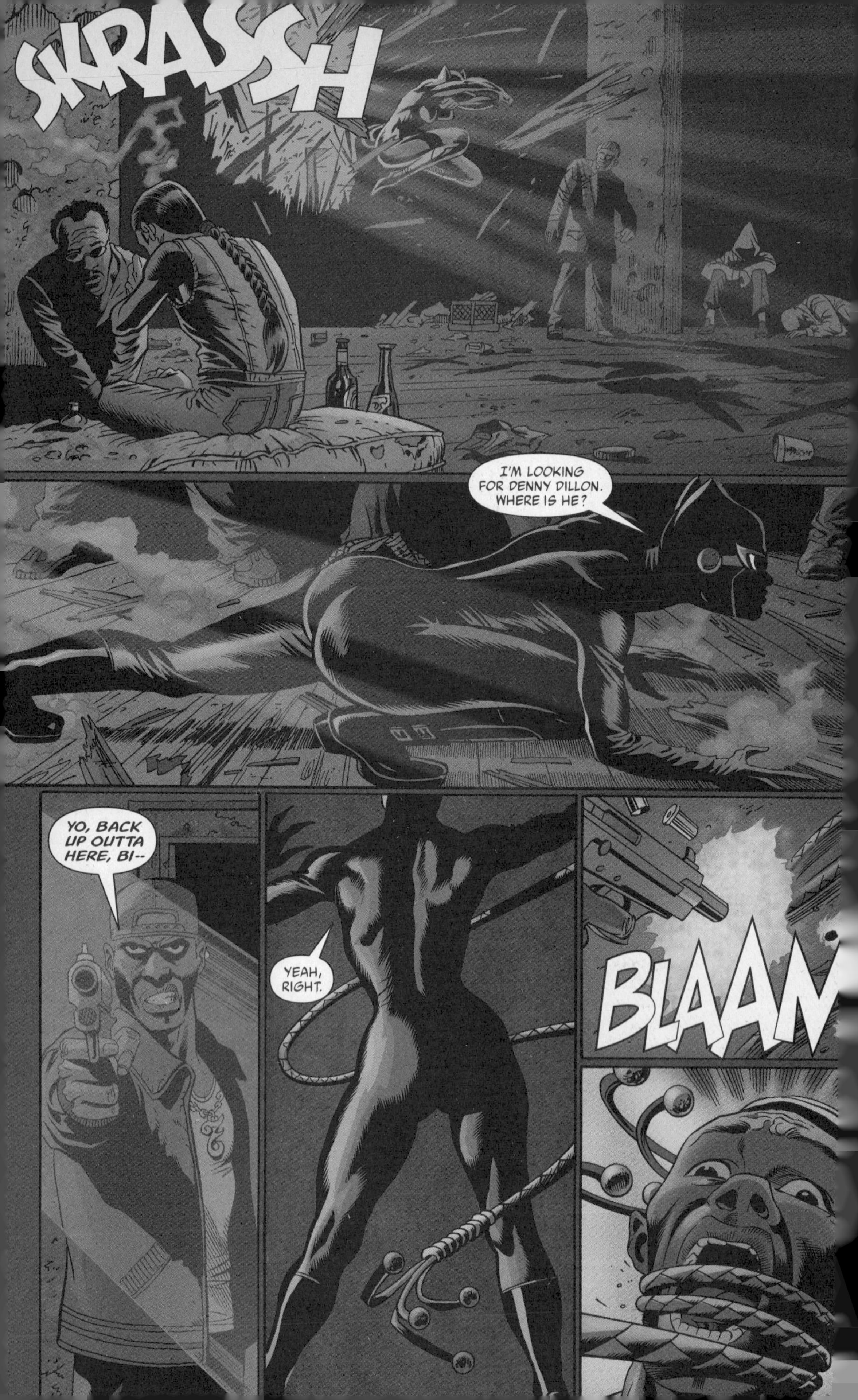
SKRASSH
I'M LOOKING FOR DENNY DILLON. WHERE IS HE?
YO, BACK UP OUTTA HERE, BI--
YEAH, RIGHT.
BLAAM

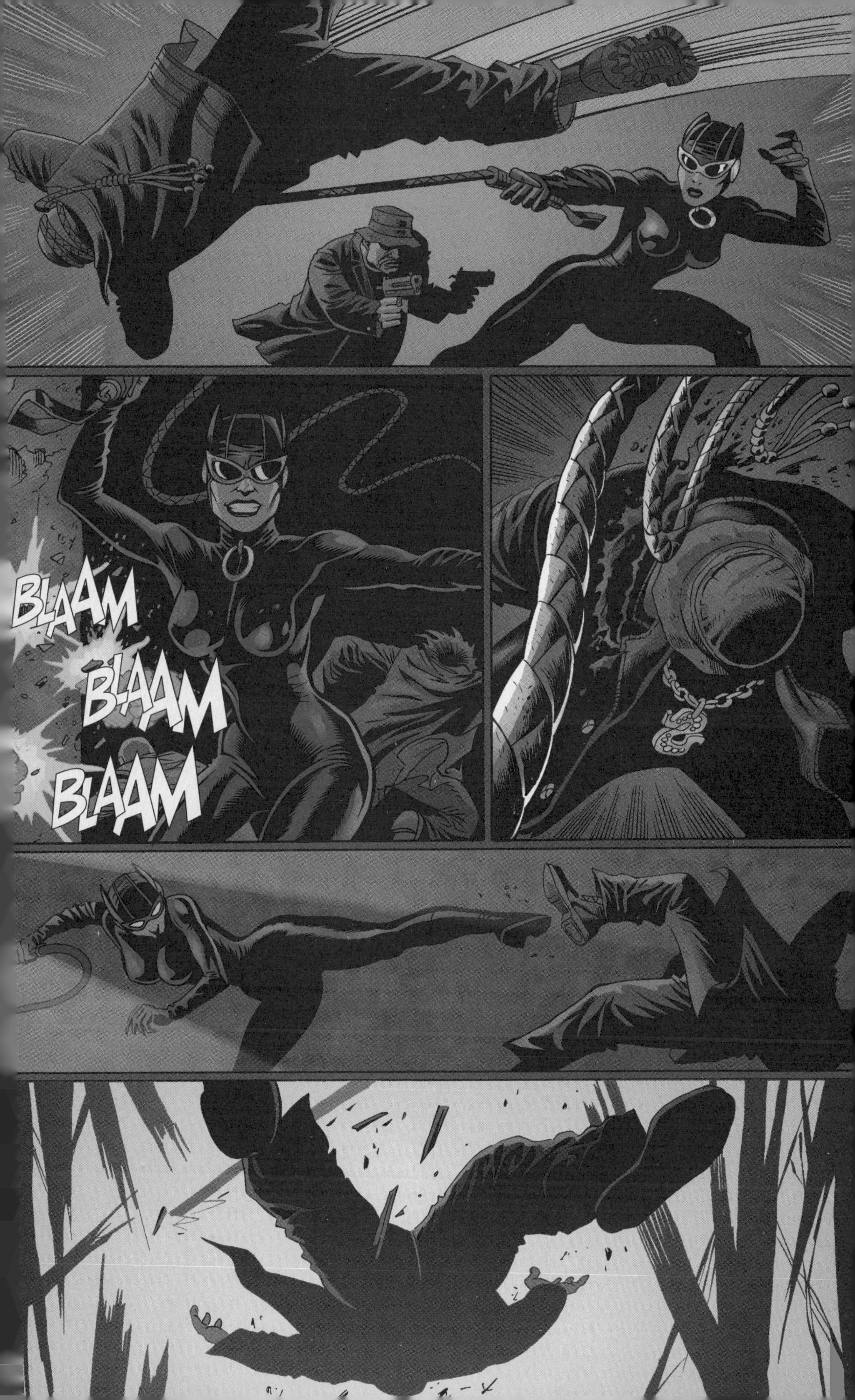
BLAAM
BLAAM
BLAAM

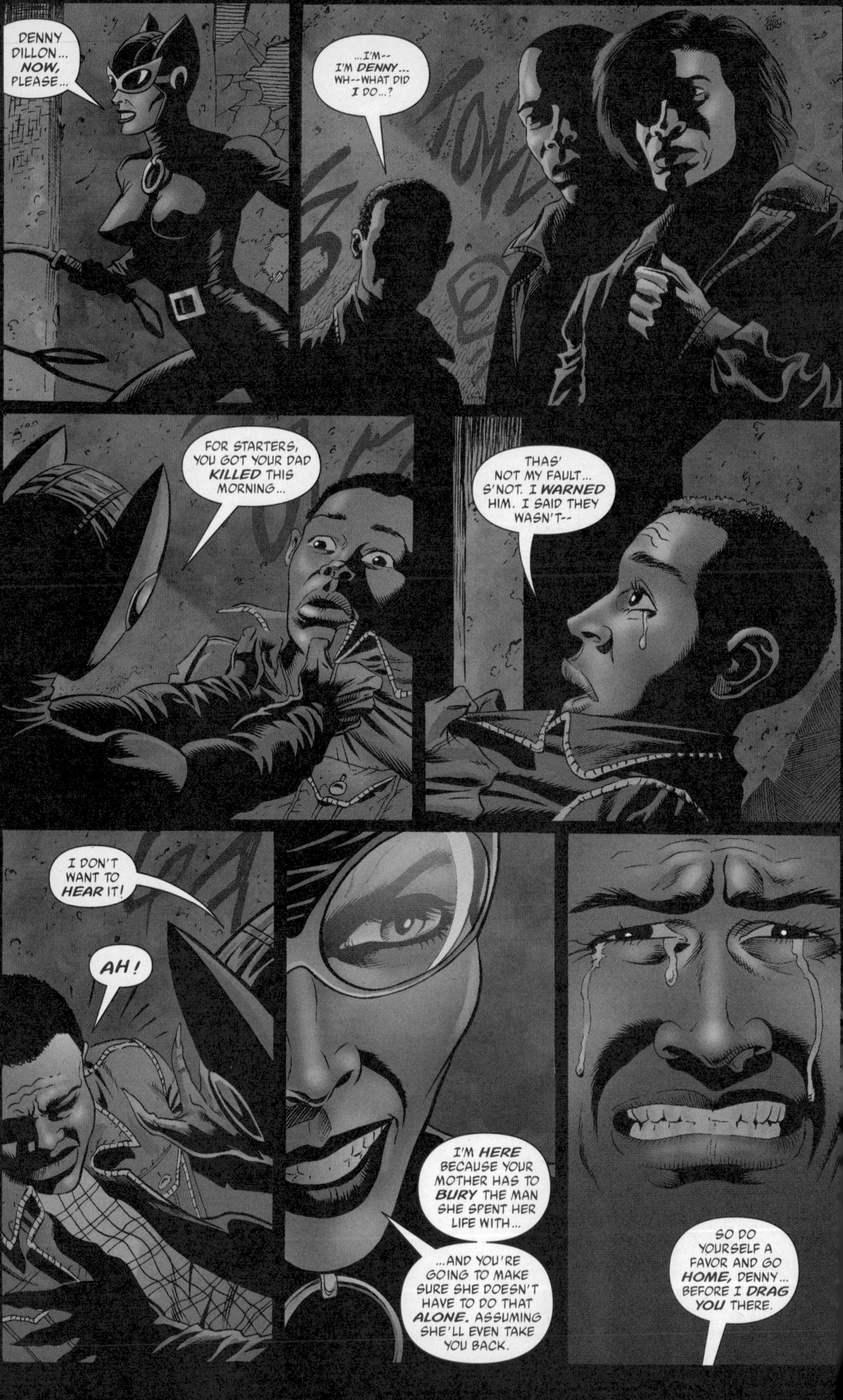
DENNY DILLON... NOW, PLEASE...
...I'M-- I'M DENNY... WH--WHAT DID I DO...?
FOR STARTERS, YOU GOT YOUR DAD KILLED THIS MORNING...
THAS' NOT MY FAULT... S'NOT. I WARNED HIM. I SAID THEY WASN'T--
I DON'T WANT TO HEAR IT!
AH!
I'M HERE BECAUSE YOUR MOTHER HAS TO BURY THE MAN SHE SPENT HER LIFE WITH...
...AND YOU'RE GOING TO MAKE SURE SHE DOESN'T HAVE TO DO THAT ALONE. ASSUMING SHE'LL EVEN TAKE YOU BACK.
SO DO YOURSELF A FAVOR AND GO HOME, DENNY... BEFORE I DRAG YOU THERE.

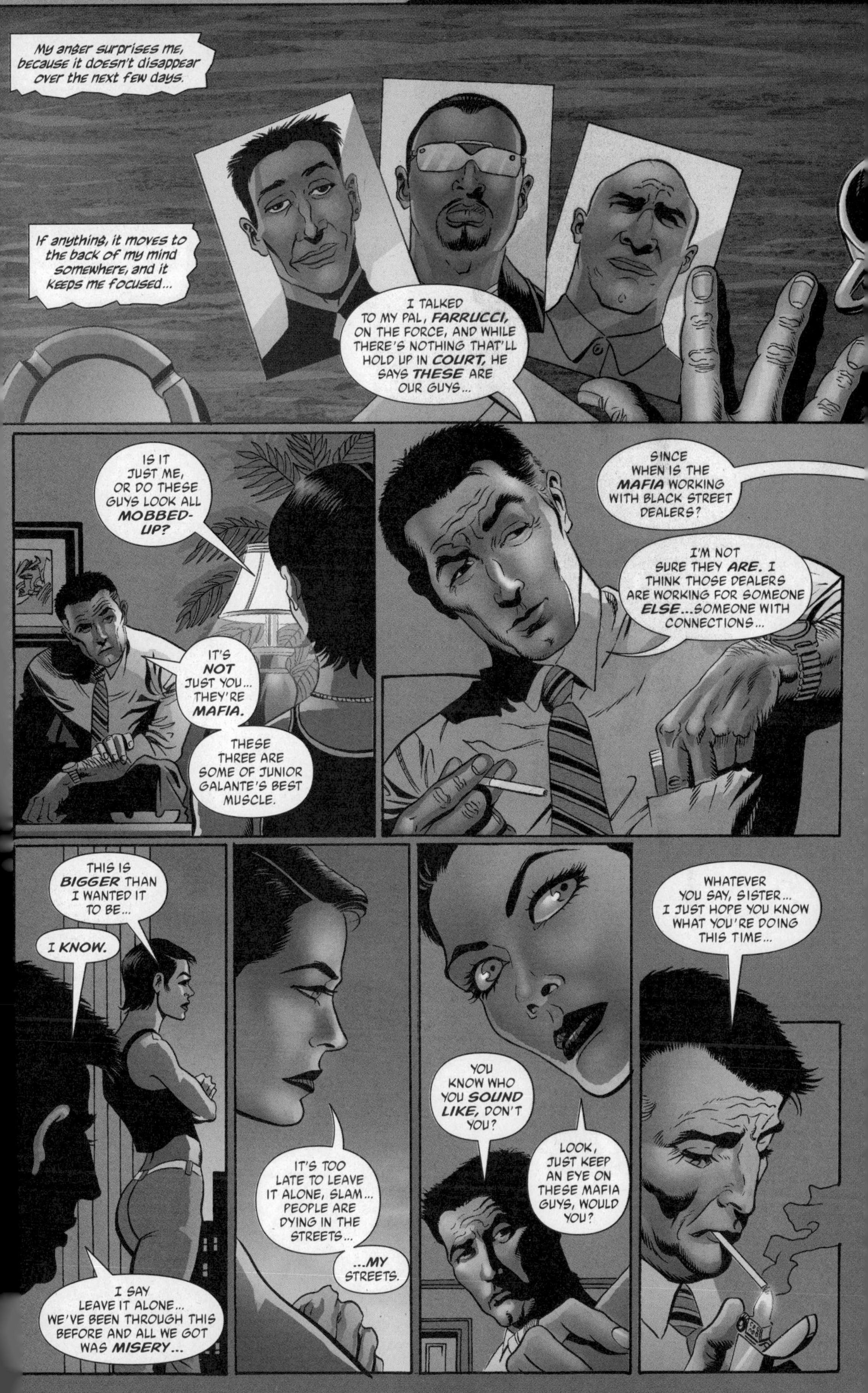
My anger surprises me, because it doesn't disappear over the next few days.
If anything, it moves to the back of my mind somewhere, and it keeps me focused...
I TALKED TO MY PAL, FARRUCCI, ON THE FORCE, AND WHILE THERE'S NOTHING THAT'LL HOLD UP IN COURT, HE SAYS THESE ARE OUR GUYS...
IS IT JUST ME, OR DO THESE GUYS LOOK ALL MOBBED-UP?
IT'S NOT JUST YOU... THEY'RE MAFIA.
THESE THREE ARE SOME OF JUNIOR GALANTE'S BEST MUSCLE.
SINCE WHEN IS THE MAFIA WORKING WITH BLACK STREET DEALERS?
I'M NOT SURE THEY ARE. I THINK THOSE DEALERS ARE WORKING FOR SOMEONE ELSE...SOMEONE WITH CONNECTIONS...
THIS IS BIGGER THAN I WANTED IT TO BE...
I KNOW.
I SAY LEAVE IT ALONE... WE'VE BEEN THROUGH THIS BEFORE AND ALL WE GOT WAS MISERY...
IT'S TOO LATE TO LEAVE IT ALONE, SLAM... PEOPLE ARE DYING IN THE STREETS...
...MY STREETS.
YOU KNOW WHO YOU SOUND LIKE, DON'T YOU?
LOOK, JUST KEEP AN EYE ON THESE MAFIA GUYS, WOULD YOU?
WHATEVER YOU SAY, SISTER... I JUST HOPE YOU KNOW WHAT YOU'RE DOING THIS TIME...

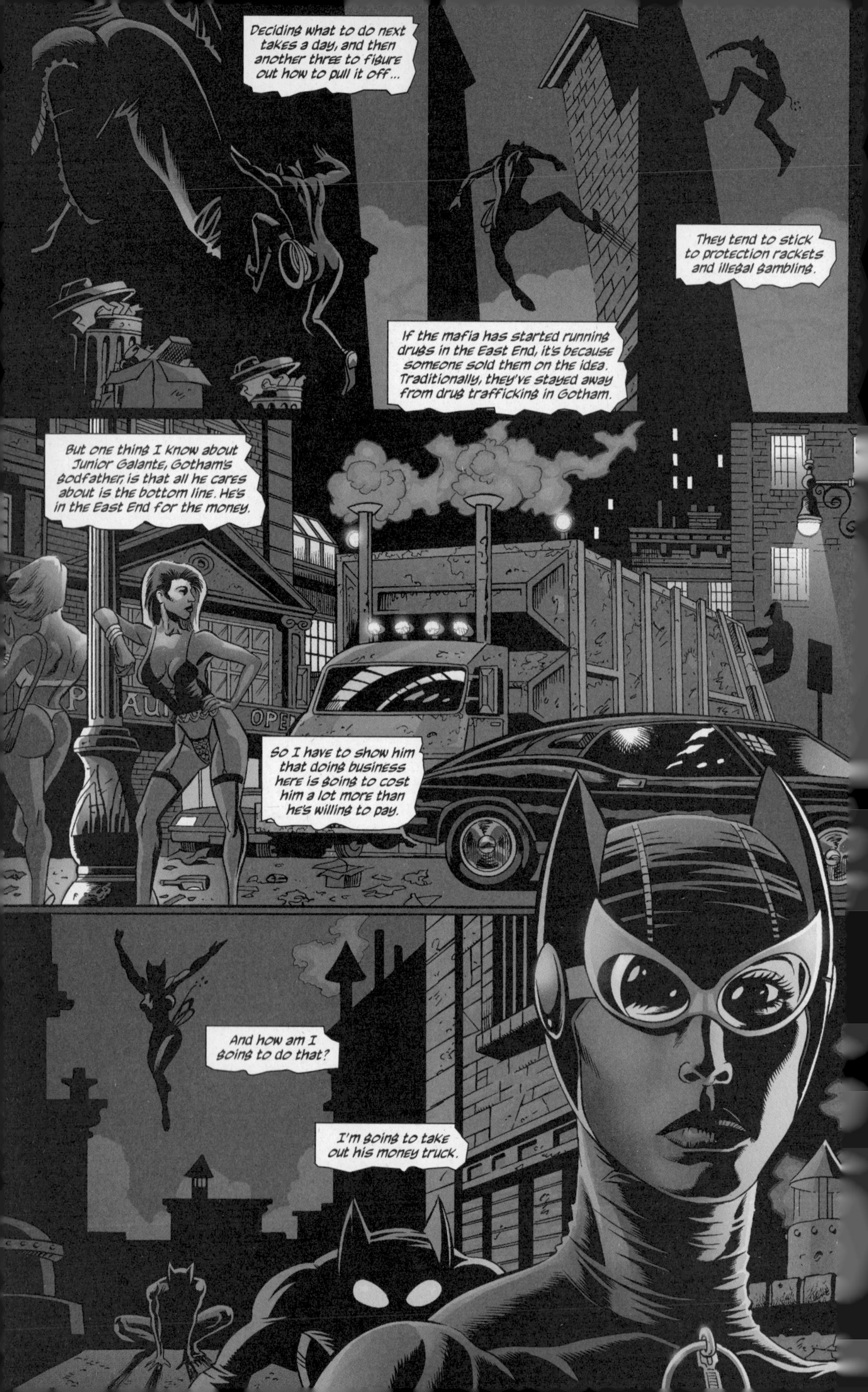
Deciding what to do next takes a day, and then another three to figure out how to pull it off...
If the mafia has started running drugs in the East End, it's because someone sold them on the idea. Traditionally, they've stayed away from drug trafficking in Gotham.
They tend to stick to protection rackets and illegal gambling.
But one thing I know about Junior Galante, Gotham's godfather, is that all he cares about is the bottom line. He's in the East End for the money.
So I have to show him that doing business here is going to cost him a lot more than he's willing to pay.
And how am I going to do that?
I'm going to take out his money truck.

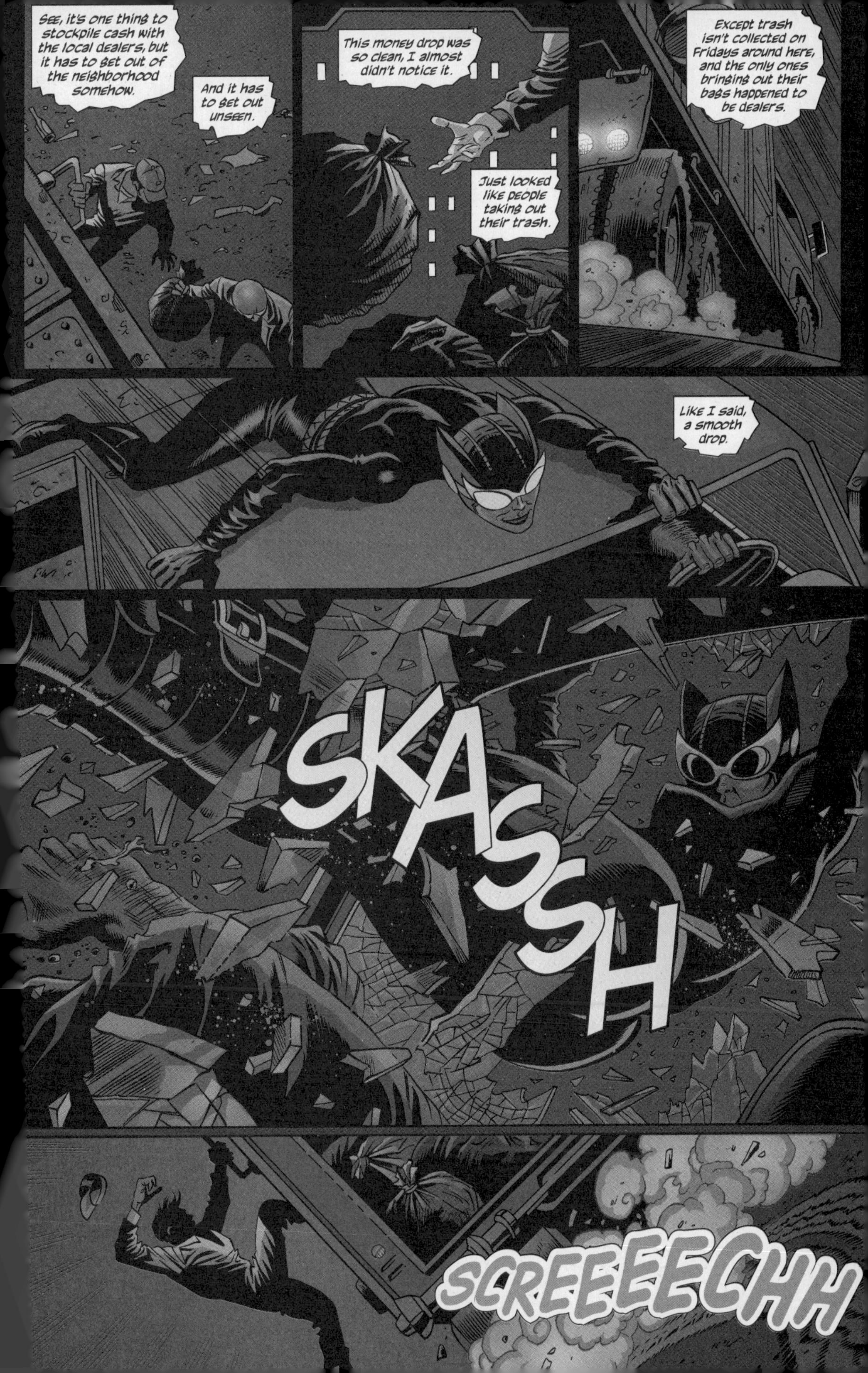
See, it's one thing to stockpile cash with the local dealers, but it has to get out of the neighborhood somehow.
And it has to get out unseen.
This money drop was so clean, I almost didn't notice it.
Just looked like people taking out their trash.
Except trash isn't collected on Fridays around here, and the only ones bringing out their bags happened to be dealers.
Like I said, a smooth drop.
SKASSSH
SCREEEEECHH

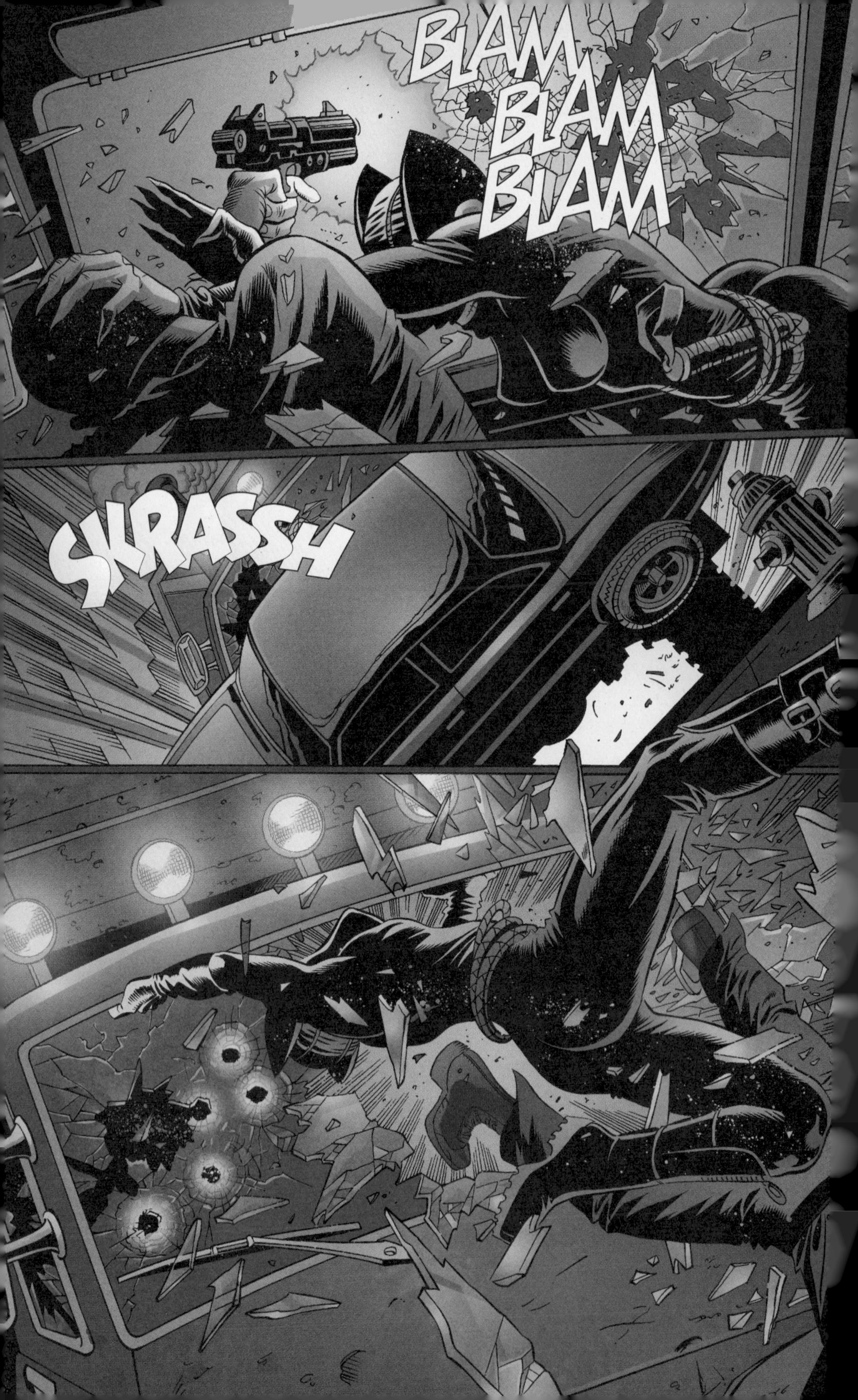
BLAM
BLAM
BLAM
SKRASSH

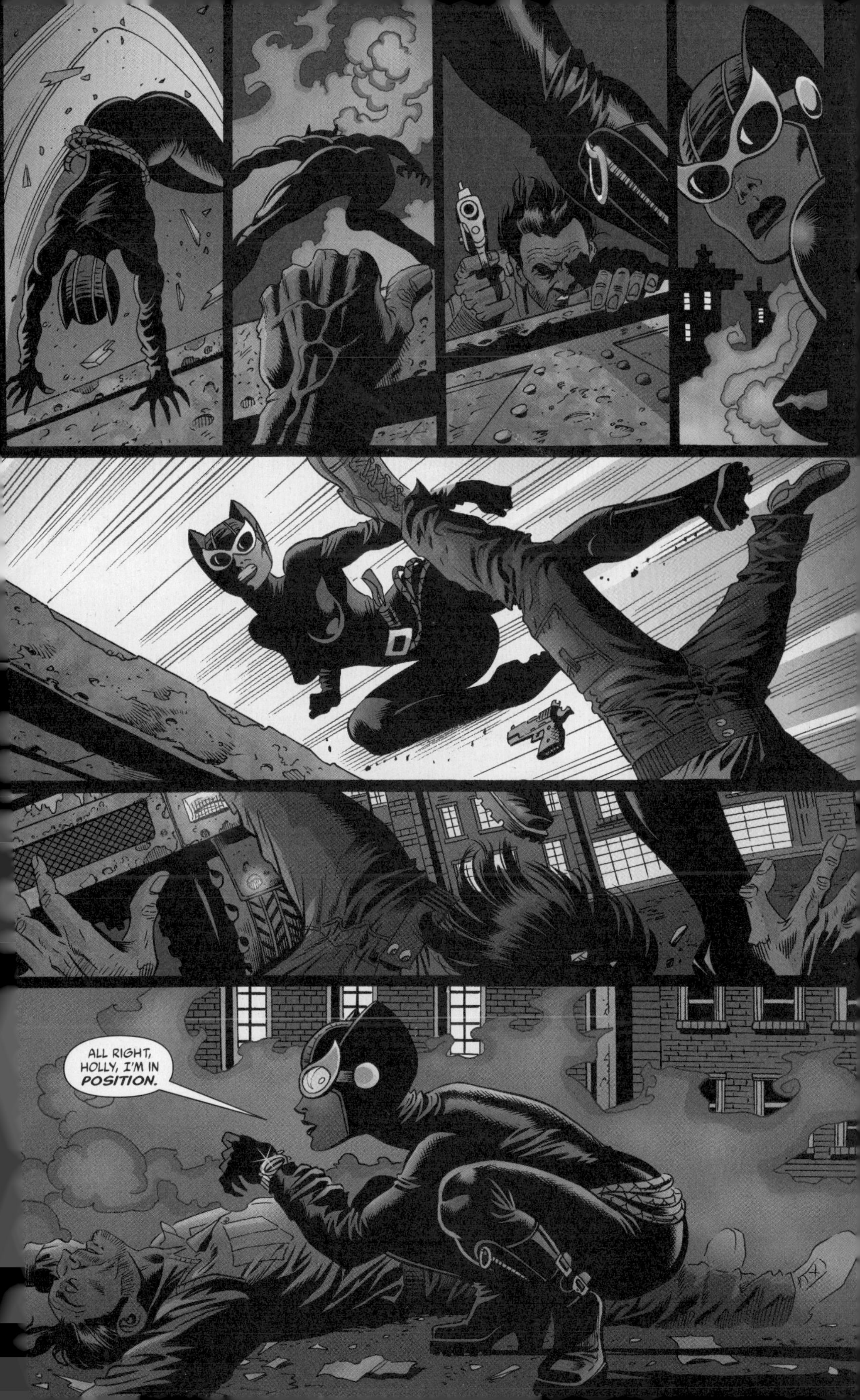
ALL RIGHT, HOLLY, I'M IN POSITION.

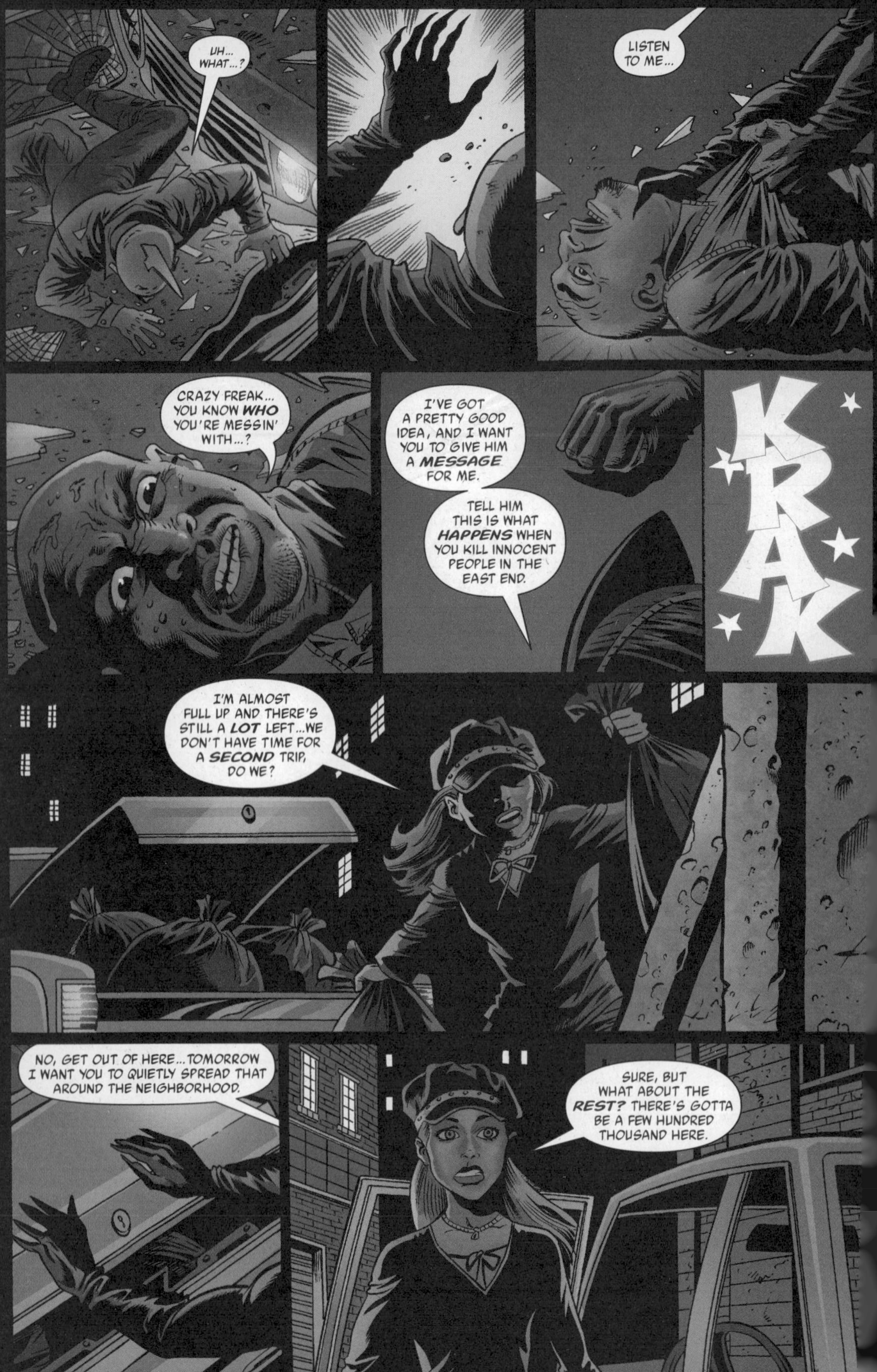
UH... WHAT...?
LISTEN TO ME...
CRAZY FREAK... YOU KNOW WHO YOU'RE MESSIN' WITH...?
I'VE GOT A PRETTY GOOD IDEA, AND I WANT YOU TO GIVE HIM A MESSAGE FOR ME.
TELL HIM THIS IS WHAT HAPPENS WHEN YOU KILL INNOCENT PEOPLE IN THE EAST END.
KRAK
I'M ALMOST FULL UP AND THERE'S STILL A LOT LEFT...WE DON'T HAVE TIME FOR A SECOND TRIP, DO WE?
NO, GET OUT OF HERE...TOMORROW I WANT YOU TO QUIETLY SPREAD THAT AROUND THE NEIGHBORHOOD.
SURE, BUT WHAT ABOUT THE REST? THERE'S GOTTA BE A FEW HUNDRED THOUSAND HERE.

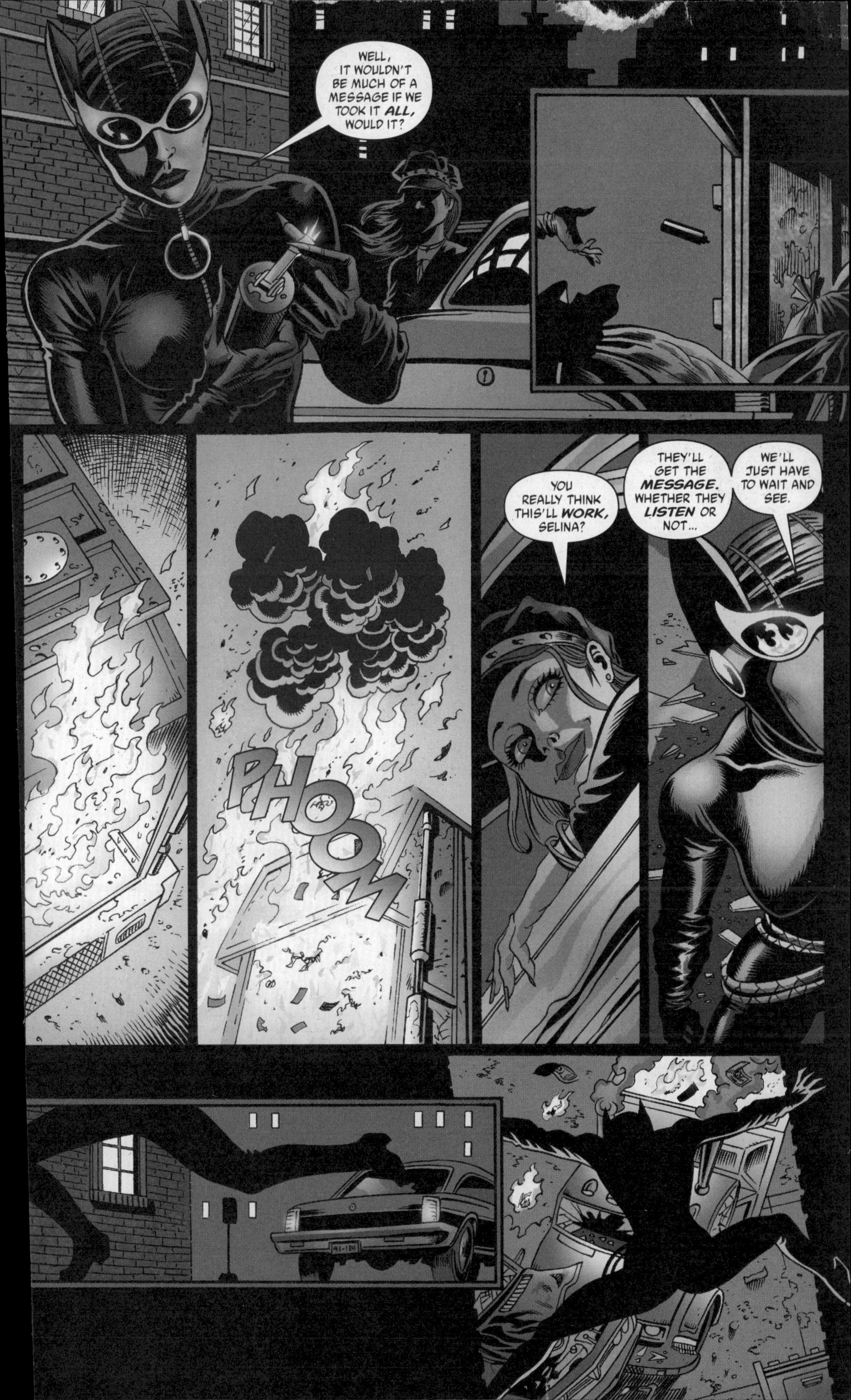
WELL, IT WOULDN'T BE MUCH OF A MESSAGE IF WE TOOK IT ALL, WOULD IT?
PHOOM
YOU REALLY THINK THIS'LL WORK, SELINA?
THEY'LL GET THE MESSAGE. WHETHER THEY LISTEN OR NOT...
WE'LL JUST HAVE TO WAIT AND SEE.

# backlist

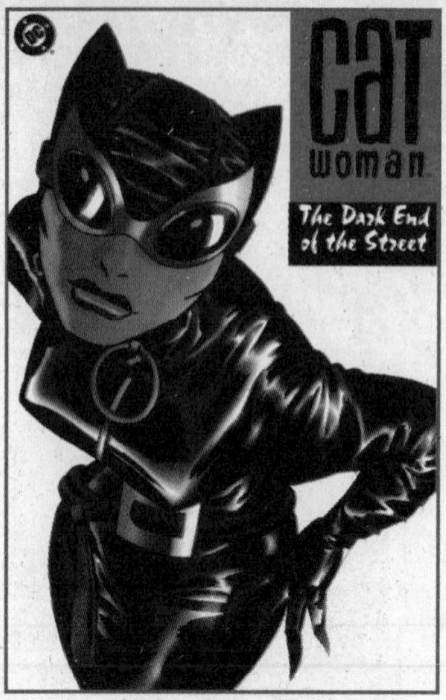
Cat
woman
The Dark End of the Street

CATWOMAN:
THE DARK END OF THE STREET
**Brubaker/Cooke/Allred**

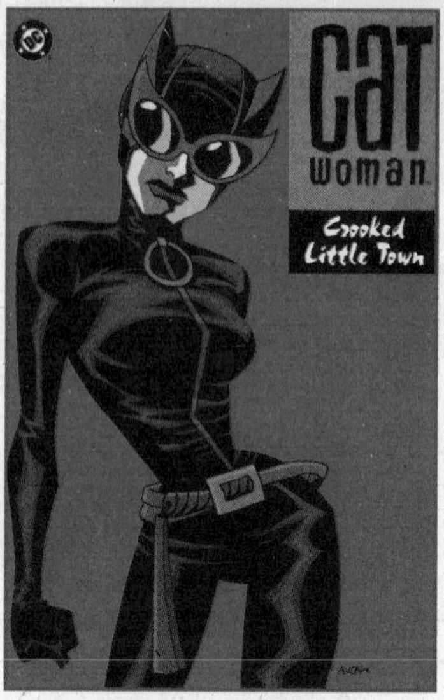
Cat
woman
Crooked Little Town

CATWOMAN:
CROOKED LITTLE TOWN
**Brubaker/Rader/Stewart/Burchett**

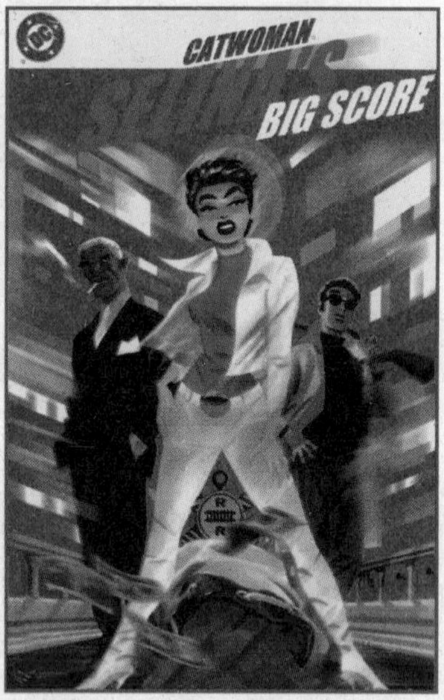
CATWOMAN
BIG SCORE

CATWOMAN: SELINA'S BIG SCORE
**Cooke/various**

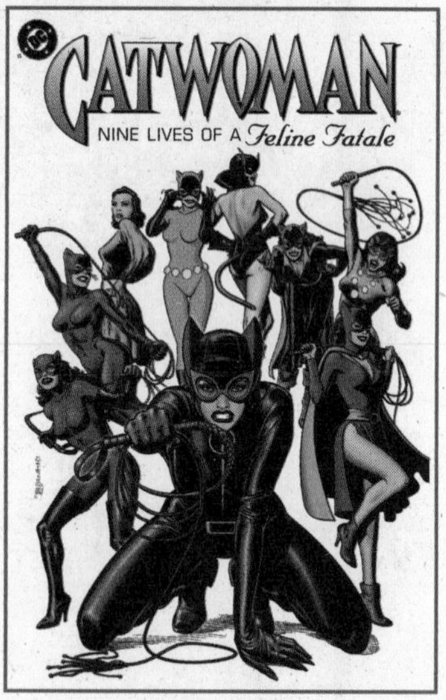
CATWOMAN
NINE LIVES OF A Feline Fatale

CATWOMAN:
NINE LIVES OF A FELINE FATALE
**various**

**Sink your claws into these dynamic collections featuring CATWOMAN!**

BATMAN: CATACLYSM
**various**

BATMAN: CONTAGION
**various**

BATMAN: DARK VICTORY
**Loeb/Sale**

BATMAN: HUSH VOLUME 1
**Loeb/Lee/Williams**

BATMAN: HUSH VOLUME 2
**Loeb/Lee/Williams**

BATMAN: THE LONG HALLOWEEN
**Loeb/Sale**

BATMAN: THE MOVIES
**O'Neil/various**

BATMAN: NINE LIVES
**Motter/Lark**

BATMAN: YEAR ONE
**Miller/Mazzucchelli**

BATMAN IN THE FORTIES
**various**

BATMAN IN THE FIFTIES
**various**

BATMAN IN THE SIXTIES
**various**

BATMAN IN THE SEVENTIES
**various**

BIRDS OF PREY
**Dixon/Haley/Frank/Raffaele/various**

CATWOMAN: THE CATFILE
**Dixon/Balent/B. Smith**

BATMAN: TERROR
**Moench/Gulacy/Palmiotti**

Visit us at www.dccomics.com for more information on these and many other titles from DC Comics or call 1-888-COMIC BOOK for the comics shop nearest you, or go to your local book store.

741.5
AUS        Austin, Chuck

           Catwoman, the
           movie

DUE DATE                      0904   12.95

| | | | |
|---|---|---|---|
| | | | |
| | | | |
| | | | |
| | | | |
| | | | |
| | | | |
| | | | |
| | | | |
| | | | |
| | | | |